Language Acts and Worldmaking

Language Acts and Worldmaking

Series Editors: Professor Catherine Boyle, Professor Debra Kelly, Dr Ana de Medeiros and Dr Carlos Montoro

This book series takes its name from the research, teaching, learning and public engagement carried out by Language Acts and Worldmaking (www.languageacts.org). By worldmaking we mean the power of language, as a material and historical force, to shape the ways we construct our personal, local and transnational identities and therefore how we live and make our worlds. Furthermore, language learning is key to understanding how societies are structured and governed and to empowering culturally aware and self-reflective citizens. Put simply, Language Acts and Worldmaking explores how the languages we use affect the way we think and feel about ourselves, about other people and about the world around us.

The series expands this work at national and international levels by inviting the contributions of researchers, teachers, learners and users of diverse languages across the world. The aim is twofold: to challenge widely held views about language learning as a neutral instrument of globalization and to innovate and transform language research, teaching and learning, together with Modern Languages as an academic discipline, by foregrounding its unique form of cognition and critical engagement.

The aims of the Language Acts and Worldmaking book series are to:

- propose new ways of bridging the gaps between those who teach and research languages and those who learn and use them in everyday contexts from the professional to the personal;
- put research into the hands of wider audiences (teachers, students of all ages, communities, those generally interested in language and culture);
- share a philosophy, policy and practice of language teaching and learning which turns research into action;
- provide the research, experience and data to enable informed debates on current issues and attitudes in language learning, teaching and research;
- share knowledge across and within all levels and experiences of language learning and teaching;
- showcase exciting new work that derives from different types of community activity and is of practical relevance to its audiences;
- disseminate new research in languages that engages with diverse communities of language practitioners.

The main focus of each volume differs. Some deal with current issues in language research, teaching and learning. Others primarily engage with practical aspects of language teaching, learning and research at varied educational levels or in contexts outside formal structures of institutions. Some focus on research and the academic discipline of Modern Languages and those disciplines most closely allied to it, for example Linguistics, Cultural Studies, History, and so on. All volumes are underpinned by research while maintaining a balance with experiences of the application of research findings.

Titles in the series:

Language Debates

Language Acts and Worldmaking

Language Acts and Worldmaking

How and Why the Languages We Use Shape Our World and Our Lives

Edited by Catherine Boyle and Debra Kelly

lãnguãgë
âçts and
worldmåkîng

First published in Great Britain by John Murray Learning in 2022
An imprint of John Murray Press
A division of Hodder & Stoughton Ltd.
An Hachette UK company

This paperback edition published in 2022

1

The acknowledgements on pp. vi constitute an extension of this copyright page.

All illustrations in Chapter 1 by Clari Searle, © Copyright 2020 by badlydrawnbirds.co.uk

Cover image: A robe of many languages created during the Worldmaking Workshop: A Stitch in Time... for the *Who Are We?* Exhibition, led by the Open University at Tate Modern London, May 2018 © Carlos Montoro, 2018

A CIP catalogue record for this title is available from the British Library

Trade Paperback ISBN 9781529372304
eBook ISBN 9781529372311

Typeface by ITC Officina Sans Std Book 11.5/13 by Integra Software Services Pvt. Ltd., Pondicherry, India

Printed and bound in Great Britain by Clays Ltd, Elcograf S.p.A.

John Murray Press policy is to use papers that are natural, renewable and recyclable products and made from wood grown in sustainable forests. The logging and manufacturing processes are expected to conform to the environmental regulations of the country of origin.

John Murray Press
Carmelite House
50 Victoria Embankment
London EC4Y 0DZ

Nicholas Brealey Publishing
Hachette Book Group
Market Place, Center 53, State Street
Boston, MA 02109, USA

www.jmlanguages.com/languageacts

Contents

Acknowledgements

The Editors wish to express their thanks to several colleagues who have worked in project management and administration roles on *Language Acts and Worldmaking* over the years and whose enthusiasm, expertise, hard work and support made this both a better project and a joy to belong to: Rhosyn Tuta, Hannah Tattersall, Emily O'Connor, Beth Martin and Felicity Roberts. We would also like to acknowledge the collaboration and valuable early research work of Dr Alice Hazard.

They also extend their most grateful thanks to the team at John Murray Learning; Alison Sharpe for her work on developing this new series and for her editorial supervision; Helen Rogers, Chloe West and Emma Green, who, in their various roles, keep the project on track; and most of all Sarah Cole who believed in our work right from the beginning and who continues to champion it in so many different ways. Our first volume, *Language Debates*, and this second volume, *Language Acts and Worldmaking*, are indebted to her vision and that of the team around her.

Chapter 1

The authors would like to acknowledge the contributions of Dr Llüisa Astruc and Dr Matilde Gallardo for their participation in the research design and data collection stages of this study. They are also grateful to all the language teachers who volunteered to take part in this research. Finally, they express their gratitude to Clari Searle for creating the illustrations in this chapter.

Chapter 3

A shorter version of Sophie Steven's piece 'Worldmaking in the imagination' was published as a blog on the *Language Acts and Worldmaking* website under the title 'Worldmaking and Imagination' (June 2020). She is grateful to colleagues from the project for helping her to develop the ideas for that blog during a writing retreat in January 2020 and to her friend and colleague Rosalind Harvey for reading through a draft of the blog and making suggestions before its publication. Her contribution to this volume has been enriched by those opportunities and by the generosity of playwright Raquel Diana in sharing her work.

Chapter 7

The authors would like to express their thanks to colleagues on the *Language Acts and Worldmaking* project, and to the participants and contributors to the workshops, publications and surveys which formed the basis of our research. Our research was immeasurably enriched by conversations in these fora and in wider debates about digital multilingualism in the digital humanities research community. Paul Spence would particularly like to thank Naomi Wells of the AHRC-funded Cross-Language Dynamics: Reshaping Community project for her partnership in developing the wider framework for 'digital modern languages' in which some of the thinking behind this chapter sits.

Copyright Chapter 1 Illustrations

Contributors

Dr Inma Álvarez, The Open University, UK

Professor Catherine Boyle, King's College London, UK

Dr Renata Brandão, University of East London and King's College London, UK

Isabel Cobo Palacios, University of Warwick and The Open University, UK

Dr Rocío Díaz-Bravo, University of Granada, Spain and King's College London, UK

Ella Dunne, King's College London, UK

Dr Mara Fuertes Gutiérrez, The Open University, UK

Isabel García Ortiz, Queen Mary University of London, UK

Professor Emerita Debra Kelly, University of Westminster, London and King's College London, UK

Dr Ana de Medeiros, King's College London, UK

Dr Carlos Montoro, The Open University, UK

Professor Emeritus Christopher Pountain, Queen Mary University of London and Queens' College, Cambridge, UK

Donata Puntil, King's College London, UK

Dr Rachel Scott, Royal Holloway University of London and King's College London, UK

Paul Spence, King's College London, UK

Dr Sophie Stevens, University of East Anglia, UK

Professor Juan Luis Suárez, Western University, Ontario, CA

AbdoolKarim Vakil, King's College London, UK

Mary Ann Vargas, King's College London, UK

Professor Julian Weiss, King's College London, UK

Dr Bozena Wislocka Breit, Polytechnic University of Madrid, Spain

Foreword

Juan Luis Suárez

I got acquainted with the Open World Research Initiative's *Language Acts and Worldmaking* research project five years ago in a small office of an old university (by North American standards) in a small city of Canada.

Since the time I was introduced to the project's title and goals the world has changed dramatically. I still live in that small Canadian city, and I work at that old university, but how I live and work in these spaces has changed dramatically. Since I first began to actively think about the *Language Acts and Worldmaking* project, the COVID-19 pandemic has radically altered the world, and, as a result, the questions I first began to ponder about this project have been brought into sharper focus. The *Language Acts and Worldmaking* project asks us to collectively think about and ask: What does worldmaking mean? Do we, human beings, make worlds? Or, do we make worlds with words, through language acts? Does language help us cope with the world there is? I think these central and fundamental questions that guide this project will become even more relevant, and more important, as we begin the complex process of accounting for what has been lost through this pandemic, and what world, or worlds, we collectively hope to envision, and create, in reaction to these losses, changes and lapses in the worlds we once lived.

From the very beginning of the pandemic, a great number of the issues humankind has faced through the many different languages we speak on planet Earth have emerged from our misunderstanding of the link that connects us to the world via our languages. Whether we think that languages make worlds or that languages support us in coping with the world, it is this link between language and reality, a link almost sacred in a profane world, that the project, and this volume in particular, has been working on.

There is nothing more impactful than our words. Even when we retreat into silence or we contend that our actions speak louder than our words, it is only after we have reconciled our human condition with our language that we act on the world. This is why this link to reality that human language re-creates every single time we speak is so important. And this always happens, as Donald Davidson would say, through our intersubjectivity, by language and interpretation of one another and the world we triangulate with.

And if this is the case, if we become humans as we interact with others and the world through language, then we must ask: How do we create the fabric (social, professional, educational, research-based) of a society in which different forms of intersubjectivity can emerge through the practice of our languages? What type of languages do we need to practise as we embark on triangulating with the world the pandemic has shattered?

The *Language Acts and Worldmaking* research project has deployed effective tools to answer these questions. It built a diverse and multidisciplinary team, it embraced activism, it engaged a wide community of practitioners and researchers, it worked on the analogue and the digital realms, and it developed communities of practice around the many dimensions of language acting: teaching, translating, community making, heritage, geopolitics and research. All of this has been done purposefully in order to bring languages and their generative and intersubjective powers to the centre of the academic research agenda.

As I look back on my first contact with the project, I keep thinking about its timeliness and also about how different things would have been since March 2020 had we cultivated, in our societies and polities, the understanding, practice and reverence of worldmaking that the use of language entails. The project is now transitioning and morphing into a different phase, one in which knowledge mobilization and application of its results will be crucial to achieve a long-lasting impact in our school systems, our university teaching and research missions, and our societal relationship with truth and trust. This volume is just one of the main actions directed towards that impact the project has sought from inception.

In terms of my own research agenda, the *Language Acts and Worldmaking* research project leaves me with a resounding reminder of the signs we need to pay attention to to understand the world we are making as we, hopefully, get out of the pandemic. Those signs we must interrogate are the linguistic signs that our politicians, leaders, institutions and communities have been using to establish our relationship with the world when this relationship was more fragile than ever. For me the message is clear: if you want to understand the world we live in, just listen to the words we use. Because it is in those words and the language acts that they entail that our sacred link to reality is destroyed or forged. Highlighting the need to enhance that sacred link is the ultimate legacy of this research project.

Introduction: The poetics of a project

Catherine Boyle

> HAMM: What's happening?
> CLOV: Something is taking its course. [Pause.]
> HAMM: Clov!
> CLOV: [Impatiently] What is it?
> HAMM: We're not beginning to mean something?
>
> Samuel Beckett, *Endgame*

This story of *Language Acts and Worldmaking* begins with two objects: a notebook and a logo. In preparing this introduction, I sat for a good while with the first notebook I used when we were preparing our bid to the Open World Research Initiative, funded by the UK Arts and Humanities Research Council (AHRC). The notebook is pretty battered and has a yellow stickie on the front cover that was put there by one of our postdoctoral researchers who was interested in the development of our thinking about worldmaking and it says: 'The original Lg Acts notebook – have a look!' The notebook has become an archive of the making of *Language Acts and Worldmaking*, made up of to-do lists, spidergrams of our meetings and of my own thinking, notes on readings, possible partners (every so often it says 'the role of Bob' – it took a while to work that out), AHRC guidance, snippets of suggestion. It is a marvellous, tactile, creative, messy, colourful reminder of how we came together as the *Language Acts and Worldmaking* team. It is a reminder that research projects usually start off as leaps of faith, as the translation of fantasy into something we can do or make, something that our expertise can make work. This then becomes the translation of that conviction into language that is legible to funders and, crucially, to the people we want to engage in our ambition. The amazing thing about reading through this notebook-archive is witnessing how the ideas, goals, objectives, ambitions and desires we formulated then have sustained us throughout these years. The notebook-archive covers from March 2015 to July 2016. Phrases emerge from it that speak of our collective thinking in that past, phrases that have become integral to the poetics of the project since then. Poetics may seem a strange word to use to describe the writing of a research project – it certainly does not figure in proposal-writing training – but it most aptly describes *Language Acts and Worldmaking* as a structure for turning our ideas into action: it speaks of the trails and traces of our research, of the concepts we discussed and returned to and came to understand from our multiple perspectives. It is an invitation into our discourse, our ways of thinking, our desire to move with and through languages and ideas. We share our worldmaking through this poetics.

Every project needs a logo. Every website needs a design. What is a project without business cards, bookmarks, pencils, tote bags? Reluctantly, we were pulled into the need for a 'brand' (not so reluctantly I was drawn into the need for good stationery). More enthusiastically, we wanted to create an image that spoke for us as a way into who we are. We met the company commissioned to do our logo, described the project to them, and a beautifully prepared book of possibilities came back. For us, the logo was about how we narrated the story of our research, about how we presented to the world a project we believed in profoundly. And we are academics: we had to be sure of what it signified beyond our immersion in the project. The most controversial logo was one with random diacritics on the letters. It provoked some consternation. A first reaction was that we are linguists and cannot present to the world an image that suggests that we do not know how to distinguish one accent from another, potentially laying bare our credentials as serious Modern Languages scholars. One extreme reaction from a non-academic passionate linguist was that they would not let their children be taught by anyone capable of choosing that logo.

Our logo considerations were, in fact, discussions about linguistics, language history, translation, teaching. I think back now and see that the discussions emerged, inevitably, from the interests across the research strands of the project, and as we discussed its use across a range of digital media, its readability for our partners and co-researchers and students, we were thinking about the community of co-researchers and partners we had already started to build around our work. We tried to read it – I have a lovely recording of Chris Pountain, the research lead of our Loaded Meanings strand, reading it phonetically – and the joy (maybe also frustration) in playing with the words brought us closer to what this sign said to us. Or rather, what we had asked the designers to return to us in their understanding of our work. The random-diacritic logo is on our webpage, where the accents dance with page changes.

This is not purely anecdotal. Our logo speaks to what *Language Acts and Worldmaking* is all about. That is, that language is not abstract; it is material, ever-changing, historically informed and constructed. Our logo represents some of our key aims for language learning: that it should be playful; that mistake-making is integral, necessary, creative and instructive; that the languages we learn are never static; that language is often unrecognizable, just out of our grasp, and that unattainability forces us to reach for meaning and understanding. As we learn languages, we are surrounded by constant prompts for our imagination, asking us to move with open minds across different realities and experiences.

I look into my notebook-archive and wonder when the concept of 'worldmaking' became so important to us. I look through the many mindmaps and remember sitting through an early-summer night bringing together a first draft of the whole project that bore the title 'Language Acts and Worldmaking'. I recall a sense of academic apprehension at using such loaded terms, without, at that point, proper reference to a theoretical framework. I had been introduced to Nelson Goodman's concept of worldmaking by the brilliant Digital Humanities scholar Willard McCarthy at a workshop for PhD students. Like all rewarding research trails, this one was immediately evocative, and led to ideas, phrases and suggestions that sparked intuitive connections with the work of languages. Goodman, writing in 1978, invites reflection on the move from a 'unique truth and a world fixed and found to a diversity of right and even conflicting versions of the world in the making' (1978: x). 'Worlds,' he says, are made 'from other worlds', from congruences of systems, and his interest was in 'the processes involved in building a world out of others' (Goodman, 1978: 6–7). These are ideas that invite wonderful creative speculation and are in dialogue with our conception of the work languages do in the world. The flip side of the idea of worlds from other worlds is an unwieldy relativism, of which he is aware and against which he warns us: 'while readiness to recognize new alternative worlds may be liberating, and suggestive of new avenues of exploration, a willingness to welcome all worlds builds none [...]. A broad mind is no substitute for hard work' (Goodman, 1978: 21). Our challenge has always been that of building from the suggestion of worldmaking into the complex practicalities that our project has at its heart.

We understand worldmaking in relation to the ways that languages work in the world; there is a concreteness to our approach that leads us beyond Goodman and prompts us constantly to work to reconfigure how we 'report' and 'remake' our research and teaching, to use Goodman's formulations; how we frame and articulate the research and events we carry out in a way that stretches our discipline, reshapes it and informs its transformation. I turn to our mission statement, written as we developed the project:

> Through six interlinking research strands we examine language as a material and historical force which acts as the means by which individuals construct their personal, local, transnational and spiritual identities. This we call 'worldmaking' [...]. Learning a language means understanding the historicity of concepts, beliefs and social practices – how they operate in the past and present. Our research and partnerships demonstrate the indispensable value of language learning for understanding how societies are structured and governed and for empowering culturally aware and self-reflective citizens.

The book you have before you is the result of our work so far. Each of our research strands shares and explores the ways in which we have developed our endeavour from our core principles, in areas of teaching and pedagogy, literary and cultural history, linguistics, Digital Humanities, translation. As we move across time and place through the myriad languages we study and bring into contact with each other, we also move across research, theory and practice. We share our practice and look to the future. We seek to be activists in the call for sustained attention to language learning in its broadest sense. 'Language Teachers as Researchers and Worldmakers', by our Diasporic Identities and the Politics of Language Teaching strand, explores how languages teachers' professional identities are shaped by their experience of diaspora. Carlos Montoro, also of our Diasporic Identities strand, connects the concept of worldmaking with activity theory and proposes ways of reshaping Modern Languages. In 'Translation Acts: the multiple possibilities of the imagination', Translation Acts strand researchers demonstrate how performance and translation are creative ways of engaging learners. 'Language and hospitality in worldmaking', by our Language Transitions strand, reflects on how the notion 'hospitality' works in the world, taking, for example, some of the many community-based projects funded as part of our project. The Travelling Concepts strand's chapter 'Worlding Iberian Studies and language literature' returns to the central goals of the project and reflects on the regeneration and transformation of language learning in terms of a curriculum to re-energize the discipline. 'How old words become new (and then old again), by the Loaded Meanings strand, shares research into 'cultured borrowings', and the chapter focuses on how these loanwords enter a language, some numbering in the most common words in the language. In 'Digital mediations and advanced critical literacies in Modern Languages and Cultures', our Digital Mediations strand surveys frameworks for critical digital pedagogies and explores principles for designing teaching programmes that incorporate Applied- and Modern Languages-driven responses to digital mediation.

The book takes the reader through the ways in which our six research strands have worked to achieve the goal of reconceptualizing our approaches to the discipline. We have done so in communication with each other, aware of each other's thinking, present at events, workshops, seminars, enjoying the constant learning process and using the experience of travelling into disciplinary contact zones that spark both recognition and discovery. I make one last foray into our pre-funding days: to our pitch to the AHRC in December 2015. We talked of our aim to build an environment that will broaden the definition of research to embrace the human potential to think creatively and critically, to produce young people with the capacity to engage fully with an open world. We said that we wanted to redefine our understanding of research itself, not as the exclusive domain of professional academics but, in its broadest and most fundamental sense, as critical thinking and the production of new ideas across a spectrum of possibilities. The community of co-researchers we have gathered around us, and who have been instrumental in shaping our thinking, attest to the power of democratizing approaches to and processes of research. You will find in this book the voices and work of our partners and our co-researchers – schoolchildren, artists, translators, community workers – all of whom have shaped our thinking. Our goal for the future remains the same: to build on what we have done and to work to ensure that what is taught in schools and universities in the discipline of Modern Languages embodies the messy, playful, plurilingual and multilingual reality that surrounds us and through which we shape our worlds, and our worlds shape us. 'Something is taking its course.'

Reference

Goodman, N. (1978) *Ways of Worldmaking*. Indianapolis, IN: Hackett Publishing.

1

Language teachers and researchers as worldmakers

Inma Álvarez, Isabel Cobo Palacios, Mara Fuertes Gutiérrez and Donata Puntil

Overview

Language teachers' professional identities are shaped and enriched by their diasporic journeys. Their teaching trajectories mix their multiple worlds on hand, enabling them to remake their personal and professional selves and making them highly skilled worldmakers. This chapter examines experienced higher education language teachers and researchers' professional journeys from their initial experiences in their home countries to the full development of their careers in the UK. Our work is based on language teachers' profiles captured via a questionnaire and their textual accounts of those journeys using a narrative framework that invited them to engage in backward, inward and outward reflection (Bukor, 2012). The language teachers' stories were analysed using a thematic networks approach (Attride-Stirling, 2001) that revealed both individual and common patterns expressed into two global themes that highlight the significance of diaspora and the teaching environments in the development of their professional identities. To complement this view, drawing on the concept of the rhizome as an epistemological model where data is not linear or hierarchical (Deleuze and Guattari, 1987), the dichotomy between researcher and researched is deconstructed, adopting an autoethnographic perspective represented in four autobiographical vignettes. These accounts constitute the basis to elaborate collaboratively on the common and different ways we are both language teachers/lecturers and researchers.

Introduction

Language has the power to shape how individuals live and make their worlds, as personal, local, transnational and spiritual identities are constructed through language in a process called throughout this book 'worldmaking'. Under this premise, language teachers are active worldmakers who move seamlessly between different linguistic and cultural worlds. From their experiences of diaspora, they are highly skilled at drawing on their own rich linguistic and cultural resources for translating and remaking cultural concepts, but also at reframing their identities. Their essential place in-between cultures has been acknowledged as exposing them to both 'meaning in disarray' and, at the same time, the possibility of finding 'rich meanings and identities in unexpected arrangements of the self' (Ros i Solé, Fenoulhet and Quist, 2020: 398).

This chapter examines experienced UK higher education language teachers' professional diasporic journeys from written narratives and from autobiographical vignettes that capture their/our trajectories from their/our initial experiences in their/our home countries to the full development of their/our careers in the UK. This close look at language teachers provides contextualized experiences of individuals who migrated and shaped their professional identities within a diasporic context, including our own. The group of language teachers described within this chapter includes professionals working in higher education contexts in the UK, both at language centres and in departments. While the intention is to reveal their individual roadmaps from the context of home to their careers overseas and how these trajectories impact on their professional identities, we also identify connecting features that can contribute to a more global understanding of the language teaching force at universities in other countries. Similarly, language teachers working at primary and secondary level or even in non-formal or informal settings may also recognize themselves in the attitudes, values and aspirations that emerge in the tightly interlinked personal and professional diasporic journeys described here.

This research journey started as a study which invited language teachers from London universities to engage in backward, inward and outward reflection (Bukor, 2012), using a narrative frame (Barkhuizen and Wette, 2008), in order to uncover the shaping of their professional selves by considering their personal entry into language teaching, their evolving attitudes as language professionals, and the impact of the wider sociocultural and institutional context. The study, therefore, intended to facilitate a depiction of their own professional portraits from their own perspective and through their own voices, and as such, it allowed for making explicit the articulation of conscious, and some unconscious, aspects of their evolving selves. In analysing the data, we explicitly add our researchers' subjectivities as data to the agency of the researched. Drawing on the concept of the rhizome (Deleuze and Guattari, 1987) as a multidimensional metaphor of subjectivity and on the nomadic positioning of the self (Braidotti, 2011) helps us deconstruct the dichotomy between researcher and researched and reveal our insider positioning as researchers investigating language teachers' professional trajectories. These findings help us introduce ourselves, authors of this chapter, by adopting an autoethnographic perspective as members of the language teaching community, and to elaborate collaboratively on the common and different ways we are both language teachers/lecturers and researchers.

Tracing language teachers' professional trajectories

Language teachers' professional trajectories are often marked by their moves from their homelands which prompt a diasporic thinking of the world (Canagarajah and Silberstein, 2012). This type of thinking brings at the same time loss from what is left behind and opportunities for new meanings and affiliations from their encounter with the new worlds. Braidotti (2011), following Deleuze and Guattari (1987), would define this process as 'deterritorialization', stepping away from a notion of stability and of unity of the self and embracing relationality and uncertainty in the mapping of new territories. In this chapter we refer to language teachers' diasporic identities not as bounded by a linguistic group and a destination but as members of one profession mostly defined by a nomadic movement (Braidotti, 2011). Although we refer to the UK higher education context, different language practitioners in other formal or informal educational settings might identify themselves within this nomadic 'deterritorialization' of the professional self. It is also important to note that by 'nomadic' Braidotti (2011) does not only refer to the physical move between countries, but also to an internal state of mind that embraces movement and fluidity across different territories within the self. For this reason, those language teachers who did not travel across countries in their professional careers might also see themselves represented in that state of mind.

Over time, language teachers develop areas of competence which directly relate to their personal migration history and to which they become accountable. It is, therefore, key to understand how language teachers express those competence areas in both their home and adopted communities so others are able to recognize them, and how their ways to participate in or reject aspects of those communities shape both their personal and professional identities. Our biographies and professional trajectories into becoming language teachers and researchers, despite being different, are similar in their non-linear unfolding and in their entanglement between the personal and the professional. They are embodied and lived professional experiences where the boundaries between present, past and future are blurred, and where the movement between the personal self, the practitioner and the researcher is never at rest. Indeed, as Gallardo has pointed out, 'the personal and the professional selves converge into oneself that results in the becoming of a language teacher' (Gallardo, 2019: 3). 'Becoming' implies movement, not stasis. It entails change, transformation, experimentation, motion, but also chaos and confusion. It is a zigzagging between different physical and symbolic territories, between disciplines and different discourses, between human and other-than-human entities that are unstable, fluid, multiple and unpredictable (Braidotti, 2013). 'Becoming' in this sense, implies the belief in the existence of deep connections between identity making and worldmaking. This is because language teachers' selves are shaped by a multiplicity of worlds, and, at the same time, they can make cultures and worlds. In exercising language teaching and research, we make multilingual worlds. Worlds for ourselves and others. Verbal and written worlds. Real and imagined worlds.

Unravelling our personas

As authors of this chapter, we position ourselves as language academics – both teaching and researching – in higher education who aim to examine the multiplicity of identities we inhabit in our professional lives. As Perez Cavana puts it, these multiple identities 'do not appear as solid coexisting identities, but as a fluid movement, continuously changing according to the context' (Perez Cavana, 2019: 84). We unravel the different personas we embody and live throughout our academic worldmaking journeys and the impact they have on the perception of ourselves as language professionals. While we work with textual articulations of individual stories, we have also included in this chapter multilingual drawings as a visual illustration of teachers' professional identities and as a way of breaking through traditional academic discourses (Richardson and St. Pierre, 2005).

Figure 1. Dual introductions.

In this chapter we attempt to break the tensions between practice and research, between personal and professional, between language and subjectivity. By exploring others' and our own life narratives and embodied experiences, and by reflecting on our research journey, we embrace the notion of multiple and rhizomatic identity (Deleuze and Guattari, 1987) in which personal, professional, material and embodied experiences challenge the linear discourse that traditionally defines the journey into becoming a researcher in education.

We argue that being and becoming a teacher and researcher is a 'guddling' business (from a Scottish term used to describe attempts to catch fish with your bare hands). It is not a linear development from A to B, but rather an embodied, lived and unstable experience that unfolds itself within many territories, across different languages, and that is rooted in personal experiences. Never finished, always in progress. It is an 'assemblage' of doing, being and becoming within a nomadic, inter- and cross-cultural framework of reference. As Haraway suggests, the search for a totalitarian and 'full' objective positioning is an idealistic quest for an unquestionable truth, while 'the knowing self is partial in all its guises, never finished, whole, simply there and original; it is always constructed and stitched together imperfectly, and therefore able to join with another, to see together without claiming to be another' (Haraway, 1988: 586). Multidimensionality and a multiplicity of visions are key aspects of our research, together with the notion of subjectivity as multiple, fluid and heterogeneous. We position ourselves within a posthuman critical discourse that considers language identities as vibrant, embodied, lived and material and that views subjectivity as an act of permanent partiality (Braidotti, 2013; de Freitas and Curinga, 2015; Pennycook, 2016; Ros i Solé, Fenoulhet and Quist, 2020). Our research implies embracing identity complexity, challenging bias assumptions and conceiving data differently as part of the research process. Moreover, we see research as worldmaking, that is, we recognize its power to generate new worlds. In this case, worlds that emerge in narrative discourses which help us articulate an understanding of our experiences and the worlds within which they take place, and potentially change them.

In outlining our journeys, we chose to represent our experiences with some vignettes whose aim is to go beyond the semantic representationality of language and discourse (Leavy, 2009; Rose, 2016). The use of drawings and of different languages within the vignettes has the main purpose of offering a visual and embodied field of representation that highlights the kaleidoscopic movements across different territories and that challenges the supremacy of one language in describing those embodied experiences (Leitch, 2006).

Becoming data

This study is, on the one hand, exploratory, given the unknown nature of the individual diasporic journeys of language teachers in the UK. On the other hand, it is underpinned by an autoethnographic approach (Pensoneau-Conway, Adams and Bolen, 2017) because it exposes our own biographies from a reflective stance towards our language professional journeys. In this section we explain our methodological approach to investigate the professional trajectories of language teachers, including our own.

Backward, inward and outward

Barkhuizen and Wette (2008) have suggested that using narrative inquiries when exploring language teaching experiences has important benefits for both researchers and teachers, compared with other methods of qualitative data collection. In particular, they advise the use of narrative frames as templates containing prompts that 'provide guidance and support in terms of both the structure and content of what is to be written' (Barkhuizen and Wette, 2008: 376) and thus help participants in their reflective and writing processes. In addition, from the researcher's perspective, these frames help control the content to ensure the focus of the story on the expected research aims (Barkhuizen and Wette, 2008). As we were looking for specific aspects of language teachers' trajectories, a narrative frame was chosen as a method of data collection for our study.

The narrative frame we designed for capturing language teachers' trajectories prompted them to reflect on their professional situation and the temporality of their personal experiences as teachers of languages. It was intended to help their reflections in various directions (Bukor, 2012):

Backward – temporal direction in their past and present experiences

Inward – internal conditions of experiences

Outward – external conditions of experiences.

Collaborative autoethnography

Our method of research is also grounded in collaborative autoethnography because it combines being self-focused, context-conscious, researcher-visible and critically dialogic (Chang, Ngunjiri and Hernandez, 2012). This research represents a collaborative effort in analysing and interpreting from inside and outside autobiographical data – from others and ourselves – as well as writing together about lived professional experiences of language teaching and research.

Figure 2. *Tutto si collega a todo lo demás* (Everything connects to everything else).

We are both researchers and researched. We first collected autobiographies from others using a narrative frame, and these findings were the basis for conducting individual self-writing. Becoming data means transgressing traditional perceptions of validity and accountability as key principles of academic research in the social sciences, and embracing instead the unknown, the marginal and the personal as counterparts of being and becoming researchers. Following this approach, we therefore present the self as data and critically interrogate it, with an inward and outward lens, in navigating contexts across cultures. In doing so we expose our researcher identity (Norton and Early, 2011) and acknowledge 'the importance and inevitability of researcher subjectivity influencing their research process and product' (Chang, Ngunjiri and Hernandez, 2012: 25).

Researching from the inside

Our research focuses on higher education language teachers' professional trajectories, and therefore we feel a strong connection with their stories. Such closeness with participants involves a relationship of trust and power. On the one hand, being part of this community of teachers makes trust easier. Transcultural skills and teaching experience helped us create an unthreatening, self-controlled, supportive, polite and cordial interaction with other teachers. On the other hand, we were aware that, as researchers, we can be perceived as having a louder voice and consequently more power over decisions taken. Our research intended to capture their words and ours, taking care to preserve and disseminate their original voices and ours. In this research about others like us, we embraced our quality of insiders. At the same time, we navigated our colleagues' narratives from the outside but with a capacity to dip inside their lived experiences, going from the detached to the attached. When carrying out research we are trained to guard ourselves against bias and to keep an outsider perspective (Miles and Huberman, 1994), but here we argue that our analysis of the professionalization process of language teachers was enhanced precisely because it connected directly to our personal journeys. Our research had the capacity of being empathetic and understanding as well as passionate and vindicating. Thus, we occupied the space between inside and outside this research (Corbin Dwyer and Buckle, 2009).

At the same time, we also examined ourselves, which inevitably happens from the inside. By engaging in self-focused writing about our own professional trajectories we wanted to be able to elucidate, discuss and visually represent collaboratively our processes of being and becoming in languages. In this way, our researching personas are visible and transparent and can be easily linked back to the experiences of those we have studied.

Language teachers' narrations

The 29 stories presented in this section come from very experienced, highly qualified language teachers like us. We are all migrant teachers from all over the world working in higher education institutions in the UK, teaching face to face and at a distance. All of the teachers' voices collected were female, except one. This pool of volunteers reflects the language teacher population in the UK which is dominated by women. This reality might, of course, be different in other educational contexts and could potentially display other movements and practices; for example, in other parts of the world, language teachers might not be mainly women due to migration or tradition.

Teachers completed narrative frames that we analysed following a thematic networks approach. Rather than focusing on the details of the individual experiences, we looked for commonalities in teachers' accounts as well as contrasting views/experiences of teaching and migration. Thematic networks techniques helped us to break up discourses and cover 'explicit rationalizations and their implicit signification' (Attride-Stirling, 2001: 388) which are then represented in an organized hierarchy of themes. The thematic networks approach requires the breakdown of the text in order to come up with a summary of the main themes and help organize the data in a visual form. Thematic networks were constructed by moving from an arrangement of basic themes to organizing themes and finally summarized into two global themes: 1) Diaspora is salient in language teachers' identities; and 2) The environment influences language teaching. Four organizing themes were identified for each global theme, so there is a total of eight organizing themes, with 25 basic themes classified within them. Figures 3 and 4 below represent the complete thematic networks.

Diaspora is salient in language teachers' identities

The global theme of 'Diaspora is salient in language teachers' identities' emerged from four organizing themes around the influence of teachers' countries of origin, their capacity to embrace opportunities beyond the comfort of their national borders, the development of their interculturality, and the evolution of their practices and feelings about the world (Figure 3).

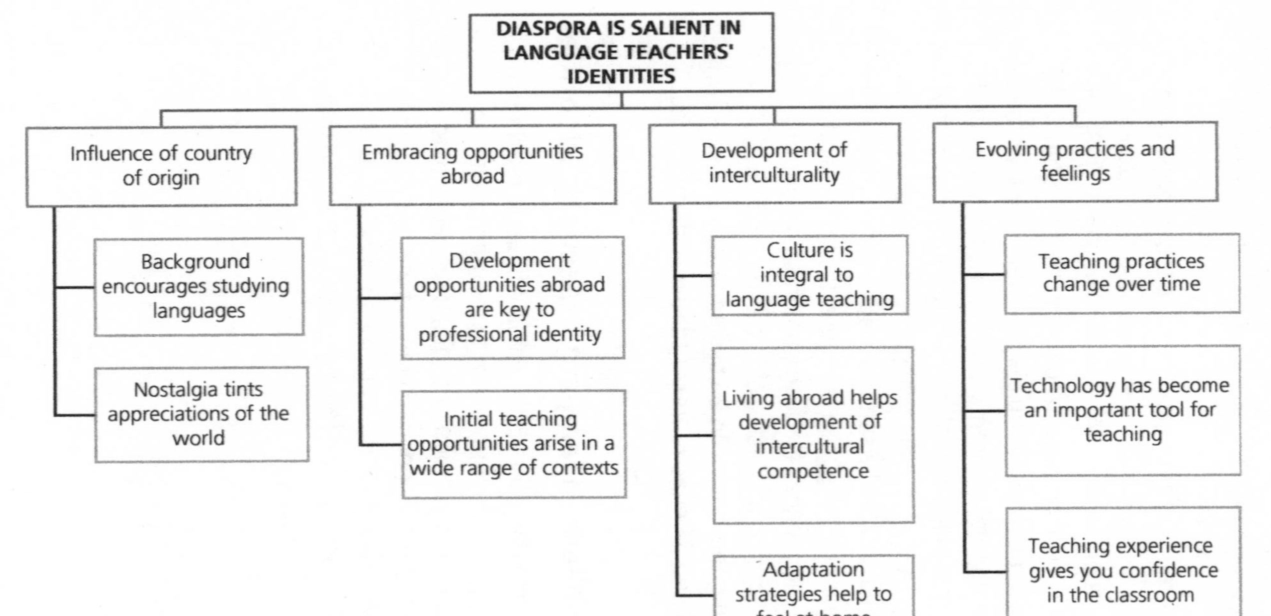

Figure 3. Thematic network for 'Diaspora is salient in language teachers' identities'.

Influence of country of origin

For many teachers, their family background before migration impacted their interest in language learning and teaching and started to shape their professional choices. One teacher expressed it this way: 'Having been raised in a multilingual, multicultural home environment, I was perhaps sensitized to the value and fun of using different languages from a very young age' (Participant 12). These findings coincide with previous research that revealed that for language teachers, 'choosing teaching appeared to be socially driven by family influences and past and present teachers as well as economic factors' (Fajardo Castaneda, 2011: 230). Once teachers start to cross borders, a well-documented sense of loss ignited by nostalgic feelings seems to arise, hence their appreciation of their new world is described by absences from their culture of origin. In their narratives, language teachers declared missing family, friends, lifestyle, food or weather. St. Pierre (1997, 2014) maps in her articles her becoming a researcher in education, and states that the land where you come from always stands as a mental and physical place of belonging. However, our evidence shows that premigration links are not necessarily strong enough to be preserved and, in fact, for two teachers there was no sense of loss at all. Their narratives exposed a unique sense of belonging in their adoptive land.

Embracing opportunities abroad

Language teaching and professional development take place in a variety of contexts, particularly at the early stages of teachers' careers abroad. Institutions seem to have a key role in providing them with relevant training which helps to establish the foundations of their teaching practices and shape their areas of expertise. Teachers expressed with words of enthusiasm their early development in the profession: as one of them put it, 'I gained an expertise in teaching languages and learned a lot from my worldwide learning and teaching experiences, and from my personal and academic educations' (Participant 1).

Not surprisingly, these first teaching experiences are not necessarily linked to higher education. Participants in our study mentioned a range of contexts in which they were exposed to diverse groups of students at the early stages of their teaching careers, including facilitating language lessons in non-accredited and vocational courses, in complementary schools or as volunteers for migrants or asylum seekers.

Development of interculturality

Teachers' narratives showed increasing awareness of the strong connection between languages and cultures, and how this seems to be an important element in their practice. For example, the idea that culture is a key area within language learning appears recurrently, with teachers seeing themselves as cultural mediators breaking stereotypes: 'What I like about teaching languages is that by teaching a language you learn a culture, you meet a new world as well' (Participant 26). This pedagogical approach is an obvious reflection on the impact of intercultural theories erupting in the teaching of Modern Languages in the past few decades, and, in particular, on the importance of supporting learners in their development of intercultural awareness and an intercultural communicative competence (Byram, 1997; Council of Europe, 2020).

The correlation between living abroad and developing an intercultural/transcultural competence was also highlighted and frequently linked to language education:

> Language teaching and learning is about, in our multicultural society, achieving successful communication, keeping an open mind and developing tolerance and respect of others [...]. I live across cultures and living in another country doesn't deprive me of one culture but, on the contrary, it enriches me of another. In our current climate of interconnectedness, it's hard to think still in terms of compartmentalized cultures. There are certainly different attitudes and approaches towards life that I carried with me when I came to the UK and

> **new ones that I have embraced even though they were not embedded in my 'original culture'. However, they are not mutually exclusive and can be reconciled or coexist in a lively yet creative opposition.**
>
> Participant 5

In connection to this, a variety of adaptation strategies, including developing social skills, embracing challenges, exploring the Anglophone cultures and multiculturalism, being empathic and tolerant, engaging with local communities or volunteering, is mentioned in the narratives as actions that have helped teachers to feel at home in the UK, and sometimes developing a new multicultural identity: 'By mixing with a wide range of people of different nationalities, understanding the British way of life with its systems, customs and traditions. I also integrated well into British culture by being open and interested in the running of the country' (Participant 20).

Evolving practices and feelings

Narratives show how teaching practices and feelings evolve as teachers become more experienced practitioners. Initial insecurities mentioned were related to lack of knowledge of the discipline, teaching practices or classroom management: 'At the beginning I felt very insecure, slow and without orientation, now I feel knowledgeable, experienced and better structured' (Participant 29). Continuous professional development and peer-collaboration seem to play an essential role in practitioners' constant modifications of their teaching techniques. It also seems that, as experience is acquired, feelings move away from anxiety and insecurity into a more enjoyable and confident status, reaching a sense of fulfilment. Professional growth seems to bring a more thorough, eclectic and flexible approach to language teaching, increased use of technologies and a better understanding of students' needs: 'Today I try to listen to learners more, try to recreate a student-centred learning environment because I am convinced of the importance to let students express and recreate meaning in their own words' (Participant 17).

The environment influences language teaching

The second global theme also emerged from four organizing themes that highlight language teachers' passion for their discipline which translates in their advocacy, a student-centred approach to their teaching but, at the same time, a great awareness of the contextual factors that make their subject fragile in the UK. The environment plays an important role in the shaping of language teachers' identities (Figure 4), as Barkhuizen (2016) has explained: their identities change 'discursively in social interaction with teacher educators, learners, teachers, administrators, and the wider community, and in material interaction with spaces, places and objects in classrooms, institutions, and online' (Barkhuizen, 2016: 4). Moreover, as Block has indicated, 'the process of becoming a teacher in a cultural setting that is different from the one in which one was educated, is a long and hard road of adaptation and re-making of who one is' (Block, 2015: 22).

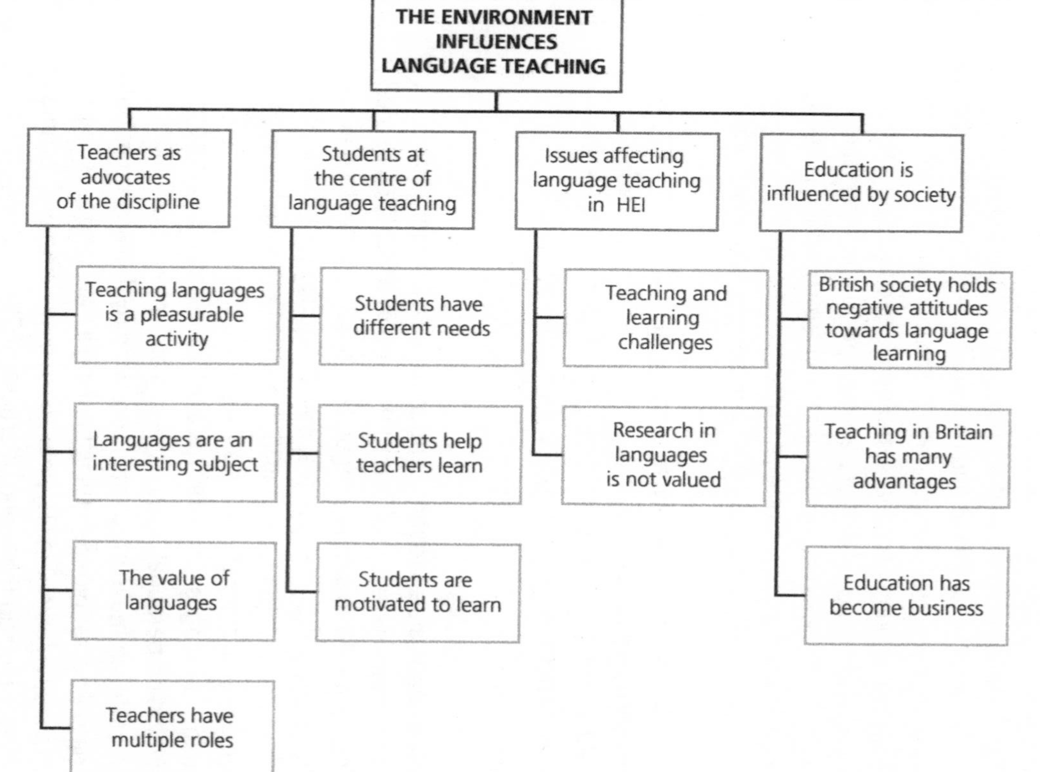

Figure 4. Thematic network for 'The environment influences language teaching'.

Teachers as advocates of the discipline

This organizing theme brings together insights on how teachers understand their discipline. As language education is an applied subject, it has links with several feeder or parent disciplines, such as Pedagogy, Linguistics, Applied Linguistics and Language Studies. Teachers' stories emphasized several pedagogical aspects that make their jobs an enriching and pleasurable activity, among others the different dynamics established with students in the classroom (for example, sharing personal experiences or observing learners' progress) and the possibility of developing and nurturing teachers' creativity. It is interesting to note that language teaching is seen as beneficial not only for students but also for teachers' personal development (mainly through their interactions with the students):

> **'It is also extremely rewarding to be able to create an atmosphere of trust in class which usually leads to teacher and students bonding and sharing personal experiences – enriching for all of us'**
>
> Participant 8

Teachers also value Modern Languages as a subject and mention their interest in different theoretical disciplines related to Linguistics: for example, linguistic typology, genealogical relationships among languages, psycholinguistics, philosophy of language or language acquisition. Other related fields such as cultural or literary studies also appeal to them. In addition, language learning is described as a valuable asset and essential in developing personal, metalinguistic and intercultural skills, some of which make students more employable and contribute to create a better world: 'I think learning a new language improve our lives, develop our skills, help us communicate with others and effectively change the world' (Participant 25).

This multiple nature of language teaching as a discipline is mirrored in the teachers' perceptions of their role; they mentioned a variety of tasks and duties conducted as part of their job, some of them related to the teaching of linguistic or cultural features and related skills, and others linked to generic teaching duties such as giving feedback or managing students' expectations and mixed-abilities classrooms. Teachers often position themselves as cultural mediators and facilitators who share their knowledge with their students and support them in approaching and mastering new languages and cultures: 'Activities are put in place to allow them to realize that everyone has different objectives, preferences and ways of learning. It reduces the potential of a student to feel alienated later on in class if/when they feel that they don't get what they want' (Participant 21).

Students at the centre of language teaching

Teachers' interaction with students has been suggested as an additional factor with an impact on their professional identities (Wilkins et al., 2011). Teachers' narratives frequently mentioned the importance of interaction in the classroom and the need to create a motivating learning environment and a flexible curriculum for students who might have different needs. More importantly, teachers feel they learn from their students, too, showing a positive and enriching teacher–student relationship, again with advantages for teachers as well: 'What I like about teaching languages is to learn about new languages and cultures when there are students from different nationalities' (Participant 11).

In connection to this, teachers seem to be aware of the main issues that students need to overcome in their learning (lack of time, lack of realistic goals, etc.). However, they believe students are usually quite motivated to learn, making teachers feel valued: 'They loved my languages and cultures (both Catalan and Spanish) and that made me feel very special and value what I do even more [...] [The way] students engage with teachers here in the UK is very rewarding' (Participant 3).

Issues affecting language teaching in higher education institutions

Teachers' accounts also mentioned difficulties attached to teaching and research. On the one hand, teachers problematized their teaching conditions such as casualization, lack of job–life balance due to problematic timetables and too many administrative duties. Other issues were specific to how higher education institutions organize and deliver their provision and programmes of study, which on some occasions does not concur with what teachers feel is needed to achieve a certain degree of language proficiency. Many teachers commented on how there seems to be too much focus on assignments, institutional targets or student satisfaction. Something quite specific to the UK that is also reported as unhelpful is the distinction between 'language' and 'content' modules, that is, modules that deal with Cultural Studies, Literature, Politics, History and other area studies linked to the target language countries against modules that teach language skills: 'The distinction between language and content modules seems quite inappropriate to me, as languages also have a content (for example, phonetics, grammar, lexis, etc.)' (Participant 11).

On the other hand, a second area of concern expressed in the narratives has to do with research in languages not being valued. In fact, this has partly to do with the distinction between language and content modules, thus quite specific to how language teaching in higher education in the UK is organized, which might not apply to other national contexts: 'Today I find that researching language can be just as stimulating as researching literature; before I gave that privilege just to Literary Studies and its abstractions [...].
I don't like, either, the feeling of superiority of some colleagues who are lecturers and who teach content subjects (different from us teaching fellows who teach language)' (Participant 15).

Education is influenced by society

Teachers' reflective narratives made reference to the negative attitudes towards language learning in UK society, and expressed surprise at that fact considering its multilingual and multicultural nature: 'I don't like that there is currently – in general – a negative attitude towards learning foreign languages' (Participant 27). Among the reasons quoted is that only a minority seems to enjoy language learning, whereas most of the population sees neither language learning as an academic subject nor its intrinsic value. In connection to this, a large number of teachers feel language learning has no prestige, which also has an impact on how the profession and professionals are perceived and considered. Interestingly, some teachers see primary and secondary school curriculum and attitudes towards language learning as part of the problem, reflected as well in the little competence that pupils achieve in the target language after years of study.

Despite these issues, teaching in the UK seems to have many advantages, too, according to the narratives. Many of them are related to the environment: teachers enjoy working in a stimulating multilingual and multicultural context, as part of a team and in well-organized, tolerant and transparent higher education institutions that respond to challenges appropriately in a very practical way. Participants also praised the lack of nepotism in UK universities, where the most suitable candidate gets the job.

A final basic theme found in the narratives has to do with a wider issue related to higher education institutions being under pressure to be more efficient, especially after the 2008 economic crisis, resulting in universities starting to adopt policies and processes traditionally reserved for companies, not educational institutions. This modus operandi is common in US universities, and some institutions from other countries are mimicking it, too (Ginsberg, 2011). In the UK, in particular, this tendency has become even more apparent after the tuition fees increased substantially in the academic year 2012–13, following the recommendations of the *Independent Review of Higher Education Funding and Student Finance* (also known as the *Browne Review*, cf. Browne et al., 2010). As a consequence, teachers find it frustrating having to treat students as clients.

Being and becoming language teachers and researchers

This section aims to expand the previous study by examining another aspect of language teachers' professional self: the development of their researcher identity. While the above study on language teachers' professional identities investigated their teaching trajectories, here we expand this knowledge by discussing the becoming of professional researchers through self-narrative writings.

Figure 5. Multiple beings.

Our research as part of the *Language Acts and Worldmaking* project suggested that it is common for language teachers and lecturers to face serious practical constraints when wanting to do research, even informal research, although many would be interested. This has also been acknowledged elsewhere: for instance, a study conducted in 2015 by Rontu and Tuomi, including responses from 129 Finnish higher education language teachers, indicated that the majority of these teachers wish to engage in research activities and would like these to become part of their work.

Diasporic identities

As in the narratives examined, the following self-writing pieces expose the stages within our professional trajectories which are parallel, rhizomatic and never completed movements between the personal and the professional. Our stories disclose the diasporic nature of, and environmental influences on, the processes of professional identity formation as shown in the findings of our study. It becomes apparent that the diasporic multifaceted nature of our professional identities is shaped by two events: moving countries and working for different institutions. Our autobiographical trajectories expose not only our physical journeys but also the processes of becoming teachers and researchers. Therefore, they relate to geographical displacements as well as the multiplicity of our identities. As previously mentioned, Braidotti (2011) expanded the concept of 'deterritorialization' to describe a move away from the centre, from the familiar, towards the marginal, the minor, the unsettled. A move that creates instability but also generates empowerment and transformation. A diversification of perspectives forms the basis for a deconstruction of the multiplicity of visions involved in ourselves. We also refer to non-human relationships that contribute to the shaping of our personal and professional identities; by non-human, we refer to the intersubjective contact and relationality (Barad, 2007) with objects, places, stories, artefacts, experiences that affected our being language practitioners and researchers. We do not claim a universal truth in the experiences outlined in the following individual stories, although readers of this chapter might find some commonalities with their own professional trajectories.

Donata

Figure 6. Donata.

My journey as a language teacher started more or less 40 years ago, when I was in primary school and I was obsessed with learning English and teaching English to my dolls, to my schoolmates and to members of my family. I carried on with that obsession later on in my life, and teaching became my profession. I have taught in different parts of the world to students of all ages, nationalities, genders and social backgrounds, and I still consider teaching languages my obsession. Instinctively, when I started this journey as a game in primary school, I was using objects, clothes, drawings, food, colours, images and other material artefacts that would evoke the idea of 'otherness' and of 'difference'. I later on developed this passion for using material objects to teach languages into a method, aligning my teaching philosophy to the communicative and task-based approach and to a holistic and sensory perception of languages as vibrant and lived entities, rather than structural lists of words and verbs. In my teaching approach, even when I was a child, I always aimed to make my students feel at home while studying a foreign language and embracing with joy and curiosity their new emerging self as a language learner. I always contested the notion of 'foreignness' attached to the study of languages, and I underlined it in everything I did in my professional career both with students and with trainee teachers. I consider language learners as translators who are inhabiting different territories at the same time and navigate across different linguistic landscapes, different semantic points of references, and different perceptions of themselves while encountering new texts.

Becoming minor (Braidotti, 2011) and making of my marginality a point of force and of empowerment has been my professional trait, my learning and teaching philosophy that found its ground also in my lived experience as a researcher. I officially started my career as a researcher in language education in 2017 when I began a Doctorate in Education (EdD). But I could say that, as in my narrative as a language teacher, becoming a researcher is something that started unofficially much earlier. While engaging with the data collection and the writing process for my thesis, I progressively came to realize that the engagement with my current research began before it officially began, as much research does, and that the investigation into language teachers' narratives is an act of research within myself. I grew up in a small village in the Italian Dolomites on the border with Austria and Slovenia. A place where multilingualism and cross-cultural contamination were/

are the norm and where I took for granted that identity is multiple and heterogeneous. A beautiful place, but a marginal place, on the borders and out of the centre. Despite having had a very happy childhood, I always wanted to escape from that place in order to explore the world and to become 'different' from its inhabitants. But I realized I always go back to that space, also in my journey as a researcher, as Elizabeth St. Pierre beautifully puts it: 'I have learned that I am much more attached to the place itself, to the land, which I now understand will always serve as the literal ground of my consciousness, the mental and physical map against which all other places collide' (St. Pierre, 1997: 366).

It is the marginality of that place I choose to embrace and that represents my standing point of academic investigation. Aligning my thinking with Deleuze and Guattari's (1987), with Braidotti's (2011, 2013) and with Barad's (2007) conceptions of becoming-marginal, becoming-woman, becoming-molecular, I embrace a decentration of the subject and of academic practice towards interactions, relationalities and mapping as guiding principles in my research. I grounded my thesis within posthuman and post-qualitative ontological, epistemological and methodological paradigms and I deliberately employed different words to describe data, participants and findings. Based on Donna Haraway's seminal article (1988), I define data as 'situated stories'. Autobiographical narratives have been assembled, mapped, discussed and analysed in an ongoing process that resembles the co-writing of this book chapter in which notions of hierarchical positioning and authorship are questioned and unsettled. The participation into my research project has been very active and embodied; participants' stories are entangled with my own personal and professional situated narrative and the findings are defined as a multi-layered 'assemblage', as a meaning-making process of collaboration and co-construction.

New materialism (Bennett, 2010) played an important role in my research, as well as in my teaching practice, acted out in the use of artefacts and personal objects as part of the self-narratives within my research project. The embodied materiality of objects allowed space for affective encounters and for lived experiences to emerge within the playfulness of the research spirit. This paved the way for the multidimensionality of the self to be emotionally displayed and shared among participants, blurring the dichotomy between researcher and researched and creating an entanglement, an 'assemblage' in Deleuzian terms, of lived experiences. In this process, I, as a researcher, have been deeply affected by the power of the shared emotions and stories, by the creative space in-between myself and participants, by the co-construction of knowledge and by the new emotional becoming it represents, which is not only academic endeavour.

Inma

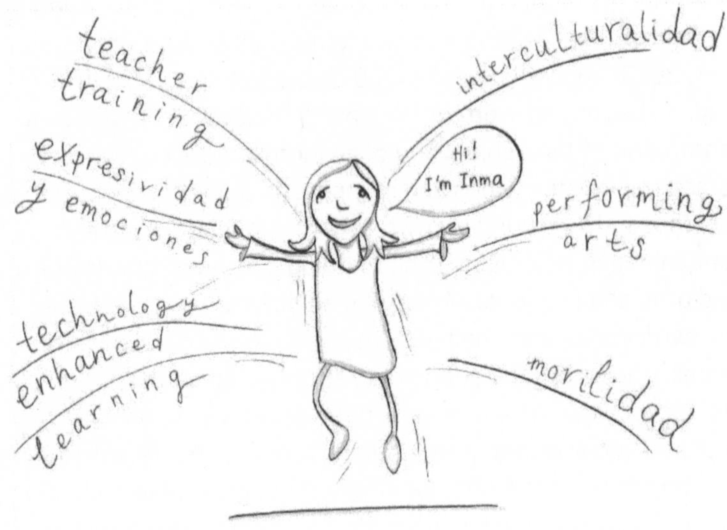

Figure 7. Inma.

When I was in school, English had become the compulsory foreign language in the primary and secondary curriculum. At university, I continued studying English, but I also needed French and German to be able to read philosophy in the original languages. Studying languages felt like very hard work, but there was something about comparing how they work that I found fascinating. I became a researcher immediately after I finished my undergraduate degree in Madrid, Spain. I had specialized in

Aesthetics and wanted to study the challenges of transmitting dance knowledge. I was interested in understanding how dance was documented and learned, and the implications of different historical methods for our capacity to reproduce and appreciate dance works. So, research came first for me, then teaching.

After my first year of my doctoral studies I was fortunate to find a job at the University of Michigan in the USA where I had access to a vast specialist library and wonderful academics and doctoral researchers. Crossing the Atlantic to take on a language teaching post was life-transforming at a personal and professional level. I was trained in situ, with many other teaching assistants from around the world, on how to teach American students, intercultural communication and language teaching methodologies. I was naive but very enthusiastic, and learners seemed to enjoy my lessons. The start of my professional career felt, however, in-between two distant worlds: my research interest in dance and my teaching responsibilities in languages. Tremendously inspirational at the time was a German colleague who invited me to be a participant observer in her classes where she was producing very successfully theatre plays with learners of German. She helped me see how my background in the performing arts could be relevant for the teaching of languages. With that in mind, I experimented with drama activities that aimed at developing learners' expressivity and emotion in the target language. Through this experimentation I realized that speaking expressively and with a range of emotions plays an important role in understanding, transmitting meaning and embodying language. Most importantly, the key to true transformation seemed to be in movement. I also noticed that these activities were producing high levels of enjoyment and satisfaction among learners. My sessions included exercises to warm up their voices, improvisation techniques to remove focus on mistakes, and movement exercises to help students breathe and relax their bodies. Later I learned that research had found that drama techniques are particularly effective and highly motivational in language education (e.g. Aita, 2010; Bernal, 2007; Department of Education, 2010).

After various language teaching jobs in different locations, I settled in England, and inevitably, I felt compelled to do research on language education. An emerging area at the time was the introduction of interculturality in the languages curriculum. Already sensitized to the challenges of working across cultures, I felt attracted to the theorization and implementation of a cultural dimension in language education that was premised on principles of social equality and justice. Intercultural competence manages individuals' perceptions, beliefs and attitudes towards culturally different others. I theorized and tested some ideas about how to develop such competence, and in particular how to deliver it at a distance. My research in this area also led to my involvement in various projects that would transform my pedagogical approaches to teachers and learners of languages. For instance, in the Lifelong Learning European-funded project *Performing Languages* we aimed at exploring the connections between drama, language learning, intercultural understanding and European identity. The focus was on enhancing language teachers' awareness of how all these aspects interrelate in the languages curriculum and the kind of pedagogical innovations these connections could bring about.

Isabel

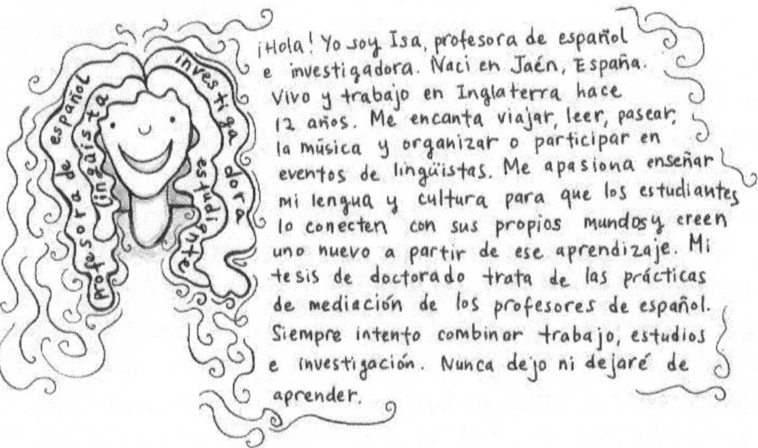

Figure 8. Isabel.

My journey as a language student, since I started my degree at university, has always been hand in hand with my journey as a teacher and, subsequently, as a researcher. The fundamental characteristic of my professional career has been its non-linearity and a constant refuelling. The first major refuelling station I recall in terms of shaping my language professional identity was my year abroad. The encounter with such a different world unveiled a stimulating and real way of living. In the process of getting steeped in that foreign community, I developed a sense of mediation, bridging and creating connections among the languages and cultures I encountered by learning about them and being critical in my comparisons. As soon as I finished my degree and PGCE in Spain, which had some other refuelling interruptions that built my curiosity about the world during other study trips, I got my first formal job at my home university to teach English. That shift from being a student to becoming a teacher in the same institution within a short time, and with some of my former lecturers as my students, made me question and accept my identity as a teacher. This first experience as a language teacher in higher education was eye-opening into my first encounter between my student-self and my teacher-self.

Facilitating knowledge through the interpretation of my lived experiences abroad brought students closer to that world they were trying to reach through language learning. When the opportunity to teach abroad arose, I embarked on it and continued my teacher career as a Spanish teacher in the UK. The threads created between my job in Spain and the different positions and institutions I was part of in England made my teacher identity stronger. Not only were parts of my students and teacher identities formed during this stage in my life but also my translingual and transcultural identities shaped themselves as I learned to reflect on my migrant position embedded into a wider scope of a new world. The fact that I was teaching my first language and culture (considering English my second, although they are not always in the same position) turned out to be a key element in configuration of my professional and personal selves. A continuous reflection on my own experiences and being able to make parallels with other cultures led me to explore and engage in further studies throughout my career.

The non-linearity characteristic of my journey is represented in the variety of paths taken on this road during my teaching years, combining student, researcher and teacher identities. A continuation in my teaching practice and my education has always been important to me as I found practice and research fed each other in each step. This is the reason why I did not stop teaching when I was accepted on my PhD course. The balance between a student life and a teaching career seemed natural to me since accumulating experience without further education was in my view not strengthening and fostering the full potential of myself. As Farrell puts it, 'the old cliché "experience is the greatest teacher" may not be as true as we think, for we do not learn as much from experience as we learn from reflecting on that experience' (Farrell, 2006: 77). These stop points to refuel my student self in my path were in fact recharging my teacher profile, keeping my student and researcher selves alive to consolidate my position as a teacher in every step taken. Becoming a language teacher has meant constant thinking and reflection. Reflection occurs when contemplating every input made to language, from my home country, from my community and from my family. I am no longer a passive speaker, but an active thinker who reflects on the use of language within its culture in ways that can be presented to my students. It is this reflective teaching approach that led me to initiate research work and become a researcher.

Bridging practice and research was my aim when embarking on a PhD as an insider researcher. During the interviews I conducted for my PhD thesis, the first question was asking teacher-participants what their different roles as language teachers were. It is remarkable how only one of them (out of ten, including the pilot answers) commented on her role as a researcher by saying that she felt she needed to be at the vanguard of not only language learning but also as an educator of younger people with all their needs. The rest of the participants focused on their role as psychologist and motivator, in-between languages and cultures, and administrative responsibilities. It is worth considering all these real constraints as limitations to language teachers becoming language researchers.

Mara

Figure 9. Mara.

My journey as a language lecturer and researcher can be described as diasporic and multifaceted. It starts as a language lover: from a very young age, I have been fascinated by languages as communication systems, and how human beings are able to convey their thoughts and express their feelings using a small range of sounds that eventually make meaning. In secondary school I was very inspired and influenced by one of my teachers, Victoria Giralda, who introduced me to key linguistic concepts and ideas, such as Jakobson's functions of language, Saussure's 'langue et parole', or linguistic variety, and encouraged me to think critically about my own language, reflecting, for example, on the tensions between norm and usage affecting Spanish. Loving languages and exploring all these areas made it very easy to choose my degree, Filología Española (Hispanic Studies), which I studied at the Universidad de Valladolid (Spain), choosing Linguistics as my path.

After finishing my degree, I was awarded a scholarship and became a research student at the same institution, where

I completed my doctorate in Spanish Linguistics (with a thesis focused on the Historiography of Linguistics) and started teaching Linguistics to undergraduate students. Later, while holding a postdoctoral research fellowship at the University of Manchester (UK), I became interested in Spanish Language Teaching, and completed several teacher training courses at the Instituto Cervantes in Manchester, where I eventually started teaching Spanish, too. This experience gave me the opportunity to become familiar with the latest methodologies related to language learning and teaching for the first time and, more importantly, to start considering language teaching as a long-term career path. I came back to teaching in academia one year later, when I was offered my first full-time permanent position as a Senior Lecturer in Spanish at Leeds Beckett University (UK). In 2015, I changed institutions and started working as a Lecturer in Spanish at The Open University (UK), where currently I am also the Head of Spanish.

Looking at my teaching experience, I have moved from teaching Linguistics to teaching Spanish, firstly face-to-face, now in an institution specialized in distance learning. With regards to my research interests, they have also been deeply influenced by the different positions that I have held over the years, as I have tried to make them fit into those different positions, evolving from a theoretical research approach to language phenomena to more applied areas and methodologies.

Despite this non-linear path, when reflecting on my professional journey up to the present, I can also identify two areas that have defined and shaped my professional identity over the years: my interest in language teaching and research and the inspiring influence that teachers, mentors, colleagues and 'mi maestro', el Dr. Emilio Ridruejo, have had on me. Moreover, my interest in language teaching and research gives me the strength to overcome obstacles: for example, the frustration that comes with Spanish Language Teaching not being recognized as a valid academic discipline and research field by some sectors in academia (Evans, 1990).

Being in languages

We are constantly reconstructing our professional identity through our teaching and research processes. Our multiple identities align with each other, although sometimes they occupy different orders. Figure 10 represents possible identarian configurations and the mutual impact of teaching and research practices on those potential ways of being in languages. We explain how our trajectories move between them. There are four positions which might include teaching and researching; each stage of these potential configurations varies in terms of commitment to teaching and research activities. Trajectories can flow from any point to any point. It is potentially possible to move between them at any point, but there are some common sequences, as we will see.

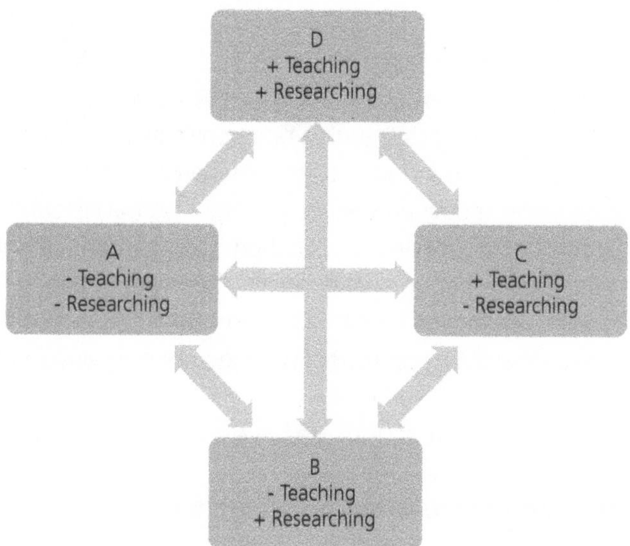

Figure 10. Being in languages.

Position A on the left represents most language students – at school and undergraduate level – who are not teaching or doing research but spending most of their time studying their courses. This learning stage is the preamble to becoming a language professional. Block has suggested that 'the move into any new occupational identity is normally marked by many ups and downs as knowledge acquired both formally and empirically mediates a transition from outsider (non-teacher) to insider (teacher) in the community of practice in question' (Block, 2015: 22). Similarly, it could be argued that the conversion from non-researcher to researcher is influenced by formal and informal learning. Position B reflects the instances where we go further with our development by continuing with postgraduate studies. If a person engages in a Master's or PhD programme, they would become language researchers who might not be teaching at that point but might have done in the past. Others may go straight from learning into teaching without enrolling in postgraduate studies. This would be the case for language practitioners who are teaching but not researching, position C. The last possible position to consider is D, which involves both teaching and researching. We realize that there is no point of return once we embark on research and start reflecting and questioning our actions as practitioners in the classroom. We also argue that this position might be occupied by practitioners who conduct informal research in their teaching that might not be necessarily articulated in a formal research output such as a peer-review publication. Our relationship with our students does change as we look at them as outsiders; we also look at ourselves as partially from the outside. But this cognitive process of critical reflection does not only emanate from our researcher persona. The type of researcher we are is also influenced by the teachers we have become and by previous professional experiences. As teachers, our research choices are permeated by our personal and pedagogic trajectories.

The examination of our autobiographies reveals that two of us – Inma and Mara – started our careers as researchers in academia, and teaching came later, so we move from A to B to D whereas Donata and Isabel went into teaching, then to researching with some teaching, therefore moving from A to C to D (Figures 11–14). Our professional engagement levels with our research and teaching roles are in constant flux between B, C and D. In our investigation we discovered that when the moves between those positions happen across cultures, critical experiences in the new environment add to the reconfigurations of the sense of self:

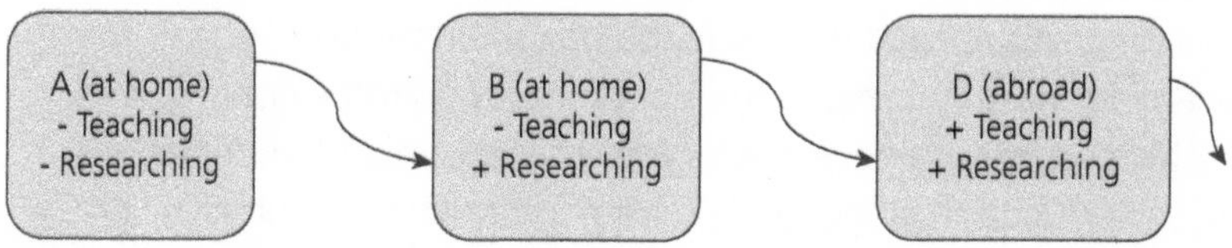

Figure 11. Inma's professional trajectory.

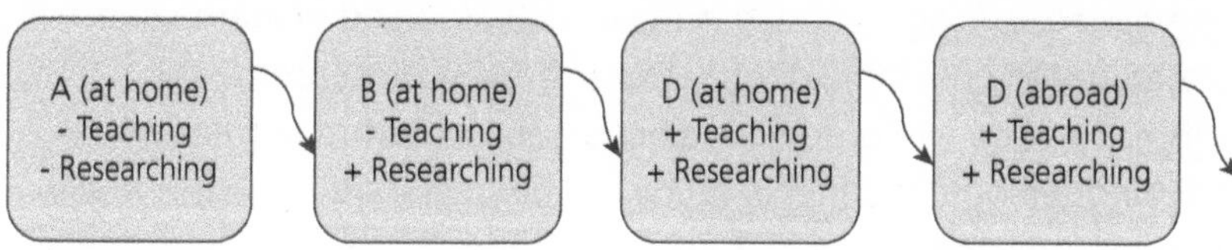

Figure 12. Mara's professional trajectory.

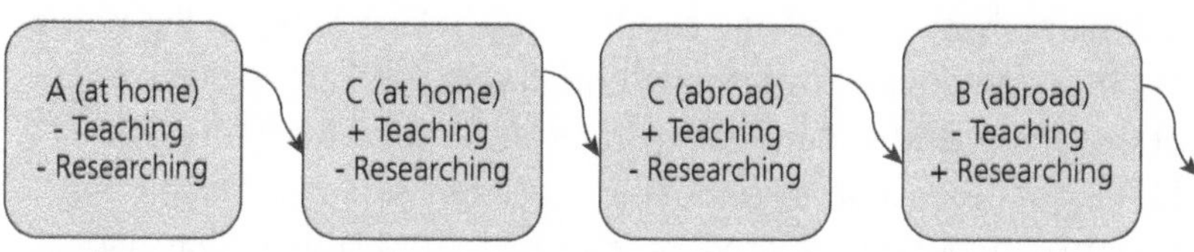

Figure 13. Donata's professional trajectory.

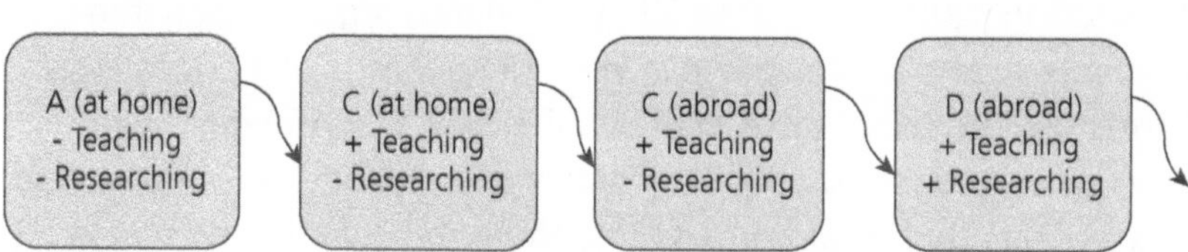

Figure 14. Isabel's professional trajectory.

We suggest that what constitutes our professional identities is not a single one of these embodied positions at any given time but rather the combination of the positions we occupied, those we are experiencing right now and those we will take on in the future.

Conclusions

Language teachers' professional identities are frequently shaped and enriched by their nomadic experiences of diaspora. Their teaching and research trajectories mix their multiple worlds, enabling them to remake their personal and professional selves. In this chapter we have presented the accounts of experienced higher education language teachers' professional journeys from their initial experiences in their home countries to the full development of their careers in the UK. Our study also includes our own autobiographical stories of teaching and research and emphasizes common identity traits marked by career paths crossing national borders. We highlighted that the nomadic trajectories outlined in this study are physical, although it is not always the case.

The professional identities of the language teachers (self-) examined here are defined by the study of languages in the home country, the development of interculturality and cross-cultural pedagogies, and experiencing students' pleasure and curiosity for languages within an educational context which provides opportunity but, at the time, is adverse to research activity. We discussed how the context might be representative of higher education institutions in the UK, but we also argued that some aspects might be recognizable in other countries and educational settings. The experience of becoming data, researching others and writing together about professional trajectories is underpinned by a vitality that is reinforced throughout the chapter and that is closely connected to the concept of worldmaking that initiated this discussion. If we consider worldmaking as both a real and symbolic act grounded in our experiences and acts of language, then language teachers can be considered worldmakers, active agents of transformation through and in language learning, teaching and researching.

References

Aita, S. (2010) 'Performing England: Language and culture in performative praxis', *Research in Drama Education*, 15(3), 361–84.

Attride-Stirling, J. (2001) 'Thematic networks: An analytical tool for qualitative research', *Qualitative Research*, 1(3), 385–405. DOI: 10.1177/146879410100100307.

Barad, K. (2007) *Meeting the Universe Halfway: Quantum Physics and the Entanglement of Matter and Meaning*. London: Duke University Press.

Barkhuizen, G. (2016) *Reflections on Language Teacher Identity Research*. New York: Taylor & Francis.

Barkhuizen, G., and Wette, R. (2008) 'Narrative frames for investigating the experiences of language teachers', *System*, 36, 372–87.

Bennett, J. (2010) *Vibrant Matter: A Political Ecology of Things*. Durham, NC: Duke University Press.

Bernal, P. (2007) 'Acting out: Using drama with English learners', *The English Journal*, 96(3), 26–8.

Block, D. (2015) 'Becoming a language teacher: Constraints and negotiations in the emergence of new identities', *Bellaterra Journal of Teaching and Learning Language and Literature*, 8(3), 9–26.

Braidotti, R. (2011) *Nomadic Theory: The Portable Rosi Braidotti*. New York: Columbia University Press.

Braidotti, R. (2013) *The Posthuman*. Cambridge: Polity Press.

Browne, J. et al. (2010) *Securing a sustainable future for Higher Education: An Independent Review of Higher Education Funding and Student Finance*.
https://assets.publishing.service.gov.uk/government/uploads/system/uploads/attachment_data/file/422565/bis-10-1208-securing-sustainable-higher-education-browne-report.pdf.

Bukor, E. (2012) *Exploring Teacher Identity: Teachers' Transformative Experiences of Re-constructing and Re-connecting Personal and Professional Selves* [thesis]. https://tspace.library.utoronto.ca/handle/1807/31700.

Byram, M. (1997) *Teaching and Assessing Intercultural Communicative Competence.* Clevedon: Multilingual Matters.

Canagarajah, S., and Silberstein, S. (2012) 'Diaspora identities and language', *Journal of Language, Identity and Education,* 11(2), 81–4. DOI: 10.1080/15348458.2012.667296.

Chang, H., Ngunjiri, F. W., and Hernandez, K.-A. C. (2012) *Collaborative Autoethnography.* Walnut Creek, CA: Left Coast Press.

Corbin Dwyer, S., and Buckle, J. L. (2009) 'The space between: On being an insider-outsider in qualitative research', *International Journal of Qualitative Methods,* 54–63.

Council of Europe (2020), *Common European Framework of Reference for Languages: Learning, teaching, assessment. Companion volume.* Strasbourg: Council of Europe Publishing. Available at www.coe.int/lang-cefr

Deleuze, G., and Guattari, F. (1987) *A Thousand Plateaus: Capitalism and Schizophrenia.* Minneapoli, MN: University of Minnesota Press (original work published in 1980).

Department of Education (2010) *Developing Drama in English: A Handbook for English Subject Leaders and Teachers.* London: Crown.

Evans, C. (1990) 'A cultural view of the discipline of modern languages', *European Journal of Education,* 25(3), 273–82.

Fajardo Castaneda, J. A. (2011) *Teacher Identity Construction: Exploring the Nature of Becoming a Primary School Language Teacher* [thesis]. https://core.ac.uk/download/pdf/40013454.pdf.

Farrell, T. S. C. (2006) 'Reflective practice in action: A case study of a writing teacher's reflections on practice', *TESL Canada Journal*, 23(2), 77–90.

Freitas, E. de and Curinga, M. X. (2015) 'New materialist approaches to the study of languages and identity: Assembling the posthuman subject', *Curriculum Inquiry*, 45(3), 249–65.

Gallardo, M. (2019) *Negotiating Identity in Modern Foreign Language Teaching*. Cham: Springer International Publishing AG. https://link.springer.com/book/10.1007%2F978-3-030-27709-3.

Ginsberg, B. (2011) *The Fall of the Faculty: The Rise of the All-Administrative University and Why It Matters*. Oxford: Oxford University Press.

Haraway, D. (1988) 'Situated knowledge: The science questioning in feminism and the privilege of the partial perspective', *Feminist Studies*, 14(3), 575–99.

Leavy, P. (2009) *Method Meets Art: Art-based Research Practice*. New York: The Guilford Press.

Leitch, R. (2006) 'Limitations of language: Developing art-based creative narratives in stories of teachers' identities, teachers and teaching', *Theory and Practice*, 12(5), 549–69.

Miles, M. B., and Huberman, M. (1994) *Qualitative Data Analysis: An Expanded Sourcebook*, 2nd edn. Oaks, CA: Sage Publications.

Norton, B., and Early, M. (2011) 'Researcher identity, narrative inquiry, and language teaching', *Research Tesol Quarterly*, 45(3), 415–39.

Pennycook, A. (2016) *Posthumanist Applied Linguistics*. London: Routledge.

Pensoneau-Conway, S. L., Adams, T. E., and Bolen, D. M. (2017) *Doing Autoethnography*. Rotterdam: Sense Publishers.

Perez Cavana, M. L. (2019) '"When I am teaching German, I put on a persona": Exploring lived experiences of teaching a foreign language', in M. Gallardo (ed.) *Negotiating Identity in Modern Foreign Language Teaching*. London: Palgrave Macmillan, 69–90.

Richardson, L., and St. Pierre, E. A. (2005) 'Writing: A method of inquiry', in N. Denzin and Y. S. Lincoln (eds) *The SAGE Handbook of Qualitative Research*. Thousand Oaks, CA: Sage, 1410–44.

Rontu, H., and Tuomi, U. (2015) 'Language centre teachers as researchers: The case of Finland', *CercleS*, 5(2), 465–80.

Ros i Solé, C., Fenoulhet, J., and Quist, G. (2020) 'Vibrant identities and finding joy in difference', *Language and Intercultural Communication*, 20(5), 397–407.

Rose, G. (2016) *Visual Methodologies: An Introduction to Researching with Visual Materials*. London: Sage Publications.

St. Pierre, E. A. (1997) 'Nomadic inquiry in the smooth spaces of the field: A preface', *Qualitative Studies in Education*, 10(3), 365–83.

Wilkins, C., Busher, H., Kakos, M., Mohamed, C., and Smith, J. (2012) 'Crossing borders: New teachers co-constructing professional identity in performative times', *Professional Development in Education*, 38(1), 65–77. DOI: 10.1080/19415257.2011.587883.

2

Ways of worldmaking in Modern Languages

Carlos Montoro

Overview

This chapter argues that languages, in and of themselves, should be the core of the politics of language teaching and learning, mainly taking the particular case of the UK. Languages, in their dual role as mediators of human activity and objects of study, can be a great force for change, meaning-making and ultimately worldmaking, if and when their remit is clearly defined within a multi-systemic, cultural-historical perspective. The current fragmentation of the Modern Languages discipline has been analysed using an expansive worldmaking framework that can shed some light into current challenges and ways in which they are being tackled, and pave the way towards future transformative interventions based upon an understanding of existing deep-seated, historical contradictions and the co-creation of new tools and concepts to resolve them.

This chapter provides theoretical and practical ways of reflecting on some of the issues affecting Modern Languages, particularly in the UK, from a worldmaking, transformative lens. The concept of worldmaking, based, firstly, on Goodman's (1978) *Ways of Worldmaking*, is presented and then expanded through a cultural-historical activity-theory perspective, this time taking the work of Vygotsky (1987), Leontiev (1978) and Engeström (1987) as points of departure. From a cultural-historical and systemic perspective, a framework is built to understand contextual, relational, mediational, political and communal angles of academic disciplinary practice, the societal need for it, and potential and expected outcomes of engaging with Modern Languages, particularly in higher education in the UK. Special attention is paid to the concept of 'object', that is to say, what 'doing' Modern Languages means and to whom, and its potential split or diffuse nature is discussed. Ways of worldmaking are proposed as threads to pull contradictions in the field in reoriented directions towards a productive future for Modern Languages. The worldmaking concept, central to the project of *Language Acts and Worldmaking*, has been expanded to tackle some of the most pressing disciplinary challenges in Modern Languages. It is argued that the force for change lies in the languages themselves, as they enable the making of new worlds, and worldmaking through languages can be a form of resistance (Phipps and Gonzalez, 2004; see also McLelland, 2017).

Ways of worldmaking

Goodman's (1978) *Ways of Worldmaking* states that there is 'a diversity of right and even conflicting versions of worlds in the making' (Goodman, 1978: x) rather than fixed worlds based on single truths. His pluralistic view argues that worlds can be built in many ways, all 'right' as long as there is congruence with the symbolic system underpinning them. Words and symbols make worlds, because we cannot conceive content without form. Yet, this conception is never free from perception, 'the making is a remaking' as worldmaking 'starts from worlds already on hand' (Goodman, 1978: 6). This process is always systemic and relational as it involves building a world out of other worlds through five ways of worldmaking: (de)composing, weighting, ordering, deleting and adding. This creative worldmaking process is closely linked to knowing and understanding because verbal accounts and experimental tests are ways of both perceiving and creating, since 'perceiving motion [...] often consists in producing it [...], [and] discovering laws involves drafting them' (Goodman, 1978: 21). In other words, 'ways of combining and constructing symbols [...] are among the instruments of worldmaking'

(Goodman, 1978: 56). Worlds are in constant flux while the 'constructional system' (Goodman, 1978: 13) remains stable, and thus acceptable worlds must be the right fit within the conceptual framework rather than 'true' to the world itself. There are no primal or essential worlds to be found as they are built only by us, often following our impulse to 'find what we are prepared to find' (Goodman, 1978: 14).

Occasionally, symbols and words (e.g. a unicorn) represent something that lies within the symbol itself rather than, as is often the case, something that exists externally. This is where a liminal or third space opens up for us to imagine new worlds and see 'what is not before us' (Goodman, 1978: 72). Metaphors, for instance, can then move from symbolic to actual worlds, to express or exemplify new possibilities. Goodman was captivated by the power of symbols, despite their transient and shifting nature, to create meaning for us through perception, even when our perception is incomplete. But he failed to understand how dogmas about 'truth' and 'reality' could prevail given how unreliable symbolization and perception are. He believed that facts are never found but made. For him, what something is matters less than what you make of it. Inevitably, this way of *rendering* (making and presenting) worlds gives rise to conflicting versions and contradictory claims. Goodman's take on conflict is that 'worlds seem to depend upon conflict for their existence' and one needs to peel the onion 'to its empty core' (Goodman, 1978: 118–19) by looking more deeply into conflict. A focus on correlations (e.g. coherence and cohesion) and purpose may reveal that even falsehoods can have a role to play.

Expansive worldmaking

Let us now look at worldmaking from an (cultural-historical) activity-theory perspective (Vygotsky, 1987; Leontiev, 1978; Engeström, 1987) with a focus on the overlaps between the approaches and aspects that can be developed further. The resulting concept of 'expansive worldmaking' denotes its transformative, developmental and expanded nature and is based on five main principles.

First, activity theory mirrors Goodman's systemic, relational and holistic approach and provides categories for each type of element in the system, as described below. Second, activity theory refers to Goodman's pluralistic view as multivoicedness, or heteroglossia (Bakhtin, 1981), which increases when various systems come into contact with each other. Third, activity theory contributes a cultural-historical perspective known as historicity whereby each voice, rule and tool in the system carries with it a cultural-historical background, as does the overall system. This was implicit in the worldmaking assertion that all worlds come from previous worlds, but it needs to be made explicit. Fourthly, Goodman's (1978) account of how change and development transform worlds relies on purpose (what for) as the main driver whereas in activity theory the purpose (known as outcomes) is closely linked to the key concept of object (what and why), as shall be seen below. Finally, Goodman's 'core of the onion', that is, what lies beyond perception, is not empty but populated by 'historically accumulating structural tensions within and between activity systems' (Engeström, 2001: 137), known in activity theory as 'contradictions', which drive change. Unlike what Goodman calls conflicts, contradictions lie at a deeper level and are not directly observable but manifest themselves only through conflicts or 'disturbances', that is, 'deviations from the normal scripted course of events' (Engeström and Sannino, 2011: 372; or what Goodman calls 'symptoms').

Finally, activity theory emphasizes the potential of activity systems for expansive transformation. As systems evolve through time, contradictions may become untenable and individuals may start questioning and deviating from the set rules. This may give rise to new collective collaboration to change and reconceptualize the motive and the object of the activity, giving birth to a new, expansively transformed activity, or, in Goodman's terms, to a new world or version of a world. Both theoretical propositions argue that a 'third space' opens up when you reimagine activity systems or worlds, making it possible for participants to see 'what is not before us' (Goodman, 1978: 68) or in Engeström's terms 'what is not yet there' (Engeström, 2014: xxxiii).

To expand Goodman's worldmaking view further, in activity theory, linguistic and other symbolic signs are also seen as mediators between the inner world of the individual and the outer world of society, and this mediation is regarded as central to any human activity (Vygotsky, 1987; Engeström, 1987). In other words, from both perspectives, we interact with the world through language and symbols rather than doing so directly. As Goodman argues, we cannot have worlds without words, without symbols, and, in activity-theoretical terms, there is no human activity without tools and signs mediating it. But Goodman's emphasis on perception would be seen by Vygotsky as an emphasis on one of the 'natural psychological functions' while Vygotsky's interest was placed on how these develop into 'higher psychological functions', such as solving problems or understanding a map, through social contact and culturally constructed artefacts that act as mediators.

In line with the worldmaking's procedural focus rather than 'finished' and 'fixed' worlds, Vygotsky also concentrated on the 'buds' or 'flowers' of development rather than on the 'fruits', which led him to define the key concept of the 'zone of proximal development', regarded as 'the distance between the actual level of development as determined by independent problem solving and the level of potential development as determined by problem solving under adult guidance or in collaboration with more capable peers' (Vygotsky, 1987: 86). This is a key concept when developing expansive worldmaking, as it has practical applications, for instance in the design and implementation of new curricula in Modern Languages, collectively and co-constructively.

Despite the focus on process, Goodman seems to suggest that worlds are unique and indivisible entities, as is an 'activity system', the 'molar unit of life [...] mediated by psychic reflection, the real function of which is that it orients the subject in the objective world' (Leontiev, 1978: 50), 'a collective systemic formation that has a complex mediational structure' (Engeström, 2008: 26). For activity theory, the scope goes beyond symbolic mediation to include explicit mediation by means of physical tools.

Goodman would probably agree, though he does not make it explicit, that any activity is driven by 'needs' that account for a general 'motivation'. Activities can be performed through different goal-directed 'actions' (Leontiev, 1978: 63). When actions are performed in routine-like, unconscious fashion, they become 'operations'. Actions do not need to be directly related to the pursuit of the general motive, in a similar way as a work of fiction can tackle an issue through another subject matter, as Goodman shows. Actions operate according to chronological, linear and finite 'action time', but 'activity time' is recurrent and cyclic (Engeström, 1999), following a chronotopic (Bakhtin, 1981) or holographic dimension, whereby different temporal and spatial sequences are overlaid. Hence, when Goodman argues that there is a propensity to resolve temporal-spatial disparities, he seems to be referring to actions (such as 'moving' dots) rather than activities, and this is where activity theory exceeds the scope of worldmaking.

Another key consideration involves whether to see worldmaking from an individual, decontextualized perspective or from a collective, socially embedded one. Activity theory sees this process as an agentive and mutually transforming subject-object interaction. 'Agency' is 'the ability and the need to act' (Kaptelinin and Nardi, 2006: 33) typical of human beings, 'his or her capacity to change the world and his or her behaviour' (Engeström and Sannino, 2011: 5) or, as Bourdieu puts it (cited in Phipps and Gonzalez, 2004: 129), 'the embodied and bodily living out of knowledges gained through experience in the world as a learned disposition for action'. Somehow, for Goodman, this ability or capacity seems to be taken for granted, or to be ever present. For activity theory, the individual's 'needs' account for an underlying 'motivation' that determines their 'orientation' to tasks (Leontiev, 1978). Motives are socioculturally determined, and human diversity triggers multiple orientations to tasks, and thus different people approach different tasks differently (see Wertsch, Minick and Arns, 1984), something Goodman did not seem to consider.

What was missing in so-called 'first-generation' activity theory (Engeström, 2001) and in Goodman's account of worldmaking was the collective dimension of human activities or worldmaking. The 'second generation' of the theory provides us with a collective model in the form of the complex structure of the activity (see Figure 1).

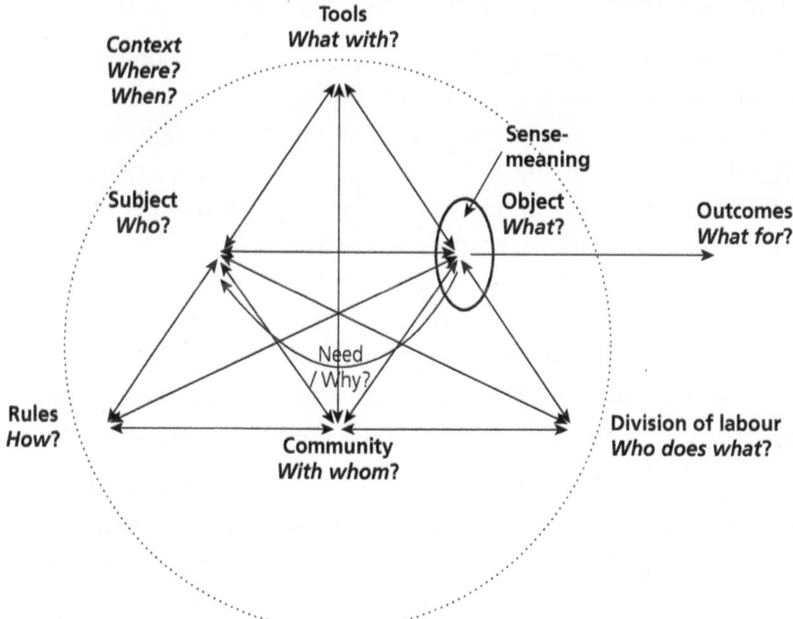

Figure 1. Complex structure of activity (adapted from Engeström, 1987: 78).

The model adds a clear focus to the 'object' that orients the activity, with its potential for imbuing actions with purpose, sense and meaning, but also opens out to ambiguity, interpretation and change. This is where Engeström's view differs from Goodman's, because the object, not the outcomes or function of the activity, is what provides sense-making and use value (intrinsic value) to the activity. In activity theoretical studies involving language learning in higher education (Blin, 2010; Montoro, 2013; Montoro, 2016), the transition from object to outcomes has been seen as problematic, and perhaps this exploration of the concept of worldmaking can contribute to a better understanding of it. In response to a certain need, the 'subject' is the individual or group of people pursuing the object, which is expected to bring about desired 'outcomes'. 'Rules' are implicit and explicit indications of how to carry out the activity. The 'community' consists of people who share to a greater or lesser extent the object of the activity. The 'division of labour' refers to how work is distributed among participants. As seen earlier, 'tools' may be material or mental, objects or signs that physically or symbolically mediate the activity.

'Third generation' activity theory (Engeström, 1987) incorporates what Goodman refers to as worlds clashing by going beyond separate collective activities to analyse how various activity systems interact, including how a current activity and a new, more advanced form of the activity contradict each other, and how some activities are subservient to others. This account of the various generations of activity theory in contrast with worldmaking principles illustrates the importance of transcending individual and even collective dimensions to move into not only systemic but also multisystemic representations of worlds or human activities, such as that of learning and teaching Modern Languages.

Yet, systemic and multisystemic models are but representations of activity systems, not the worlds themselves but versions of worlds, using Goodman's terminology. As such, they are worlds in the making or dynamic activity systems, which can be used as tools of inquiry (De Donato-Rodriguez, 2009). The power of language (and of visual representation) lies in the fact that it is with linguistic and symbolic signs that we can not only represent the world but make it, shape it and remake it – reshape it. We have almost endless potential in our hands and minds to engage in activity-making activities, in expansive worldmaking. For that, Goodman insisted on the need for a frame of reference, a theoretical framework, and it is with this expansive worldmaking framework that a review of the issues in Modern Languages has been conducted.

Understanding Modern Languages

In this section, each of the systemic elements of the Modern Languages activity is analysed from an expansive worldmaking perspective. The assumption is that, collectively, linguists (the subject) engage in teaching and researching language, linguistics and literature (the object) (Pountain, 2017) for the benefit of students who may or may not be specialists (the indirect object). The crisis consists of receding student numbers (i.e. a 'runaway object'), which have resulted in department closures in higher education (i.e. austerity 'rules' regarding resource allocation) and an expansion of the object of study, for instance, by offering more 'open' or *ab initio* modules to attract more students (i.e. a more 'diffuse' object of study). The following sections will take each of the elements of the system in turn to analyse them. The example of the UK is used for comparative purposes, but the 2020 Joint Statement issued by the British Academy, the American Academy of Arts and Sciences, the Australian Academy of the Humanities, the Academy of Social Sciences in Australia and the Royal Society of Canada demonstrates that the same or similar issues regarding languages exist in Anglophone countries globally:

> The challenge of providing education in multiple languages has proven especially complicated in primarily Anglophone nations and even in countries whose English-speakers are co-citizens with important populations speaking other languages. Today, Anglophone communities in particular are not producing enough speakers of languages other than English to meet 21st-century needs, arguing that multilingualism is too difficult to achieve or that English should be treated as a lingua franca [...]. Although our countries have different linguistic communities and official languages, our academies stand together in recognizing a common challenge and the shared need to support the enhancement of language education in schools, colleges and universities, and the workplace [...].
>
> British Academy
> www.thebritishacademy.ac.uk; www.amacad.org

Contextual issues

Modern Languages in the UK, modelled on the Classics, with its emphasis on literature, dates back to eighteenth- and nineteenth-century interest from the wealthy in European art and commerce (Kelly, 2017). The scope has broadened to include politics, popular culture, cultural history, cinema and the visual arts, among other areas, but the European focus has largely remained (Álvarez et al., 2018). National ambivalence in the UK, especially at government level since 2010, about the European Union project has affected the discipline in higher education. Student numbers peaked in the 1990s (under pro-European governments) and have since been in sharp decline.

Reasons for the lack of students transitioning to higher education programmes in Modern Languages (entrants in the UK have more than halved since 2000 – British Academy, 2016) and closures of the relevant departments have dominated disciplinary debates in the recent past. A poor Research Excellence Framework (the REF; an exercise undertaken approximately every five years on behalf of the four UK higher education funding councils to evaluate the quality of research conducted by British higher education institutions) in Modern Languages in 2014 and the decision to invest more heavily in Science, Technology, Engineering and Mathematics (STEM) nationally are blamed for underfunding (Tinsley, 2013).

The high point for languages in the UK was in the late 1980s and 1990s with the introduction of 'languages for all' programmes (McLelland, 2017) at a time when languages were compulsory for all pupils aged 11–16. The removal of compulsory languages in post-14 GCSE (the main qualification taken by 14- to 16-year-olds) in 2004 may have created a break in the transition between educational levels that the introduction of the English Baccalaureate (EBacc) with a compulsory language element may not have managed to bridge sufficiently. There is no unanimity in the UK Modern Languages sector around making languages compulsory again for 14–16 pupils.

Short of closing down departments and programmes, universities have been downscaling or merging language units, often language centres or similar entities, offering more 'open' modules to both linguists and non-linguists and increasing the number of *ab initio* language modules. In other words, to respond to the 'runaway object' issues (i.e. the lack of students) universities are expanding the object of study to include a greater diversity of students, possibly producing a diffuse object in the process.

As most of the 50-plus departments that have closed in the last two decades (Coussins and Harding-Esch, 2018) existed in post-1992 universities (sometimes also referred to as 'new' or 'modern' universities; these are former polytechnic or central institutions in the UK that were given university status through the Further and Higher Education Act 1992 or are institutions that have been granted university status since 1992), accessing research-intensive and Russell Group universities (a self-selected association of 24 public research universities in the UK established in 1994) where the language programmes are still offered has become harder, especially for less privileged students (McLelland, 2017; British Academy, 2016). Four in five Modern Languages students are now in pre-1992 institutions (Tinsley, 2013) and between one in three (Tinsley, 2013) and one in four students (British Academy, 2016) doing Modern Languages at university in the UK come from private schools.

Finally, Modern Languages is a heavily gendered subject (Phipps and Gonzalez, 2004; McLelland, 2017; Tinsley, 2013), and GCSE and A level (the main qualification taken by 16- to 18-year-olds) language exams are perceived by students and schools as harsh, creating further barriers for uptake (severe grading was finally, partly, accepted by Ofqual, the English examination regulator, as an issue and grading standards adjusted in French and German, but not Spanish, in November 2019). Modern Languages is therefore becoming one of the most class- and gender-marked subjects, which adds to the perception that the British are bad at languages and only high achievers can learn them (University of Cambridge, 2015), and a regression to access for the elite prevalent a century ago (McLelland, 2017).

Given the prolonged duration of the crisis, a generation has been 'lost to languages' (British Academy, 2009), making it harder to improve the recruitment of teachers and students, as departments keep closing at an alarming rate (Polisca et al., 2019). Without clarity about the history of Modern Languages, history keeps repeating itself in a circular manner (McLelland, 2017) and old approaches are recycled again and again. To gain some sense of progression and movement, the study of the discipline could be divided into generations, as is common practice in other areas and disciplines (see, for instance, the generations of activity theory described above). This would provide historical perspective and the potential for renewal and rebirth in the form of a new generation that can reinvigorate Modern Languages. Paradoxically, as noted at the beginning of the chapter, the force for change lies in the languages themselves, as they enable the making of new worlds, and worldmaking through languages can be a form of resistance (Phipps and Gonzalez, 2004; see also McLelland, 2017).

Relational issues

Some staff in Modern Languages feel vulnerable because the discipline is undervalued (Worton, 2009). Greater collaboration between units, institutions and disciplines could be beneficial (Worton, 2009; AULC, 2015) but the division of labour poses unique challenges, as working conditions vary significantly between those teaching and researching specialist content, such as literature, and linguistic skills. This 'false dichotomy' (Worton, 2009: 4) seems 'fairly unbridgeable' (Pountain, 2017: 269) and results in a 'split object' of study. The various languages offered (52 at the last count; Polisca et al., 2019) and the interdisciplinary push to open up Modern Languages modules to more *ab initio* and non-specialist students spreads the discipline thinly, creating a more 'diffuse object' of study.

From an activity-theoretical perspective, education is a subject-producing activity (Engeström, 1987), but the challenge and opportunity for Modern Languages is perhaps to raise the disciplinary standard to become an activity-producing activity, developing students as whole social beings who can not only interact with multiple worlds but engage in worldmaking, crossing boundaries and borders in fluid and dynamic encounters, learning in action, as a way of overcoming current limitations. This would set the teacher and the learner in co-learner roles co-creating knowledge, as Phipps and Gonzalez suggest (2004), in a context of crisis that can generate transformative agency in them and change in the system using forces born out of disturbances and contradictions. Yet, this risk-taking approach may not suit an already vulnerable workforce 'with a siege mentality' (Phipps and Gonzalez, 2004: 33).

Mediational issues

From a utilitarian perspective, languages are increasingly instrumentalized, viewed as commodified sets of skills for employability (Phipps and Gonzalez, 2004). This perception of languages has historically (not just recently) assigned an ancillary, 'service' role to them (McLelland, 2017) that could lead to the disappearance of language programmes in the future (Kelly, 2001, cited in Phipps and Gonzalez, 2004), other than as language for specific purposes in combination with disciplines like business. Against this, Modern Languages fights to maintain a status of being a full intellectual discipline (Phipps and Gonzalez, 2004; McLelland, 2017; AULC, 2015).

Uniquely, in Modern Languages, language is both the vehicle for knowledge exchange and the subject matter, which raises questions about whether to teach and read in the original language or in translation. McLelland (2017) sees this combination of mastering a practical skill and theory as a strength with no parallel in any other subject in the humanities. In this sense, the concept of mediation from activity theory could 'breathe life into languages' (Phipps and Gonzalez, 2004). For instance, if we see translation as mediation (Kelly, 2018; Bauckham, 2016), accepting that 'we all live in translated worlds' (Phipps and Gonzalez, 2004: 154), translated texts hold expansive worldmaking potential, at best if parallel translations could be reintroduced (McLelland, 2017). What translation should not be is the assessment method whereby a single, fixed version is correct (Phipps and Gonzalez, 2004; Forsdick, 2018), as this would amount to confusing a tool with the object of study, the means with the end, in an unproductive and inhibiting way.

As for pedagogical methods, student engagement should be active and agentive, less scripted and teacher-led, more fluid and mobile, linking content to life to transform each student as they engage with it (Phipps and Gonzalez, 2004; Ros i Solé, 2016). Language teaching has the potential to transform the discipline if it transcends the 'Cinderella of Modern Languages' status (Phipps, 2016: viii) by moving away from its mainstream communication ideology to a sociocultural and personal approach (Ros i Solé, 2016; Kelly, 2018). The two main challenges are overcoming the pendular movement of recycling old methodologies (e.g. from emphasis on grammar to neglecting it and back) (McLelland, 2017) and contending with the fact that grammar, near-native fluency and accuracy are still regarded as a marker of prestige, and lack thereof is still stigmatized (McLelland, 2017: 124). In line with widespread reviews of assessment methods in higher education, Worton (2009) argues that assessment should be more integrated with teaching and be a part of the learning process. Developing a new pedagogical approach is sometimes presented as a potential solution to tensions in Modern Languages (Coleman, 2001, cited in Phipps and Gonzalez, 2004) and the increasing use of English as 'the language of pedagogy' (Phipps and Gonzalez, 2004: 14) is called into question.

Finally, classroom-ready learning materials seem to be scarce and inconsistent (Dobson, 2018; AULC, 2015; Worton, 2009), creating an urgent need for systematic production and sharing of readily available resources. New media and computer-assisted language learning (CALL) have provided new technological tools, but their impact is hard to determine (McLelland, 2017). The Open University in the UK is an exception in that it is said to be the only institution in the country that is constantly producing new, updated materials (AULC, 2015) and sharing them online. Worton (2009), University of Cambridge (2015) and AULC (2015) suggest that digital technologies can improve the language provision and free up assessment time that lecturers could use to conduct research, which is scarce in the areas of language and language pedagogy, as language teachers are often paid hourly and have little time to spare other than their personal time (AULC, 2015).

Political issues

The various 'rules' applied in the field hold expansive and restricting potential, such as University College London's (UCL) language strategy (supported by Coussins and Harding-Esch, 2018) that imposes a GCSE-level language requirement on all its students to be fulfilled at the start or end of their studies (commended by the British Academy, 2009). Different versions of these requirements have been presented by the Nuffield Foundation (2000), Bone (2008), the British Academy (2011) and HEFCE (2011) but so far do not seem to have gained much traction in the higher education sector. Structural issues plaguing the sector, such as department closures, mergers, curriculum reforms and the collapse of support structures such as the National Centre for Languages (CILT), have been well documented by Phipps and Gonzalez (2004) and Dobson (2018). The net result is the so-called 'languages deficit' in the UK that forces employers to deal only with English-speaking staff and clients or to recruit abroad (almost twice as often as their European counterparts do; Tinsley, 2013).

Perhaps as a result of the scarcity of graduates with languages, these have a greater salary-earning potential than graduates in Maths, English and Physics (British Academy, 2009). The opportunities for those possessing the 'soft' power of languages (University of Cambridge, 2015) are clear in international trade and diplomacy (Worton, 2009; Coussins and Harding-Esch,

2018; Norton, 2018) as well as in defence and security (British Academy, 2013). Paradoxically, this is a message that has not reached a critical mass because there is still a widespread negative belief about the career prospects of language graduates (McLelland, 2017).

The decentralized nature of the education system in the UK complicates evaluation of language policy and advocacy efforts (McLelland, 2017). Advocacy has recently been led by the British Academy, the British Council and the University Council of Modern Languages, along with the Association of University Language Communities and the Association for Language Learning (McLelland, 2017). The UK was involved in the creation of the European Centre for Modern Languages in Graz, Austria, in 1994, but withdrew in 2011. In that same year, the National Languages Strategy for England, launched in 2002 (DfES, 2002), which had introduced the notion of 'Languages for All', ended.

In terms of resource allocation, the British Academy (2009, 2011) states that resources are now tied to student intake and that therefore dwindling student numbers cause programme and department closures. Uptake of language subjects remains low at both primary and secondary levels (Worton, 2009; British Academy, 2011). In contrast, languages in private schools are still in high demand (Worton, 2009), though they account for only 5 per cent of pupils overall (McLelland, 2017). When it comes to assessment, an issue that concerns many is that of 'harsh marking' of GCSE and A level exams for language subjects, with hard-to-predict results.

As for labour issues, Modern Languages departments have been reducing their teaching staff (Worton, 2009) while more of that teaching is being done by PhD students working as postgraduate teaching assistants (PTAs) and through casualization of contracts (see Álvarez et al., 2018; AULC, 2015). In broad terms, funding for languages is problematic because no single government department is responsible for languages (Coussins and Harding-Esch, 2018;

McLelland, 2017), and companies are not yet investing in languages despite their clear need for multilingual employees (Coussins and Harding-Esch, 2018; Norton, 2018; Tinsley, 2013), as they could do through corporate responsibility programmes (Norton, 2018) or tax breaks (Coussins, 2014; Hogan-Brun, 2018), perhaps because they prefer to hire employees who already have languages rather than train them on the job (British Academy, 2016).

Communal issues

In terms of the 'community', in 2010 the Higher Education Academy stopped funding subject area centres, including the Centre for Languages, Linguistics and Area Studies (LLAS), which had to close soon after. Its associated scheme to promote language uptake, Routes into Languages, now operating under the auspices of the University Council of Modern Languages, is also struggling to raise funding for its operation, despite its valuable regional approach to student recruitment (Worton, 2009; DfES, 2007). Generally speaking, Worton (2009) argues that the loss of students has led to a loss as a field, a loss of status and a loss of funding.

Another (false) dichotomy exists between language centres (seen as 'language providers' and offering language courses mainly to students not taking Modern Languages as their degree, also known as Institution-Wide Language Programmes) and Modern Languages departments (perceived as teaching language through 'content', e.g. literature, cultural history, cultural studies) as explored in the previous chapter here (see also Worton, 2009). Language centres keep increasing their student numbers (AULC-UCML, 2018), while Modern Languages departments struggle to recruit (British Academy, 2016). Collaboration between both units takes different forms, but closer collaboration (and even full integration) seems to be increasing (Álvarez et al., 2018; Polisca et al., 2019), for instance by delegating language teaching in language departments to language centre staff who are arguably less expensive to pay, have specialized language training, and are more open to collaboration, innovation and use of technology.

However, Modern Languages departments are concerned that this may lead to loss of income, programme incoherence and student disenfranchisement (Worton, 2009; Álvarez et al., 2018).

As for the all too crucial transition from school to university, Tinsley (2013: 18) clearly shows that an inverse-pyramid shape exists whereby the higher the education level, the more opportunities to study a diverse range of languages there is, even though 80 per cent of the Modern Languages programme offerings focus only on the ten most popular languages (Álvarez et al., 2018). Yet, if we consider where universities are located, Hutchings and Matras (2017) suggest that focusing on local community languages would be a wise strategy as the drop-out rate in community language subjects is nowhere as marked as that of Spanish and French at AS level (an examination at advanced subsidiary level, representing the first component of an A level qualification) and A level, for instance.

Productive issues

The purpose of Modern Languages is seen by some as leading internationalization efforts in higher education (Bone, 2008, cited in Worton, 2009), improving business opportunities (Coussins and Harding-Esch, 2018) and social cohesion (Norton, 2018), the last being a more solid foundation for growth of the discipline than a business focus, in McLelland's (2017) view. A new approach to highlighting the value of languages has been making the case for its cognitive benefits of engaging with other languages (McLelland, 2017, citing Tinsley and Comfort, 2012; Bak, 2018; Norton, 2018; Hogan-Brun, 2018). Alternatively, Hutchings and Matras (2017) present a broad worldmaking approach to overcome national and global tensions.

However, some students have shown that interest in the target culture and countries is their prime motivation rather than improving employment prospects (LSE Language Centre, 2015). This would favour a focus on interculturality, criticality and global citizenship (Phipps and Gonzalez, 2004). From this perspective, 'fluency' understood not in a technical way but as 'living and dwelling' is a more desirable outcome than becoming native speakers (Phipps and Gonzalez, 2004: 117), having instead a 'learned disposition for action' (Phipps and Gonzalez, 2004: 161). Jenkins (2018) even argues that being a native speaker (let alone becoming one) is problematic because they struggle to be understood locally in increasingly superdiverse and translanguaging communities. As Coussins (2014: 1) argues, 'speaking only English is as much of a disadvantage as speaking no English'.

The object of Modern Languages

As discussed earlier, the decrease in student numbers (i.e. a 'runaway object') has led to a more 'diffuse object' of study to attract non-specialists to Modern Languages. This seems to be the primary contradiction in the discipline, as it may have been sacrificing 'use value' (i.e. intrinsic value) to increase its 'exchange value' (i.e. societal value). One could argue that the object of study is diverse and therefore diffuse as a result of the multiple languages involved (52 in higher education; Polisca et al., 2019), far greater in the UK than in non-English-speaking countries where efforts are mainly concentrated on learning English. In contrast, Hutchings and Matras (2017) advocate for the creation of modules and programmes that cut across languages and nation states in multilingual and transnational ways. In turn, Pountain argues that the teaching and learning of a language is a 'non-negotiable core' (2017: 268) of the discipline combined, 'as a minimum requirement' (269), with two other 'Ls' – Linguistics and Literature. Phipps and Gonzalez (2004) propose the concept of 'languaging' to define 'a pursuit of human growth through exchange (...) [and] action in the world' (2004: 14).

Another option seemingly in the agenda of higher education institutions comes in the form of so-called research-led teaching. Worton (2009) argues that this should not consist in simply teaching what you are researching, but that it should go more deeply, including, for instance, student-led research. We could see this movement as a 'reorientation' of the overall activity, potentially turning students into producers of their own object of study, shifting the educational emphasis from being a traditional subject-producing activity to an activity-producing activity. In addition, 'learning' as an 'act of critical appropriation of the world and of ourselves' (Phipps and Gonzalez, 2004: 143) should be at the heart of the discipline, but as 'communal exploration', 'collective inquiry' (Phipps and Gonzalez, 2004: 145–6) rather than individually or unidirectionally, not so much with a focus on individual identity (Ros i Solé, 2016) but in spaces where 'each person in each classroom experiences what it is to be both teacher and learner' (Phipps and Gonzalez, 2004: 168). Recognizing the value of the community of learners and the multivoicedness and pluralism intrinsically present in every classroom (even more so in language classrooms where foreigners exceed the already high national average; Worton, 2009; HEFCE, 2011) would shift texts from the position of object of study to that of learning tools creating space for a relational approach that values intercultural, interpersonal meaning-making exchanges.

Given the diversity of views, an expansive worldmaking approach represents a dynamic, systemic and flexible way of accommodating all languages, traditions and objects of study. With this approach, Modern Languages can adapt to changing times and allow flexible configurations and various entry points for an increasingly diverse body of students. Embracing the inevitability of an expanding object of study may be the only way of bidding farewell to the equally inevitable runaway object, the specialist students, moving away from diffuse or split perceptions of the object of study to the constant creation and re-creation of a new integrated, diverse and inclusive expanding object.

Conclusion: ways of worldmaking in Modern Languages

In his final remarks, Worton's (2009) conclusions seem to pivot around a general theme of collaboration, that is, collaboration between the programmes, languages, institutions and external agencies. Even though the report contains practical recommendations on how to move this integrative agenda forward, as Kelly argues (Phipps and Gonzalez, 2004: xi), 'however versatile individuals might be, they need the resources of shared reflection and collective imagination to respond creatively to new and daunting demands'. Precisely the point here is what these resources might be.

I suggest that expansive worldmaking provides a framework to, for instance, effect transformative curricular change. Using a Change Laboratory-inspired (Engeström et al., 1996; Virkkunen and Newnham, 2013) intervention method (Worldmaking Labs), staff, students and wider community members could co-construct curricula (from shorter or longer sessions or modules to entire programmes) following an expansive, diverse, inclusive, unifying and boundary-crossing approach. From conception to teaching, delivery and assessment, expansive worldmaking principles can be applied to model systems in action, by doing. Centrally, this would involve joint efforts between Modern Languages departments and language centres, and collaboration with other departments and institutions, external and multicultural agents, to the extent possible depending on the phase of development of the institution. By embedding as an additional layer a formative and transformative intervention method in curriculum design, an area academics still exert control over, following this expansive worldmaking approach, collaboration might become a reality as it would be born out of disciplinary, collective practice.

References

Álvarez, I., Montoro, C., Campbell, C., and Polisca, E. (2018) *Language Provision in UK MFL Departments 2018 Survey.* Available from: https://ucml.ac.uk/2018/11/02/new-report-on-language-provision-in-modern-foreign-languages-departments-2018/ (Accessed: 24 July 2021).

AULC (2015) MFL report to the Higher Education Academy *Teaching and Learning Issues in the Disciplines* project.

AULC-UCML (2018) *AULC-UCML survey of Institution-Wide Language Provision in universities in the UK: 2017–2018.* Available from: https://university-council-modern-languages.org/wp-content/uploads/2019/08/ad65a-aulc_ucml_2017-2018.pdf (Accessed: 24 July 2021).

Bak, T. (2018) Can speaking multiple languages keep you sharp?' Available from: https://www.ageuk.org.uk/information-advice/health-wellbeing/mind-body/staying-sharp/thinking-skills-change-with-age/cognitive-reserve/# (Accessed: 24 July 2021).

Bakhtin, M. M. (1981) *The Dialogic Imagination: Four Essays.* Austin, TX: University of Texas Press.

Bauckham, I. (2016) *Modern Foreign Languages Pedagogy Review. A Review of Modern Foreign Languages Teaching Practice in Key Stage 3 and Key Stage* 4. Available from: https://tscouncil.org.uk/modern-foreign-languages-report/ (Accessed: 24 July 2021).

Blin, F. (2010) 'Designing cybertasks for learner autonomy: Towards an activity theoretical pedagogical model', In M. J. Luzón, M. N. Ruiz-Madrid, and M. L. Villanueva (eds) *Digital Genres, New Literacies, and Autonomy in Language Learning.* Newcastle upon Tyne: Cambridge Scholars Publishing, pp. 175–96.

Bone, D. (2008) *Internationalisation of HE: A Ten-Year View.* London, UK: Department for Innovation, Universities and Skills (DIUS).

Braidotti, R. (1994) *Nomadic Subjects: Embodiment and Sexual Difference in Contemporary Feminist Theory.* New York: Columbia University Press.

British Academy (2009) *Language Matters.* Available from: https://www.thebritishacademy.ac.uk/sites/default/files/LanguageMatters2_0.pdf (Accessed: 24 July 2021).

British Academy (2011) *Language Matters More and More.* Available from: https://www.thebritishacademy.ac.uk/sites/default/files/LMmm%20-%20A%20Position%20Statement.pdf (Accessed: 24 July 2021).

British Academy (2013) *Languages: The State of the Nation.* Available from: https://www.thebritishacademy.ac.uk/sites/default/files/State_of_the_Nation_REPORT_WEB.pdf

British Academy (2016) *Born Global: Implications for Higher Education.* Available from: https://www.thebritishacademy.ac.uk/sites/default/files/Born%20Global%20-%20Implications%20for%20Higher%20Education.pdf (Accessed: 24 July 2021).

British Chambers of Commerce (2012) *Exporting Is Good for Britain – Skills, 2012.* Available from: http://www.goingglobalskills.com/pdfs/skills.pdf (Accessed: 24 July 2021).

Coleman, J. (2001) 'What is residence abroad for? Intercultural competence and the linguistic, cultural academic, personal and professional objectives of student residence abroad', in R. Di Napoli, L. Polezzi, and A. King (eds) *Fuzzy Boundaries? Reflections on Modern Languages and the Humanities.* London: CILT, pp. 121–40.

Coussins, J. (2014) *Manifesto for Languages.* Available from: https://www.britishcouncil.org/sites/default/files/manifesto_for_languages.pdf (Accessed: 24 July 2021).

Coussins, J., and Harding-Esch, P. (2018) 'Introduction', in M. Kelly (ed.) *Languages after Brexit: How the UK Speaks to the World.* Cham, Switzerland: Palgrave Macmillan, pp. 1–9.

De Donato-Rodriguez, X. (2009) 'Construction and Worldmaking: The significance of Nelson Goodman's pluralism'. *Theoria,* 65, 213–25.

DfES (2002) *Languages for All: Languages for Life. A Strategy for England.* Available from: https://www.languagescompany.com/wp-content/uploads/the-national-languages-strategy-for-england-1.pdf (Accessed: 24 July 2021).

DfES (2007) *Languages Review.* Available from: https://webarchive.nationalarchives.gov.uk/20070706163848/http://www.teachernet.gov.uk/_doc/11124/LanguageReview.pdf (Accessed: 24 July 2021).

Dobson, A. (2018) 'Towards "MFL for all" in England: A historical perspective', *The Language Learning Journal*, 46(1), 71–85. doi: 10.1080/09571736.2017.1382058

Engeström, Y. (1987) *Learning by Expanding: An Activity-Theoretical Approach to Developmental Research*. Helsinki: Orienta-Konsultit.

Engeström, Y. (1999) 'Activity Theory and transformation', in Engeström, Y. Miettinen, R., and Punamäki, R. T. L. (eds.), *Perspectives on Activity Theory*, Cambridge: Cambridge University Press, pp. 19–38

Engeström, Y. (2001) 'Expansive learning at work: Toward an activity theoretical reconceptualization', *Journal of Education and Work*, 14(1), 133–56.

Engeström, Y. (2008) *From Teams to Knots: Activity Theoretical Studies of Collaboration and Learning at Work*. Cambridge: Cambridge University Press.

Engeström, Y. (2014) *Learning by Expanding: An Activity-Theoretical Approach to Developmental Research*. 2nd edn. Cambridge: Cambridge University Press.

Engeström, Y., & Sannino, A. (2010). Studies of expansive learning: Foundations, findings and future challenges. *Educational Research Review*, 5, 1–24. DOI: 10.1016/j.edurev.2009.12.002

Engeström, Y., and Sannino, A. (2011) 'Discursive manifestations of contradictions in organizational change efforts: A methodological framework', *Journal of Organizational Change Management*, 24(3), 368–87. DOI: 10.1108/09534811111132758

Engeström, Y., Virkkunen, J., Helle, M., Pihlaja, J., and Poikela, R. (1996) 'Change Laboratory as a tool for transforming work', *Lifelong Learning in Europe*, 1(2), 10–17.

Forsdick, C. (2018) 'Science and languages', in M. Kelly (ed.) *Languages after Brexit: How the UK Speaks to the World*. Cham, Switzerland: Palgrave Macmillan, pp. 75–83.

Goodman, N. (1978) *Ways of Worldmaking.* Indianapolis, IN: Hackett Publishing.

HEFCE (2011) *Strategically Important and Vulnerable Subjects: The HEFCE Advisory Group's 2010–2011 Report.* Available from: https://dera.ioe.ac.uk/10338/1/11_24.pdf (Accessed: 24 July 2021).

Hogan-Brun, G. (2018) 'This post-Brexit linguanomics', in Kelly, M. (ed.) *Languages after Brexit: How the UK Speaks to the World.* Cham, Switzerland: Palgrave Macmillan, 49–59.

Hutchings, S., and Matras, Y. (2017) 'Modern languages: Four reforms to reclaim the future of our discipline', *Times Higher Education,* 26 June. Available from: https://www.timeshighereducation.com/blog/modern-languages-four-reforms-reclaim-future-our-discipline (Accessed: 24 July 2021).

Jenkins, J. (2018) 'Trouble with English', in Kelly, M. (ed.) *Languages after Brexit: How the UK Speaks to the World.* Cham, Switzerland: Palgrave Macmillan, pp. 25–35.

Kaptelinin, V., and Nardi, B. A. (2006) *Acting with Technology: Activity Theory and Interaction Design.* Cambridge, Mass.: MIT Press.

Kelly, M. (2001) '"Serrez ma haire avec ma discipline": Reconfiguring the structures and concepts', in Napoil, R. D., Polezzi, L., and King, A. (eds), *Fuzzy Boundaries? Reflections on Modern Languages and the Humanities.* London, UK: CILT National Centre for Languages, pp. 43–56.

Kelly, M. (2017) 'True is it that we have seen better days', in 'Do we need modern language graduates in a globalized world?', *Times Higher Education, 23 February.* Available from: https://www.timeshighereducation.com/features/do-we-need-modern-language-graduates-in-globalised-world (Accessed: 24 July 2021).

Kelly, M. (2018) 'Why are many people resistant to other languages?', in Kelly, M. (ed.) *Languages after Brexit: How the UK Speaks to the World.* Cham, Switzerland: Palgrave Macmillan, pp. 13–24.

Leontiev, A. N. (1978) *Activity, Consciousness, and Personality.* Englewood Cliffs, NJ: Prentice Hall.

LSE Language Centre (2015) Every Graduate a Linguist – Building Strategic Language Capability through IWIP – Research Report on a Case Study Carried Out at the LSE Language Centre. Available from: https://www.thebritishacademy.ac.uk/sites/default/files/5.%20LSE%20IWLP%20Cohort%20Study%20-%20Every%20Graduate%20a%20Linguist%20Full%20Report.pdf (Accessed: 24 July 2021).

McLelland, N. (2017) *Teaching and Learning Foreign Languages: A History of Language Education, Assessment and Policy in Britain.* Abingdon, Oxon: Routledge.

Montoro, C. (2013) *The Language Learning Activity of Online Individual Learners Using Online Tasks,* unpublished doctoral thesis. The Open University, Milton Keynes.

Montoro, C. (2016) 'Learn or earn? Making sense of language teaching and learning at a Mexican university through a Change Laboratory intervention', *Learning, Culture and Social Interaction,* 11, 48–57. DOI: 10.1016/j.lcsi.2016.05.001

Norton, M. K. (2018) 'A language-rich future for the UK', in Kelly, M. (ed.) *Languages after Brexit: How the UK Speaks to the World.* Cham, Switzerland: Palgrave Macmillan, pp. 35–45.

Nuffield Foundation (2000) *Languages: The Next Generation.* Available from: https://www.nuffieldfoundation.org/sites/default/files/languages_finalreport.pdf (Accessed: 24 July 2021).

Phipps, A. (2016) 'Foreword', in Ros i Solé, C., *The Personal World of the Language Learner.* London: Palgrave Macmillan, pp. vii–ix.

Phipps, A., and Gonzalez, M. (2004) *Modern Languages: Learning and Teaching in an Intercultural Field.* London: SAGE.

Polisca, E., Wright, V., Álvarez, I., and Montoro, C. (2019) *Language Provision in UK MFL Departments 2019 Survey. Report no. 2,* December. University Council of Modern Languages (UCML), United Kingdom. Available from: https://university-council-modern-languages.org/2019/12/24/ucml-language-acts-report-2019/ (Accessed: 24 July 2021).

Pountain, C. J. (2017) 'The three Ls of Modern Foreign Languages: Language, linguistics, literature', *Hispanic Research Journal,* 18(3), 253–71. DOI: 10.1080/14682737.2017.1314096

Ros i Solé, C. (2016) *The Personal World of the Language Learner.* London: Palgrave Macmillan.

Tinsley, T. (2013) *Languages: The State of the Nation. Demand and Supply of Language Skills in the UK.* Available from: https://www.thebritishacademy.ac.uk/sites/default/files/State_of_the_Nation_REPORT_WEB.pdf (Accessed: 24 July 2021).

Tinsley, T., and Comfort, T. (2012) *Lessons from Abroad: International Review of Primary Languages: Research Report.* Reading, Berks: CfBT.

University of Cambridge, Cambridge Public Policy SRI (2015) *The Value of Languages.* Available from: https://www.languagesciences.cam.ac.uk/national-languages-policy/report-the-value-of-languages/at_download/file (Accessed: 24 July 2021).

Virkkunen, J., and Newnham, D. S. (2013) *The Change Laboratory: A Tool for Collaborative Development of Work and Education.* Rotterdam: Sense Publishers.

Vygotsky, L. S. (1987) *The Collected Works of L. S. Vygotsky: Vol. 1. Problems of General Psychology.* New York: Plenum.

Wertsch, J., Minick, N., and Arns, F. (1984) 'The creation of context in joint problem solving', in Rogoff, B. and Lave, J. (eds) *Everyday Cognition: Its Development in Social Contexts.* Cambridge, MA: Harvard University Press.

Worton, M. (2009) *Review of Modern Foreign Languages Provision in Higher Education in England.* Available from: http://www.hefce.ac.uk/media/hefce1/pubs/hefce/2009/0941/09_41.pdf (Accessed: 24 July 2021).

3

Translation Acts: the multiple possibilities of the imagination

Catherine Boyle, Ella Dunne, Sophie Stevens and Mary Ann Vargas

Overview

This chapter explores the ways in which creativity and imagination are at the centre of the approaches, methodologies, research questions, practices and collaborations developed by members of the Translation Acts research strand. In the four interventions, we demonstrate how creative translation enables us to reflect on, share, imagine and understand the experiences of others and to make connections with them. The chapter illustrates how, as researchers, practitioners and translators, we use a range of source texts, including poetry, song (lyrics) and theatre scripts, as vehicles for seeing and being in the world that question who we are, and the ways in which we relate to the communities of which we are part.

Introduction

The translation processes outlined in this chapter, which often take place in groups and draw upon insights gained from working collectively and collaboratively, illustrate how translation allows for an in-depth and critical understanding of a text. In our work we develop translation methodologies which focus on encountering texts in many ways: by reading, listening, repeating, embodying and speaking aloud. The act of listening is prioritized in many of the workshops we do because listening alerts us to rhythms, repetitions and lyrical qualities. The questions posed as we translate take us deep into a text and allow us to discover its richness. At the same time, the different translation processes take us beyond the text as they spark our imagination, enabling us to make connections with others across time and space, and giving rise to multiple interpretations of any one text. This chapter advocates for creative translation as a way to engage a range of community groups, students and researchers as collaborators. It shows that, by listening and focusing on how we experience the source text, we can encourage playfulness through experimentation with language, sounds and images as we encounter a different language. We facilitate workshops and collaborations in which we allow creativity and worldmaking to underpin the translation process. We believe that we can inspire confidence among students and community groups, enabling them to create their own processes for translation.

In the first part of the chapter, 'Creative translation in the classroom', Catherine Boyle explores how using theatre translation techniques encourages playfulness and error-making and can facilitate the development of a metalanguage that provides insight into the processes of language learning and includes examples used in the school classroom. In 'Worldmaking in the imagination', Sophie Stevens goes on to explore how playwrights construct imagined worlds on stage. She demonstrates the importance of creative responses to source texts and proposes that theatre translation entails acts of worldmaking as we imagine the worlds of others and are inspired to rethink and reimagine our own world. In 'Tambobamba: bringing an Andean carnival to the city', Ella Dunne describes a workshop with university students and wider community groups, translating Quechua, the most widely spoken indigenous language in Peru, through sound, song, image and written word. She offers a methodology for introducing audiences to unknown, minority languages, bridging the gap between oral and written, minority and dominant, local and global. Finally, in 'Making song', Mary Ann Vargas examines and proposes alternative ways to conduct research with Latin American communities in south London, defying the extractive and very often unequal power relations associated with conventional forms of fieldwork.

Creative translation in the classroom

Translation is about many things – communication, connection, curiosity, empathy, sharing. We act, move and invent through translation as second nature. In growing into our first language we play with words, inventing tirelessly and deliberately, learning through the mistakes we make, and pushing the limits and limitations of our personal linguistic worlds. The underlying idea that informs Translation Acts is that our relationship with words and the world around us is about movement: between languages and cultures; between research, theory and practice; between the academy and classrooms, social settings, community groups and performance. We aim to create spaces for experimentation for practices devised in the context of the study of international methods and research in order to test and share the potential of translation and to inform our broader engagement with language learning.

In *Why Translation Matters*, Edith Grossman refers to 'Ralph Manheim, the great translator from German' and his suggestion that 'translators are like actors who speak lines as the author would if the author could speak English' (Grossman, 2011: 11). Grossman goes on to say that she sees the translation process as 'essentially auditory, something immediately available to other people, as opposed to a silent, solitary process. I think of the author's voice and the sound of the text, then of my obligation to hear both as clearly and profoundly as possible, and finally of my equally pressing need to speak the piece in a second language' (Grossman, 2010: 12). This is interesting as an allusion to a mode of translation: it is not Grossman's aim to illustrate what it means to say that 'translators are like actors'; what this implies is how the translator embodies the process or how they might follow an actor's method. Grossman evokes how the translator is forced to think about what they are doing, how the alchemy of translation actually works, step by step. It is an interesting anchor for our thinking: what might it mean to think in this way, to ask how the lines would be if they were spoken in another language: what would that process look like?

The intersections with the theatre translation process and the metaphor of the translator as actor provide a set of initial references for posing questions related to the ways that we make words act. In this sense, the understanding of the auditory, of hearing, is an indicator for translation, aspects of what we learn about how words function in a text. There are, here, resonances of speech act theory and John Austin's insight about the 'performative sentence or a performative utterance': 'The name is derived, of course, from "perform", the usual verb with the noun "action": it indicates that the issuing of the utterance is the performing of an action – it is not normally thought of as just saying something' (Austin, 1962: 6–7). In literary criticism a process of identifying speech acts can help us when closely analysing a text for meaning, understanding how the author constructs what is happening in the text. It plays a different function when approached as an insight that might inform the production of dramatic discourse, or the performance itself. Keir Elam directs us here:

> it was Austin's aim to show that in issuing utterances we are not only or always producing a certain propositional content but are, above all, doing such things as asking, commanding, attempting to influence or convince our interlocutors, etc. Austin brings philosophical attention to bear, therefore, on the pragmatic status of speech as an interpersonal force in the real world.
>
> (Elam, 1980: 157)

How do we conceptualize what we do as translators? How do we name the act of translation? What do we carry over from one method to another to develop ideas and action? When do we forget that even the simplest utterance does something, produces meaning? How can we bring this awareness into the classroom as an incentive to language learning? These are some of the questions and theories that have haunted my thinking about how to engage young people in active, engaged language learning in the classroom. The point here is not to be reductive in the ways the questions are posed or in responding to them. Rather, the aim is to set up a series of ways into the key preoccupations that inform workshops developed for schools. So often, young people who are not engaging with language learning, or are having difficulty doing so, are not aware that when they speak, their words will be received as utterances that their interlocutor will attempt to understand within a set of linguistic and cultural procedures. They have missed the first step, the first instruction in language learning – words act in the world – and it is impossible to move on from there. The other language does nothing, plays no function, has no use. When this happens, language learning has become 'deadly'. 'Deadly' is used here in the terms of Peter Brook's 'deadly theatre', one in which rules and convention prevail, established forms preside over innovation, and the only outcome is deemed to be transactional. 'In a living theatre, we would each day approach the rehearsal putting yesterday's discoveries to the test, ready to believe that the true play has once again escaped us. But the Deadly Theatre approaches the classics from the viewpoint that somewhere, someone has found out and defined how the play should be done' (Brook, 1990: 17). Language learning suffers in this way when the learner has a sense that the language is somehow already known by others and there is little point in their learning, nothing they can add. There is, then, little sense of how they will create, invent or improvise with the language, of how language will act on another person or situation. Language learning can be difficult and slow; structures have to be learned, vocabulary remembered, new sounds absorbed, understood and reproduced. Frustration sets in because starting from scratch is infantilizing, and this is exacerbated if the only reward is seen to be success or, perhaps more often, failure in assessment. The learning of a new language remains futile (deadly) if it is not understood to land somewhere, produce meaning, take the speaker elsewhere, and enunciate words and structures that can be understood within certain language conventions. This is where the practical insights of theatre translation might have an impact. Translation is at the core of all language learning: from the moment we start to say words in another language we are producing meaning, translating emotions, desires, fears, ideas, asking someone to receive what we say and make sense of it, even in a classroom setting.

In the project 'Creative Translation in the Classroom', the goal was to bring insights from the theatre rehearsal room into the classroom, as part of the wider call to encourage language learning in young people who are learning a second language for the first time at the worst possible time: early teenage years, when the infantilizing effect of the early stages of a new language is quite simply mortifying. More specifically, the insights are informed by the processes followed in the Head for Heights Theatre Company, where the line-by-line exploration of the translated text provides the basis of the information for the actor in how they will construct their role and how the character they create will connect with the other characters in the play and the other elements of the stage production. The 'system' developed by the great Russian theatre director and theorist Konstantin Stanislavski towers over this method and is too complex even to start to explain here. However, his method sought to systematize the creative force of acting, and Eric Bentley's simple description helps us here by posing the essential questions:

> What makes every performance of a play, no matter how many times it may be repeated, always fresh, sincere, truthful, and, above all, quite surprisingly different? [...] The actor who repeats himself is lost; for there is nothing more unendurable than a well-drilled performance in which everything has been thought out beforehand. It is the actor who can invest his 'now' with

> ever new and ever fascinating properties who is the creative actor par excellence.
>
> (Bentley, 1990: 269–70)

The system devised, which, in short, aimed to identify the ruling idea of the play, connect it to the actor's lived experience and bring it to life through improvisation, is now commonly known as 'actioning'. It is familiar to most British actors and directors and is used differently and to varying levels of intensity, but to the same end, which is to understand what the text is doing:

> put simply, the Actioning technique requires you, the actor, in early stages of rehearsing a play, to divide up your lines into separate phrases or thoughts, to assign each thought an 'action verb' which expresses the underlying intention of the line, and then, having assembled this series of verbs, to attempt to speak and act each thought in the manner of the chosen verb.
>
> The verbs themselves must be 'transitive' – in other words, something your character can do to another character [...]. This means that each thought, spoken with a particular action in mind, becomes an attempt to affect another character in the manner implied by that verb.
>
> (Moseley, 2016: vii–viii)

As Moseley goes on to say, the beauty of the technique is that the actor begins to 'own the text' (ix). The process brings the theatre collective – the actor, director, translator, designer, producer – close to the text and sets up a means by which the text is set in motion for performance. The text is brought to life through questioning, discussion, exploration, repetition, trial, error and change, as the director, actors and (in this case) translator understand more about its workings. Above all, there is a desire to bring the text to life, not theoretically but practically, by using the technique to start to embody it: the actions of each unit of text will become what is enacted on stage.

This parallels what we aim to do as teachers, which is to bring all sorts of texts to life for and with our students. But it is difficult; reading, analysing and bringing to life complex texts in a foreign language is difficult. So, what might happen when we transfer this method to the classroom? This is not to suggest an exactly parallel process for approaching a text as language learners. The important aspect of these insights into a particular form of textual analysis is that the system creates a transferable skill that can encourage students to think actively, creatively and analytically with a text in a foreign language from the point of view that it is doing something, something is happening through language. The process brings together skills that students already possess and often brings in languages that they are not formally learning. It might contribute to an awareness that they can acquire the ability to create something new in language and not only repeat what is already known by others, with little use for them. How do we convince our students that there is something at stake in the act of learning a new language?

This is what we wanted to test in the classroom in the 'Translation without Translation' workshops with secondary school pupils using methods of creative translation through theatre. In the workshops we ask our participants to complete a translation of a short poem, an extract from a play, or a song. The extracts are not 'easy', but we start from the trust that the translation is possible, no matter what the level of the student. The idea is very simple and is at the heart of *Language Acts and Worldmaking*: words do work in the world. So, the question that we pose in our workshops is equally simple: what work does each word do in the text? This approach has an important function, which is to distance the pupil from a sense that the text they are studying is somehow already 'found out and defined', as Brook would have it, and equally to distance them from the purely external aspects of the text, from the imperative to impose meaning on language they barely understand, typically by looking for themes or key messages. Neither do we 'translate' immediately by looking for unfamiliar words, or by seeking out coherence. We play and we make mistakes, and we try to break down the barriers caused by shame and embarrassment, or by indifference. In a typical workshop, what we do is to start with the simplest of language exercises: playing with words. We use (and invite) tongue twisters in a number of languages to limber up, make sounds we don't recognize but that make us listen, laugh, hear, copy, repeat. And learn that we all make mistakes.

Our next activity further develops simple language exercises: repetition; rehearsal of the words. Reading, for example, a short poem a number of times creates a sense of sonic familiarity, and in this way we incorporate the auditory into the translation process through listening out for patterns of sounds, repetitions, cadence. We do this in different ways: the workshop leader reads; a teacher reads; we go around the group, each participant reading a line. Each repetition brings the poem closer to the student-translator. In these repetitions, we add new elements: the participants pass the lines on from one to the other, and each time we do this, we give the lines different actions: the protagonist of the poem is angry/sad/happy; they are telling someone off; they are recounting a memory; they are warning someone about something; they are encouraging other people; they are expressing disbelief. The idea is not to translate but to start absorbing the language, to use previous knowledge to start recognizing language as emotion and to find out the questions to ask about what is unfamiliar. The purpose of these exercises is to create familiarity with the work, as the words are brought towards the student, to illustrate the mobility and fluidity of language as it moves from one place to another. Students are invited to question what happens when we 'refix' the language through translation. That is, how we give it new meaning in the words we choose to put on paper as a translation, knowing (or learning) that the next translation might be different.

In each repetition of the poem, we stop to find out what new things the students have discovered. These are related to, for example, rhythm, repetition, sound, rhyme. They are also related to words that the students are beginning to realize they understand, or, crucially, that they might find access to through the other languages they speak, given that these classes are happening in multilingual classrooms. Then we deal with the 'doing' words. If we are taking the approach that language always does work, the verbs are a great way to start. The students are asked to clap or hit the desk every time they recognize a verb. They are then asked to identify the root, the meaning and the tense the author is using. In doing this, they are being asked to think about the actions in the poem (which relate to the actions we have developed in the repetitions), about temporality, about grammatical structure and about the purpose of tense shifts. There is little room here for the idea that there is no meaning in a work, or that the writer did not mean to say what we think they are saying. We are showing, little by little, that we make meaning out of understanding and trusting that the words have something to say to us. And that we can make them say things to other people.

This process works. With a class of students with only a few months of Spanish, we translated Lorca's 'Nana del caballo' ('Lullaby of the Horse'). One pupil, after a couple of readings, said that they did not understand the poem yet, but that they knew it was sad and would not end well: this is a wonderful insight into the context of Lorca's *Blood Wedding*. Another pupil said they would rather draw their response and drew a horse's head with tears, uncannily like Lorca's own drawings. In another school, translating Gabriela Mistral's 'Balada de la estrella' ('Ballad of the Star'), pupils created a poetic language of translation that drew on their home languages, using memories of older relatives singing to them in the languages they brought with them in immigration, and that allowed access to the poetics of the voices and questions of childhood. Older pupils did a fabulous translation of Rafael Alberti's 'Nunca vi Granada' ('I Never Saw Granada'), which drew on the way that they started to perceive languages of memory, regret, guilt, brotherly love and bloodshed emerge from their repeated readings which drew the text closer to them. A translation of the Jacques Prévert classic, 'Le Déjeuner du matin' ('Breakfast'), used so often in schools to study and understand the present perfect, was enlightened by the pupils' willingness to play a game that gave the well-known poem a new vitality as they filtered it through a number of actions that made it strange every time we read it to each other: the upset partner; the enraged partner; the partner who is bored by it all; the partner who finds the man's actions hilarious and recounts them on the top of a bus to a friend; a waiter viewing the scene. And in a workshop based on Eugène Ionesco's *La Cantatrice chauve* (*The Bald Opera Singer*), the absurdity of the encounter between M. and Mme Smith was brought bang up to date in London by the translation of 'Mon Dieu' as 'Oh, my days!' (a current slang term often used by young people in Britain). Translation at its best.

One aim is to create a metalanguage for the process of language learning; one which the students put into practice through the frustrating first stages of the encounter with a new language. By articulating the pocess, and providing some strategies for action, the aim is to keep a focus on process. One strategy for the creation of the metalanguage is a simple and effective method used by Doris Sommer in her Pre-Texts programme (https://www.pre-texts.org/) and that comes from the practice of forum theatre developed by the Brazilian practitioner Augusto Boal. The strategy is to ask the students not 'What did you learn?' but 'What did we do?' The answers to this question are always enlightening and take us to the heart of what we believe in *Language Acts and Worldmaking*: that language is play, mistake-making, invention and creativity. Here are some things that we did:

'We laughed.'

'We played.'

'We exercised our face muscles.'

'We repeated the poem/play/song.'

'We thought about words.'

'We tried out new sounds.'

'We played with ideas.'

'We made mistakes.'

'We listened'

'We repeated'

'We practised'

'We improved'

'We looked at verbs'

'We learned new words'

'We translated'

'We used our imagination'

We used our imagination. In the next part of the chapter, some ways in which imagined worlds come into being in the theatre are explored, together with examples of how theatre and the processes of theatre translation can be used in the classroom.

Worldmaking in the imagination

Inútil decir más. Nombrar alcanza.

It's pointless to go on. It's enough to name.

Idea Vilariño

On naming

Written by the Uruguayan poet Idea Vilariño (1920–2009), these words end the play *Si muriera esta noche* (*If I Die Tonight*, taking the title of one of Vilariño's poems) by the Uruguayan dramatist Raquel Diana. Artists have always done more than simply name. They have created, critiqued and imagined. And in many cases, they have taken their own or others' life experiences as a basis for their work. There are many examples of this on stage throughout the world and through the work of the Out of the Wings Theatre Collective (www.outofthewings.org), these lives have been presented through translation for London audiences as part of the annual Out of the Wings Festival. In a workshop led by the theatre-maker and academic Almiro Andrade at the 2019 Festival held at the Omnibus Theatre, we explored some of the challenges, questions and tensions that arise when actors, directors and translators are 'Playing the Real', that is, dealing with plays based on the lives of real people ('Out of the Wings presents its 2019 Festival', 2020).

Creating and playing people on stage

Si muriera esta noche was written by Diana in 2017, directed by María Clara Vázquez, and premiered at the Ellas en la Delmira festival held at the Teatro Solís, Montevideo, in 2018. The festival presents a series of monologues by women to celebrate the 'month of women' throughout March and International Women's Day on 8 March. Diana weaves together extracts from Idea Vilariño's poetry, essays, letters, articles and songs to create a dramatic narrative about the poet's life. Performed by the playwright as a monologue, the play deals with the poet's artistic practice, her work, her conflicts, her health and her relationships, including her relationship with Uruguayan author Juan Carlos Onetti. For Uruguayan audiences, those throughout the Spanish-speaking world, as well as students and researchers in the field of Hispanic Studies, both writers and their relationship are well known. So, in the first instance, naming Vilariño is enough to attract an audience. But what else happens when you name a real person as the subject of a play? It can evoke a sense of familiarity, of connection with someone we know. It can also provoke certain expectations because the person has been captured in a particular way in cultural or historic memory. And it can cause anger and frustration that they should become a character, a representation, subject to the imagining of someone else.

In one scene in *Si muriera esta noche*, Vilariño waits for Onetti to come to visit her at her home; she has prepared everything down to the last detail so now all she can do is wait, and she gradually becomes transfixed on the sliver of light beneath her front door. He never arrives. Yet Vilariño does not seem to resent him but rather to relish the intensity and integrity of the wait. On seeing the play in 2019, I was struck by the way in which Diana depicted this scene as very sensual: Vilariño's senses were heightened by her desire, which seemed to transcend her desire for her lover, enabling her to experience and appreciate the beauty of the situation, of the moonlight, and of her own body. It was a captivating scene which was about Vilariño and not about Onetti. But how did she experience that night? How did she wait? Did this really happen during their relationship? I remember wondering: did Vilariño thank Onetti for this time spent waiting so that she did not have to forgive him for not turning up (which, I suspect, would have been more difficult)? We can only imagine the answers, based on Vilariño's account which is used in the scene, and Diana's sensual portrayal is just one possible depiction of that night. It is how Diana (as playwright and protagonist) imagined the evening, and, crucially, it made me imagine and reflect on what I might have done. If the play challenges our expectations and provokes us to reflect on them, I would argue, it is doing a good job.

Theatre and imagination

In the case of *Si muriera esta noche*, this imagining is amplified because the basis for the play already comprises a lot of creative work: the corpus produced by Vilariño. When Vilariño wrote in her poetry about herself and her experiences or those of others, she, too, was constantly representing, imagining and experimenting in her own work. *Si muriera esta noche* received excellent reviews, and theatre critic Leonardo Flamia (2018) praised the play for making the audience forget that it was a play at all, so that, in the end, their applause was for Vilariño. This is testament to Diana's decisions when creating the world of Vilariño on stage and her creative choices in constructing a captivating dramatic narrative. It is well-deserved praise for the evocative ways in which Diana recites poetry, sings and argues, as well as for the empathy she evokes for suffering, illness and heartbreak. The range of work demonstrates the vitality and agility of Vilariño as a creative artist and of Diana as an actor. But this is not Idea Vilariño. It is one possible imagining of her.

The capacity to imagine is at the heart of theatre and the work that playwrights, actors, directors and ultimately audiences are involved in. Even when the work is based on the real life of a person, what we witness on stage is one playwright's imagining of that person's life and experience. Even when this is based on historical accounts or documents, recorded footage or transcripts from court proceedings, there is still selection, interpretation and creativity involved. This is then amplified when a dramatic script is developed by actors and directors who also interpret and imagine. And there is further amplification when a play is translated, as the translator works to 'imagine, and imaginatively discard, a range of potential performances for each moment; to rehearse and reassess, to reassemble and redress' the possibilities for creating the play in the target language (Versényi, 2007: 433).

Worldmaking on stage

A concept at the heart of our work in Translation Acts is 'worldmaking on stage'. This is because the processes of theatre-making and making theatre in translation involve a series of collaborative and creative acts which provide new insights into worlds constructed and depicted on stage. While the worlds depicted on stage are imagined, they can nevertheless make connections with and help us to reflect on the world beyond the stage. 'Worldmaking on Stage' has also been a central theme of two forums organized by Translation Acts, Out of the Wings and Translation Studies at Goldsmiths, University of London. The title of the 2018 Forum was 'Worldmaking on Stage: Theatre Translation Research as Practice', and in 2019, 'Worldmaking on Stage and the Work of Theatre Translation beyond the Stage'. The forums explored questions about how practice and research are interlinked, how theatre translators work in a range of professional settings, and how theatre translation can be used to approach topics of diversity and inclusivity. The discussions, partnerships and methodologies that emerged from these encounters demonstrated how translating theatre can inspire us to make new connections to the situations in which we live, work and learn, and this can inspire new types of worldmaking. It is for these reasons that theatre and creative translation are fundamental in Translation Acts' work with language students in schools.

Contact with theatre from a different country and culture takes us outside ourselves and beyond our current surroundings. The process of theatre translation can help to develop a sense of awareness, empathy and curiosity about others. This is important for helping students to learn about and understand others but it is also vital for those students who, for whatever reason, do not want to be the subject of their language learning but would rather focus on the life experience of a character, perhaps even one based on a real person. This is essential for students who are vulnerable, lacking in self-confidence or have unstable and even dangerous home situations. In fact, exposure to the experiences of others, through theatre from a different cultural context, may help them to reflect on and articulate their own experiences in different ways and to seek support if they need it.

Working with an extract from a script in a different language offers multiple possibilities for engaging students: acting it out to imagine what the performance would be like and focusing on the emotions of the characters can help to improve confidence and fluency in speaking another language. Using an extract as a basis for improvisation so that students creatively imagine what might come next as a way to extend the narrative can spark creativity and storytelling through theatre. By translating an extract into English, students apply their language skills to enable the text to travel into the target context and they imagine how it might be played in translation.

Creative responses

Author and teacher Kate Clanchy discusses how she always begins classes and workshops with secondary school students with a poem: 'This is an exciting piece of writing; the best thing you'll hear all week, I say' (Clanchy, 2019: 195). I find this approach energizing and enticing and, as a translator, teacher and researcher, it has made me reflect on how I present creative and literary work to students and provide them with an insight into creative processes. Clanchy is reflecting on teaching English in the UK education system with students working towards GCSE (14–16-year-olds) and A level (16–18-year-olds) secondary school qualifications, not on teaching English as a Second Language. However, it is important to acknowledge, as she does in her book, that for many of her students, English is not their first language.

Having introduced and read the poem, Clanchy asks students to write a poem in response. Sometimes she gives them formal pointers, a structure or a theme to focus on but, ultimately, students each respond in their own way through creative writing. The poems produced are 'a reading of the source poem' (Clanchy, 2019: 199), and here she refers to the poem with a term used in translation: the source text. In the act of writing a new poem, in deciding how to respond to the ideas and qualities of the source poem, and the aspects of it that they might want to incorporate or adapt, students are identifying, engaging with, and experimenting with metaphor, rhyme and rhythm. They are also activating their own creative and imaginative capacities while performing a process that authors, poets and playwrights constantly undertake: using the work of others as inspiration and starting point (Clanchy, 2019: 203). In this we can make a link back to *Si muriera esta noche* in which Raquel Diana adapts and transforms Vilariño's writing by imagining it for the stage.

In 'doing' something in response, in producing a poem, students begin to understand the source poem by imagining it anew. The same applies in translation – as students carry out the acts of translation, and make decisions about how to render the text into English, they are constantly responding to the source text and, in doing so, they are deepening their understanding of the language, ideas and references that it contains, as well as how they relate to it. Writing, translating, creating a new text in response to a source text underpins a critical understanding of that source text which can be deepened through close reading, analysis and research. This, in turn, can equip students to articulate the stylistic features of the original and their own work. Therefore, creative, imaginative work is also critical work which instigates processes of worldmaking.

Worldmaking and imagination

Through theatre translation we bring texts, characters and concepts into a new cultural context where they enter into dialogue with issues in the target situation. Through the imagined world depicted on stage, ideas are generated because we encounter new perspectives, and this enables us to begin to imagine possible solutions to the challenges faced by the characters and the challenges we ourselves face. Imagination plays a crucial, critical and productive role in engaging with theatre from another language and culture and then responding by relating it to our experiences. Imagination also plays an essential role in producing new creative writing, poems and translations. But, too often, imagination as a critical and creative skill is undervalued: it might be viewed as daydreaming, as ignoring reality through time-wasting and escapism. Imagination helps us to project ourselves into new situations, to envisage solutions and to envision new ways of working. Imagination allows us to think without restrictions about possibilities for the future, to think about how the world could be and to visualize the changes that need to happen; these are all aspects of worldmaking. A further aspect of worldmaking is explored in the following part of this chapter, this time developing creativity and understanding between people and languages, and again illustrating ways in which the approaches of worldmaking can enhance learning in the classroom.

Tambobamba: bringing an Andean carnival to the city

Translating and exploring the work of José María Arguedas published in *La Prensa* (Buenos Aires, 1938–1948), I have become aware of my own position as researcher and translator, in time and space. As part of Translation Acts, this awareness sparked a series of workshops, exploring how listening to and reading Quechua, the indigenous Andean language, could encourage creativity, learning and understanding between people beyond the need for mutual language. My project, drawing on similar techniques to the 'Translation without Translation' workshops discussed in the first part of this chapter, worked with university students and with wider members of the public, exploring a language which, in the context of London and the UK, represents unfamiliar sounds and shapes to a huge majority. Participants created artworks, reflections and reactions to the texts and sounds that Arguedas uses, revealing a sensory interpretation of the 'Carnaval de Tambobamba' in London and reflecting upon the translation experience. Arguedas's essay 'Carnaval de Tambobamba' is among the shortest of his articles for the Buenos Aires Sunday newspaper supplement; it describes Tambobamba's setting – 'en la provincia más oculta del Ande peruano' ('in the most hidden province of the Peruvian Andes') – and the 'canción [...] cruel y hermosa' ('cruel and beautiful song') of the Tambobamba carnival (Arguedas, 2012: 355). The same song reappears in parallel text between Quechua and Spanish in the original edition of *El sueño del pongo. Canciones tradicionales Quechuas* ('The Servant's Dream. Traditional Quechua Songs') (1969) with a recording of Arguedas singing the song in the back sleeve of the publication. The 'Tambobamba Workshops' use this song as corpus, exploring its format as written and sung, Quechua and Spanish, in five stages. Through the stages, the participants see and hear the song in different ways, accumulating a familiarity with and an understanding of the text, through different research approaches. The aim is to create a journey of discovery, a hermeneutic journey that maps the important stages of translation when approaching a multilingual, multicultural and multimedia corpus. Here, the stages of the workshop are traced, noting my position and its relation to that of the participants and to Arguedas, as this micro study maps on to macro concepts, vocabularies and research questions that characterize the *Language Acts and Worldmaking* project.

Introducing translation and analysis of sound and song

The workshop begins with an introduction to understandings of translation. It is important for participants to recognize their own position in relation to the text, to acknowledge any preconceptions of the text and of the process of translation and analysis that they will undertake throughout the workshop. First, then, participants are asked what they understand by 'translation', creating a mind map of ideas and impressions, forming links and creating a visual map of ideas. Ideas of movement, transition from A to B, distance between A and B, 'us' and 'them', have arisen in every workshop, to then be challenged, with my encouragement, by questions of migration, orality and the 'in-between' of post-colonial translation, as coined by Bhabha (2000).

This wider exploration is then brought into focus through establishing an understanding of the 'text' involved in the translation. In her introduction to the edited anthology *Creating Context in Andean Cultures*, Howard-Malverde explains that in the edition:

> The notion of text was taken in its very broadest sense: thus the text of textiles – two words with a common root in Latin *texere* meaning 'to weave' – could be as valid an object of our interests as the alphabetic script of the seventeenth-century Huarochirí manuscript or the oral discourse of speech makers and dramatists in modern day Peru and Colombia.
>
> (Howard-Malverde, ed., 1997: 3)

Her broad outlook allows an unrestricted understanding of the term 'text' that participants are encouraged to adopt in the workshop, allowing space for the oral, the visual and the written that constitute Arguedas's corpus, and that are involved in his translating process, my own translation and that of the workshop participants. Arguedas's 'reader' should also be considered the 'listener' and 'interpreter' of sounds and song. And then, this 'reader' and 'viewer' becomes the 'listener' and 'interpreter' of two languages – Spanish and Quechua – and a multiplicity of contexts and cultures. The movement across and between the indigenous, oral and the written, colonial language characterizes Arguedas's work and reveals the complex colonial, socio-cultural history of the text, as the oral is transcribed and translated. In understanding this, the workshop participants can become involved in this exchange between oral and written, between dominant and indigenous, and between language and place. The text in the workshop is the written Quechua text, the sung Quechua text and the visual translation responses created by the participants, and the written Spanish text. It is this expansive understanding of the text, and hence of the 'reader' and 'translator', that forms a basis through which the participant of the workshop understands their interaction with the 'text'. From here, the 'text' can be analysed.

Reading the Quechua text aloud without translation

Having introduced the participant's role as translator, and a flexible understanding of the text, we then read the Quechua text aloud. At this stage, as workshop facilitator I also become a participant, working with the group as we each read a line aloud. I am completely aware that I am throwing the participants in at the deep end, reading an unfamiliar language aloud among an often unfamiliar group. By taking part myself, a sense of inclusivity and acceptance develops so that participants can become more confident and free to experiment.

This step importantly recognizes the process of transcription undertaken by Arguedas, and other writers of oral literary and cultural traditions. Through transcribing the oral song, Arguedas allows the vocalization of the song, years later in an urban context. What happens when we can see and capture the sounds on the page, linguistically? Participants read the text aloud and discuss repetition, sound and syntax. What can we notice on the page? I encourage the participants to explore the alphabetization of the oral language – what alphabet is used? How are the words pronounced? According to what language system? Here, through their own exploration of vocalizing the unfamiliar language, the participants vocalize and perform the song and the language used. As a language that came into contact with the Romance languages of Europe – and was made written – only with colonization, Quechua language presented on a page reveals a complex colonial history with which the participants of the workshop are forced to engage.

This stage of the hermeneutic journey reveals, then, that without necessarily understanding the sounds they are making by reading aloud, the participants can begin to connect with the complex socio-cultural act of transcription and translation.

Listening to the recorded song and creating visual responses

The process of exploring the Quechua in this way prepares participants for the next stage, which is listening to the song interpreted by Arguedas. This recording is now available on YouTube. Where before, in the reading, I encourage participants to discuss reactions together, the aim is to encourage a different form of engagement with the 'text'. The famous example of Clive Scott's intersemiotic translation of Apollinaire (Scott, 2014) is introduced, together with a description of the process of 'intersemiotic' translation, to ask the workshop participants to explore what they hear through a visual interpretation. Each participant is then given a piece of paper the size of a CD case, and I ask everyone to listen to the song and to design the cover art for the song from what they hear, if it was to be re-released as a CD. Putting the exercise into this context bridges the gap between the participant and the exercise: it gives them inspiration from something familiar to our everyday and so makes the activity focused but approachable and contextualized. Cover art ranges from very literal, photographic or lifelike to very symbolic and abstract – the participants are given the same free rein.

At this stage, participants explore how the unknown language can be understood only as music and sound. Using Treece's insistence on understanding the song through all of its elements helps to guide their listening, and to explain the exercise. In his description of his own workshops Treece asks: 'But what becomes of the lyrical, thematic dimension of the repertoire, and of its contribution to meaning, when the songs are heard abroad by non-speakers of Portuguese?' (Treece, 2018: 69). As translator into English of the collection of resistance songs, Treece explores the change in reception of the songs as their audience changes from Brazilian to non-Portuguese speaking. My exploration of the 'Carnaval de Tambobamba' asks a very similar question of the Quechua song. If we, in London, do not speak Quechua, what meaning is found in the Quechua song? Treece goes on to explain:

> The lyric has no greater or lesser claim than the melody to be the heart of a song's 'content' or meaning; yes, it may be the bearer of verbal information, as narrative, declamation, conversation, confession or wisdom, but as language materialized sonically in time it is also so much more than mere 'text'. However intense our appreciation of a song's inventive use of melody, rhythm, and harmony, it is only when those musical

> **structures become voiced, intoned linguistically as discourse, that their full meaning becomes realized.**
>
> (Treece, 2018: 70)

Lyric and melody, music and language, exist together in song and should not be isolated. At this stage, then, participants are encouraged to embrace the melody and music of the song. A non-linguistic corpus is paired with a non-linguistic response, engaging the senses, with a conversion of the song into imagery. The text multiplies into written word, sung song and drawn images, expanding the translation process.

Where earlier in the workshop I join in with participants to create a sense of security, here I ask participants to work alone, and most likely to step out of their comfort zone. This is an exercise I have undertaken myself, throughout translating Arguedas's articles, and it is a capturing of first impressions, emotions and ideas.

Comparing and discussing responses

Having listened to the song three times, to allow time for reflection, participants are then asked to reveal their visual responses. Here, in asking participants to explain their reactions, to guide others through their CD covers, the vocalization of impressions draws links between the different reactions. With the previous stages of the journey building up, this point of discussion is an important stage in beginning to recognize the multiplicity of the corpus, and the flexibility and creativity of the task of translation.

Within the space of the discussion, as participants speak to each other, they bounce ideas around and they adapt the meaning of their personal visual responses. The visual responses themselves become flexible and moving, as their creators' eyes are opened to how others have heard and interpreted the same song. The discussion and the reflection on impressions begin to form associations as participants make links and this next stage of the journey becomes invaluable. Here, I ask questions about colours, shapes, impressions, to encourage the movement of impressions and ideas throughout the group. This is the convergence of imaginations and creative responses to form a communal translation and understanding of the 'text'.

Reading translations of the Quechua song and discussing impressions

After a discussion of the visual interpretations, the translations of the song lyrics are then shared with the participants. This is the final stage of the interpretative journey in the workshop, offering an opportunity for reflection on the previous stages. It is here that, having employed other forms of interpretation and encouraged listening, we return to an approach of textual analysis and comparison with which university students are more familiar.

Arguedas translated the same 'Carnaval de Tambobamba' twice, and in two quite different styles. The first translation appears in an article written for *La Prensa* in Buenos Aires in 1942, now published as part of the collection that makes up *Indios, mestizos y señores* ('Indians, Mestizos and Masters') (1989). The second translation was part of the publication of *El sueño del pongo* that also includes the recording of the song. It is important here, I felt, for the reader of this chapter to have the same texts at hand as the workshop participants in order to trace the hermeneutic journey of the workshop.

In *El sueño del pongo, canciones quechuas tradicionales* (Chile: Editorial Universitaria S.A.: 1969) [Translation A]		**In *Indios, Mestizos y Señores* (Lima, Editorial Horizonte: 1985) [Translation B]**
Tambobambino maqtatas yawar mayu apamun; tambobambino maqtatas yawar unu apamun.	A un joven tambobambino el río de sangre* lo arrastra; a un joven tambobambino el río de sangre lo arrastra; a él no se le ve,	El río de sangre ha traído a un amante tambobambino. Sólo su tinya está flotando, sólo su charango está flotando, sólo su quena está flotando.
Tinyachallanñas tuytushkan qenachallanñas tuytushkan charangollanñas tuytushkan birritillanñas tuytushkan	Sólo su tinya flota en la corriente sólo su quena flota sólo su charango flota en la corriente. a él no se le ve, sólo su birrete flota en la corriente·	Y la mujer que lo amaba, su joven idolatrada, llorando llora mirando desde la orilla sólo la tinya flotando, sólo la quena flotando.

¡Wifalitay wifala wifalalalay wifala wifalitay wifala!	¡Wifalitay wifala** wifalalalay wifala wifalitay wifala!	El río de sangre ha traído a un amante tambobambino; sólo su quena está flotando, él ha muerto, él ya no existe.
Kuyakusqan pasñarí waqayllañas waqaian, wayllukusqan pasñarí llakiyllañas llakisian, tinyachallanta qawaspa charangollanta rikuspa qenachallanta qawaspa wirritillanta rikuspa	La muchacha que él amaba llorando llora, ya no más; la mujer que él amaba sólo el sufrimiento sufre, no más, viendo flotar sólo la tinya viendo flotar sólo el charango viendo flotar sólo la quena viendo flotar sólo el birrete	La tormenta cae sobre el pueblo; el cóndor está mirando desde la nube; la joven amante, la joven idolatrada está llorando en la orilla
¡Wifalitay wifala wifala wifala wifala wifalitay wifala!	¡Wifalitay wifala wifala wifala wifala wifalitay wifala!	¡Wilfalalalay wifala wifalitay wifalaáá!
Cundurllañas muyusian tambobambina maskaspa, manapunis tarinchu yawar mayus chinkachin manapunis tarinchu yawar unus apakun.	Un cóndor da vueltas en la altura buscando al joven tambobambino; no lo encontrará nunca, el río de sangre lo sepultó; no lo encontrará jamás el río de sangre lo arrasrtó	
¡Wifalitay wifala wifalalalay wifala wifala wifala wifala wifala wifalitay wifala!	¡Wifalitay wifala wifalalalay wifala wifala wifala wifala wifala wifalitay wifala!	

* Yawar mayu (río de sangre) se llama en quechua al agua de los ríos recién cargada de barro con las primeras lluvias. Esa agua es pesada y turbia, deneralmente algo rojiza.

** ¡Wifa! Grito de triunfo o de desafío

I direct the textual analysis within the workshop to notice differences, similarities and translation techniques. Through this detailed analysis participants are encouraged away from a simple search for meaning, and towards an exploration of the translation process. The translation is also always published as a parallel text, alongside the Quechua transcription. And so, I ask about the difference between seeing the Spanish translation alone and seeing the Quechua and Spanish alongside each other in parallel text. I want the participants to consider the interaction between the different versions of the song, between the different media and languages, returning always to the multiplicity of the 'text', oral and written.

The 'Tambobamba Workshops' continually allow my own research approaches to come into contact with different audiences. Through directing participants through a hermeneutic journey, I myself learn from their reactions and responses. A broad understanding of the 'text', and so the corpus, allows for a creative understanding of the process of translation, bringing the Andean carnival to the urban environment of twenty-first-century London. For me, as workshop facilitator, translator and PhD student, the process has brought to light the underlying tensions of my position in relation to Arguedas's corpus, undeniably pertaining to the act and process of translation that forms the foundation of all of our work in the Translation Acts. Leading on from this Quechua song, this chapter now closes with further reflections on song and on writing about songs. Here, the language act of making song examines what can be brought into being and experienced through this creative form of worldmaking.

Making song

London, 19 October 2020. Going through my final draft for this volume, I realized something might be missing about the way in which I have been reflecting on and writing about making songs as a methodology. So, before concluding this piece, I contacted a colleague back home in Peru in yet another attempt to grasp the significance contained in the process of song making. This quest is central to my practice-based PhD in the shape of questions. The following three are perhaps the most relevant in the context of this chapter. What is song? Why do we need to sing? What does song do? I should have known Olinda Silvano would not give me straight answers. Instead, she sent me five songs and sang a capella via WhatsApp at five in the morning in Lima, her favourite time to work. 'When everybody else is still asleep and the day is bursting with potential, that's when I like to work,' she often tells me. Olinda is an Amazonian artist, activist and community leader in

Cantagallo, a Shipibo-Konibo settlement on the outskirts of Lima. Olinda's third song is explored in more detail later.

As the poet Kae Tempest suggests,

> Stories and songs bring us into contact with our best and worst natures, they enable us to locate ourselves in other people's experience and they increase our compassion. But these things in a vacuum are useless. A story doesn't cultivate empathy just by virtue of its having been thought up; it must be engaged with to become powerful; the story must be read, the song must be listened to, in order to acquire its full charge.
>
> (Tempest, 2020)

The moment of reception Tempest is referring to brings me back to Olinda's song, and to the aural qualities singing can foreground. Walter J. Ong's thoughts are resonant in this respect:

> Sight isolates, sound incorporates [...]. Vision comes to a human being from one direction at a time [...]. When I hear, however, I gather sound simultaneously from every direction at once; I am at the centre of my auditory world, which envelops me, establishing me at a kind of core of sensation and existence [...].'
>
> (Ong, 2002: 72)

Despite the 10,164 km between Lima and London, blind to the boundaries set by the North Atlantic Ocean, Olinda's singing transports us to another world, immediately and completely, albeit through the prism of a digital device, immersing us in the vanishing act of listening.

How my research began

I am above all a theatre maker, a researcher and translator, currently engaged in theorizing on the process of making live performance collaboratively. When I began working on my thesis, the first task was to find methodologies that could be of interest to the people I was hoping to work with: Latin American theatre practitioners, local schools, and traders from the Latin American and Caribbean community at the Elephant and Castle Shopping Centre in south London. When the Centre's demolition was announced in December 2018, it seemed intrusive and unhelpful to gather information through formal interviews or written questionnaires. The sense of disorientation felt by many traders, local residents and activists at the time was captured by Latin Elephant's members Patria Román and Santiago Peluffo: 'The knock-on effects of [Mayor of London] Sadiq Khan's final decision are yet to unfold. It saddens us profoundly to have to be witnesses to the inevitable consequences' (Peluffo and Román, 2018).

How could I unsettle the inherently extractivist nature of conventional methodologies at such a critical moment? Writing a song came to mind as a possible, alternative way forward. A song could potentially embody and reframe the sudden erasure of someone's workplace, through the lens of their lived experience, without prowling into their lives. Songs are pockets of life that can be shared and revisited in performance – this complicity continues to be vital to fellow collaborators/researchers, and to the work we do together.

The traders at the Elephant with whom I have been in contact for the last three years left their shops a fortnight before the UK's 'lockdown' in response to the global COVID-19 pandemic was formally announced on 23 March 2020. At the time, they were uncertain whether they would be able to return to work in the foreseeable future. When restrictions began to ease off over the summer, some of them did manage to return, but only temporarily. By the end of the week of 21 September 2021, the shopping centre had closed its doors permanently. By then, only 40 out of 130 traders at the Elephant had been successfully relocated, thanks to the sheer determination of charities such as Latin Elephant and local resident Jerry Flynn's 35% Campaign (a campaign set up in 2016 to hold the local council, Southwark, to account on its promise to deliver 35 per cent affordable housing on any regeneration scheme).

The Elephant's closure, its impending demolition, together with new waves of COVID-19 hovering over the winter and months ahead, magnified a sense of loss and displacement for many local residents, traders, customers and passers-by. In response to these events, I engaged in the process of making a song called 'Elefan' (phonetic Spanish pronunciation for elephant), working with two Latin American colleagues, musicians and researchers, Eliane Correa and Camilo Menjura. Our intention was to capture the spirit of resilience, joy and commitment to social justice we have witnessed over the past few years. The process of making 'Elefan', the score, has been possible thanks to the support of VEM (Visual Embodied Methodologies Network) at King's College London, in collaboration with Arts Cabinet, an online curatorial platform that 'functions as a space to experiment with different forms of artistic knowledge production' (Arts Cabinet, 2020; www.artscabinet.org where 'Elefan' is available online).

'Barrio', the song

Why do we sing?

To address this question, I will outline the process of gathering information to write 'Barrio' ('Neighbourhood') during the early stages of my research, in collaboration with composer Eliane Correa. This song evolved as a result of observational fieldwork and countless informal conversations with one seamstress at the Elephant and Castle Shopping Centre, Claudia Bernal. Although 'Barrio' contains biographical references, it is above all a fictional, multilayered account of a 45-year-old Colombian seamstress who arrives in London in the early 1990s, escaping civil conflict. The song was sung twice within the context of a Latinx variety night by the same name at the Southwark Playhouse (3 March and 3 November 2019). 'Barrio I' and 'Barrio II' are fundamental references within my corpus and were possible thanks to the support of *Language Acts and Worldmaking* in collaboration with Southwark Playhouse. The lyrics for the recording reproduced below are the version of 'Barrio' sung by Dunia Correa, this time on 19 November 2019.

Dunia Correa is a talented, skilled performer. Although I wrote 'Barrio' mostly in English, some words and expressions are in Spanish. When Dunia performed at the Playhouse, she took the song to another level, adding fresh new phrases (musical and textual), improvising with the crowd in a playful exchange of complicity. The energy in the room was so contagious; audience members rose to their feet and danced together, something which seems otherworldly, even dreamlike, in pandemic times. The fluency with which Dunia crossed linguistic thresholds brought to my attention the central premise underpinning the work we do as a team in Translation Acts. Language, whether spoken, written or sung, as we say in our mission statement, 'is a material and historical force [...], enabling us to construct our personal, local, transnational and spiritual identities', as explored in the introduction to this volume. Today, perhaps more than ever before, the immersive quality of song – paradoxically evanescent by nature – may prove to have a unifying pull as sound resides in the aural traces it leaves behind in its reception.

The lyrics for 'Barrio'

In 1993
I came to live in London
I set up my small shop
With one thing on my mind
To have my child in peace
Away from all the troubles
I was young back then
I had big dreams then

I named my shop Nicole's
In Elephant and Castle
Sewing day and night
To lead a decent life
I'd left my war-torn country
All my friends and family
Closed the door behind me
Let the future
Set me free

This is my barrio
Esta es mi historia (This is my story)
The place where I belong
The place that I call home
This is my barrio

So here we are tonight
Change is coming
Our shops might be demolished
But our dreams will carry on
Our livelihoods are right here
with our children's promises
So no matter what the future brings
This is who we are

This is my barrio
This my story
The place where I belong
The place that I call home
Este es mi barrio (This is my barrio)

'Barrio', the song, spans a period of 27 years. The first verse establishes the crossing from a world in conflict to another, more stable world, where it is safe for a child to be born. The protagonist recounts her journey across the sea in the early 1990s, a time when many Latin Americans arrived in London. Quite often, their first port of call would be the *Elefan,* a fast-growing Latin American hub, where economic rentals were still possible. Support networks, Colombian coffee shops and beauty salons like La Bodeguita and Lucy's were quickly beginning to establish themselves, creating a sense of community, and a place to belong to away from home.

On 2 July 2018 Colombia played against England in a football match that could have been legendary, especially for Colombians living in London, still the largest Latin American community in the UK. England's victory, however, meant Colombia was disqualified from the World Cup. By pure chance, that Friday happened to be the day when Claudia listened to an early recording of 'Barrio' for the very first time, sung by Eliane, the composer. The match was happening that evening, so the Elephant was jubilant with yellow flags, laughter, and a festive feeling of joy and expectation. Claudia was standing next to her sewing machine, behind the counter of her minuscule shop, wearing my headphones. Yellow T-shirts with Colombian flags hung close behind her like bunting. Claudia is a woman of few words, but I will never forget how listening to 'Barrio' moved her to tears. However, although the experience seemed to have filled her with happiness, paradoxically, it also revealed her predicament. Claudia, like her fictional counterpart, was feeling numb with uncertainty, unsure whether she would have anywhere to go if the shopping centre were to close. The song had crystallized this tension, which was also felt by many of her colleagues at the time.

Claudia and her family were in the audience at Southwark Playhouse when *Barrio* first took place in March 2019. Her response to the song, in the context of a public event this time, brought to my attention the transformative experience which stories can bring about when they cross borders in live performance. From fiction, through personal to local history, across the physical dwellings inhabited by both seamstresses, the living person I know and the imaginary one come to life each time the song is sung. I have asked Claudia several times if she could describe what it feels like to listen to 'Barrio' in English, a language she had to learn from scratch decades ago. After a pause, her answer is always the same: 'Orgullo' – pride.

Olinda's third song

I went back to Olinda to ask if she could please translate her third song so I could share it in this chapter. This is her response: 'Este es el canto del anaconda. El anaconda te puede agarrar y te puede llevar. Entons' ten cuidado, ten cuidado, dice, ¿no? Este es el canto del anaconda' ('This is the anaconda's song. The anaconda can grab you and take you away. So, be careful, be careful, it says, you know? This is the anaconda's song').

For Olinda's Shipibo-Konibo community, the anaconda, or water boa, has a mythic dimension, representing the origins of life and the spirit of water. I cannot tell if the song holds a warning for these troubled times, or if it is just waving to life itself, mirroring the undulating rhythms of the anaconda as it moves silently under the water, along the riverbed. I imagine Olinda would reply, 'The answers lie somewhere in between.'

References

Arguedas, J. M. (1969) *El sueño del pongo, canciones quechuas tradicionales*, Chile: Editorial Universitaria S.A

Arguedas, J. M. (1985), *Indios, Mestizos y Señores*, Lima, Editorial Horizonte

Arguedas, J. M. (2012) *Obra Antropológica*, vol. 1, Lima: Editorial Horizonte.

Arts Cabinet Doing Research. Available from: https://www.artscabinet.org (Accessed: 6 January 2020).

Austin, J. L. (1962) *How to Do Things with Words*. Cambridge, MA: Harvard University Press.

Bentley, E. (1990) *The Theory of the Modern Stage*. London: Penguin Books.

Bhabha, H. (2000) 'How newness enters the world: Postmodern space, postcolonial time and the trials of cultural translation', *Writing Black Britain, 1948–1998*. Manchester: Manchester University Press, pp. 300–7.

Brook, P. (1990) *The Empty Space*. London: Penguin Books.

Clanchy, K. (2019) *Some Kids I Taught and What They Taught Me*. London: Picador.

Elam, K. (1980) *The Semiotics of Theatre and Drama*. London and New York: Methuen.

Flamia, L. (2018) 'Ideas', Semanario Voces, 10 April. Available from: https://semanariovoces.com/ideas/ (Accessed: 20 October 2020).

Grossman, E. (2011) *Why Translation Matters*. New Haven, CT: Yale University Press.

Howard-Malverde, R., (ed.) (1997) *Creating Context in Andean Cultures*. Oxford: Oxford University Press.

Moseley, N. (2016) *Actioning and How to Do It*. London: Nick Hern Books.

Ong, Walter J. (2002) *Orality and Literacy: The Technologizing of the Word*, 2nd edn. New York: Routledge.

'Out of the Wings presents its 2019 festival', *Out of the Wings Festival*. Available from: https://ootwfestival.com/out-of-the-wings-presents-its-2019-festival/ (Accessed: 20 October 2020).

Peluffo, S., and Román, P. (2018) 'Sadiq Khan is no force for change in London – just look at his terrible record on housing', *The Independent*, 15 December. Available from: www.independent.co.uk/voices/sadiq-khan-housing-elephant-and-castle-development-delancey-social-affordable-a8684776.html (Accessed: 4 December 2020).

Scott, C. (2014) *Translating Apollinaire*, illus. edn. Exeter: University of Exeter Press.

Sommer, D. *Pre-Texts*. Available from: www.pre-texts.org/ (Accessed: 10 February 2021).

Tempest, K. (2020) 'Kae Tempest: What I have learned from 20 years on the mic', *The Guardian*, 3 October 2020. Available from: www.theguardian.com/books/2020/oct/03/kae-tempest-what-i-have-learned-from-20-years-on-the-mic (Accessed: 4 December 2020).

Treece, D. (2018) 'Bringing Brazil's resistance songs to London: Words and music in translation', *Veredas: Revista da Associação Internacional de Lusitanistas*, 27, 68–84.

Versényi, A. (2007) 'Translation as an Epistemological Paradigm for Theatre in the Americas', *Theatre Journal*, 59(3), 431– 47. DOI: 10.1353/tj.2007.0173.

4

Language and hospitality in worldmaking: how languages act in the world

Debra Kelly with Ana de Medeiros [1]

Overview

The work of *Language Acts and Worldmaking* became increasingly politicized, in a way not originally conceived at the project's outset, through its development of counter-narratives to the hostility often shown towards the 'other', the stranger, the foreigner, as the political and social context presented here demonstrates. This chapter therefore begins by considering well-established definitions of the concept of hospitality and poses the question of how the work of languages can extend notions of hospitality, for example through the creation of 'xenodochial spaces' in language, and ways to counteract entrenched discourses of xenophobia. This is a pressing question given the particular nature of the inhospitable geopolitical context of

[1] This chapter takes its inspiration from Ana de Medeiros's idea to use the concept of hospitality in order to frame the work of the Language Transitions research strand of *Language Acts and Worldmaking* and of the Small Grants Award Scheme. This approach proved transformative in our thinking about the work we carried out within the project.

the first decades of the twenty-first century, and, as is shown, we are not alone in trying to think about what forms contemporary hospitality may take. The chapter then takes case studies based on the work of members of those communities of language teaching, learning and research which were created, and organically developed, around *Language Acts and Worldmaking,* considering six (from over one hundred) community projects funded through our own Small Grants Award Scheme. The principal criterion for selection here was the way in which hospitality was offered and received, how our 'hospes', in every meaning of the word – our guests, hosts and strangers – exchanged hospitality, and, above all, how notions of hospitality were thereby developed and extended by this worldmaking and these language acts.

Introduction: rethinking hospitality in the twenty-first century

How can the work of languages, whether in private or public use or in language teaching, learning and research, extend notions of hospitality? Set against an inhospitable, indeed hostile, geopolitical context at a time when many Western nation states were restricting hospitality to those outside their borders, the work of *Language Acts and Worldmaking* increasingly became a form of resistance, developing counter-narratives to the political hostility which echoed around the public and media domains. When thinking about and dealing with the political, social and cultural contexts of 'the other', the stranger, the foreigner, intrinsic to the work of languages, we increasingly found ourselves working with and within diverse and complex conceptions of hospitality. Consequently, while explicitly thinking about the meanings of 'language acts' and about how language acts in the world, we also developed our own strategies of hospitality within the work of languages. It is striking how frequently the concepts of hospitality and hostility rub up against each other in the public arena in a real-world manifestation of what is thought to be the related etymology of these two words: *hospes* – the host; guest, visitor; stranger, foreigner – and *hostis* – the enemy of the state; stranger; the enemy in its plural form, *hostes* (both deriving from the double meaning of Latin *hostio/hostire*, to make even, recompense, strike) – the link being the core meaning 'stranger' which develops in *hostis* as 'enemy'. This etymology and that of other words which come to mean host, guest and enemy in various languages is complex. The notion of 'enemy', for example, comes to be distinguished early by the use of the Latin *inimicus*. The word 'guest' also comes to be distinguished, not only in English but, for example, in the French *invité* and the Spanish *invitado*. It would seem that although Latin *hospes/hostis* are etymologically related, Romance languages needed to distinguish the notions of host, guest and enemy, army.[2] In his frequently cited treatments of the ethics of hospitality, Jacques Derrida argued finally that there is necessarily hostility in all hosting and hospitality (hence his term 'hostipitality') given the impossibility of 'unconditional', or pure, hospitality (Derrida, 2000). It should be further noted that in French (hence in Derrida's writing and thinking about the term), the word *hôte* can be used for both the guest and the host. Derrida's background is also important to his work. Born in colonial Algeria into a French family of Sephardic Jewish origins, Derrida was a 'stranger' and a 'host' in many different ways. A well-known French literary example of the word gives its title to a short story by Albert Camus, another Algerian-born Frenchman: 'L'Hôte' (usually translated in English less ambiguously as 'The Guest' which privileges one reading of the text) in *L'Exil et le Royaume* [Exile and the Kingdom] (1957), a collection in which many of the protagonists are 'strangers' in colonial Algeria.[3] In Greek etymology, the prefix *xeno* comes from the Greek word for strange or foreign and is encountered today mainly, often only, in the word 'xenophobia' and in 'xenophobic' behaviour and attitudes. Xenodochy, the reception of hospitality or the offering of hospitality to strangers, is one of its overlooked and underused opposites (we may think also of xenophilia in the same way). When thinking about

[2] With thanks to our colleague Chris Pountain for his clarifications on this etymology.
[3] For an analysis in English of Derrida's thinking on hospitality, see, for example, Still (2010).

how languages act in the world, such linguistic precisions are essential. They tell us so much about the circulation of ideas and attitudes, the prevalence of some, the relative absence of others, in real-world contexts.

In the political and social contexts of the early twenty-first century, governments across Europe and across the world failed to implement genuinely welcoming policies towards migrants and refugees, and hospitality as a political value was increasingly replaced by individual acts informed by private ethical values, sometimes coming together in grassroots movements and as associations of volunteers, which provided assistance and solidarity. For example, interviews with French citizens showed that private citizens in liberal democracies offer hospitality to undocumented migrants for three reasons: out of a care and concern for vulnerable and precarious migrants (widely acknowledged in the scholarly literature), but also out of a desire to uphold the basic principles and ideals of their own society and a desire on the part of citizens themselves to become a different and better kind of person by practising hospitality (Taylor and Lefebvre, 2020). Such acts, however, remain ambiguous in their effects. They provide help, relief and hope and sometimes save lives. But they can also paradoxically limit the possibility of long-term welcome, although it should also be recognized that they may lead to movements which force governments to rethink their policies. Such actions resulted in a new politically informed discourse around conceptions of hospitality, what Anna-Louise Milne has called 'a more pragmatic rethinking of hospitality' and for which Derrida's ethical and theoretical approach serves as 'a negative foil' (Milne, 2020) and what Corina Stan has termed 'a realism of hospitality' (Stan, 2018). This is apparent in the work of, for example, Guillaume Le Blanc and Fabienne Brugère's *La Fin de l'hospitalité. Lampedusa, Lesbos, Calais … jusqu'où irons-nous?* [The End of Hospitality. Lampedusa, Lesbos, Calais … How Far Will We Go?] (2017) and also in Benjamin Bouda's *Politique de l'hospitalité* [The Politics of Hospitality] (2017). Le Blanc and Brugère argue that the practice of hospitality needs to be rethought in 'an age of camps, of fear of foreigners and the suspicion of neighbours who can turn out to be enemies from within' (206).[4]

The concerns of such thinking indicate that we are not alone in trying to think about what forms contemporary hospitality may take, for example through the creation of 'xenodochial spaces' in language (referencing the Greek etymology above), and about how to counteract entrenched discourses of xenophobia. Le Blanc and Brugère argue that the European tradition of hospitality (from the Middle Ages to the twentieth century and as presented in the work of, for example, Rousseau, Kant and Arendt) and the 'metaphysical figure of the foreigner', received as guest of the community, has been erased and replaced with 'new figures of social disorder', the migrant, the refugee, the immigrant (Le Blanc and Brugère, 2017: 170). Within the Modern Languages community itself, and while we were thinking about our own work in terms of hospitality, the concept of 'Being Hospitable: Welcoming the Other across Languages' was chosen as the unifying theme (a theme conceived in March 2020) for the 2021 MLA (Modern Languages Association of North America) International Symposium in Glasgow, a place described by the organizers in their call for proposals as 'one of the most hospitable, welcoming and multicultural of cities, the ideal venue for a sustained reaffirmation of hospitality in all its forms in our times'. The theme of this major international conference resonated compellingly with the *Language Acts and Worldmaking* project, with the concerns of this book more widely, and with this chapter in particular. Our work as presented here, then, counters in different and varied ways prevalent narratives around 'the other'. Our engagement with and commitment to 'otherness' encompass a range of perspectives including multilingualism, multiculturalism, and the transformative nature of linguistic and cultural exchange, not least in the languages of the arts and of creativity, and is offered here, then, as a xenodochial space.

[4] Le Blanc and Brugère also advocate the use of the term 'refuge seekers', rather than refugees, thereby emphasizing the individuals' needs rather than their status. Earlier work includes Lynch, Morrison, and Lashley, (eds) (2007), and Baker (ed.) (2013).

Why and how worldmaking creates hospitable spaces and how languages act in the world

Before presenting and discussing examples of our hospitality within and through languages in one specific area of the work of *Language Acts and Worldmaking,* it is important, as noted in the introduction to this chapter, to set that work within, and against, the real-world contemporary context because this demonstrates very explicitly how our project of worldmaking became increasingly politicized from its inception in 2014/15. The Open World Research Initiative (OWRI) programme funded by the UK Arts and Humanities Research Council sought initially to address issues of language learning and teaching in the higher education sector in the UK and how these were linked to languages in schools, business and the community. Political events across the world soon made the research initiative ever more urgent in ways not originally envisaged. From its inception, the ethos of *Language Acts and Worldmaking* ran counter to prevalent public, political and media narratives. In Europe, notions of hospitality perhaps inevitably became caught up in debates around migration and immigration, conflicts between those who welcome others and those who reject them, and concerns around security and borders. The Mediterranean and the English Channel were put under increasing surveillance, frontiers were tightened, and camps, walls and refugee centres were built. Prominent examples include, first, the controversy which overtook Chancellor Angela Merkel's government in Germany in 2015 when she maintained her open-border migration policy, welcoming more than a million refugees (notably in response to the ongoing Syrian conflict and continuing turmoil in Iraq and Afghanistan) and bringing her into conflict that year with other European countries and then once again in 2018; and second, the unresolved tensions concerning migrants and asylum seekers landing on Italy's southernmost island, Lampedusa, which intensified during the 2020 global pandemic after the country's ports were ordered to close. To take the particular example of the United Kingdom in recent years: in the periods before and after the referendum on continued membership of the European Union held in June 2016 (which became known as the 'Brexit' vote and subsequent policy) and the political decisions taken by a series of Conservative governments in its aftermath, particularly those of the government led by Prime Minister Boris Johnson from December 2019, issues of migration, of those to whom hospitality was and was not to be extended, and who was and was not 'at home' in the UK, were constantly at the fore in public and political discourse. This was just one British example of a populist politics which took on various national forms across the world.[5] Previous aligned policies in the UK concerned the 'hostile environment for illegal immigrants' developed by Theresa May as Conservative Home Secretary under Prime Minister David Cameron in 2012, one tactic of which included the UK Home Office sending vans to areas with high migrant populations. The vans were equipped with slogans on the side instructing 'illegal immigrants', including homeless citizens of other European countries, to go home or face arrest. The hostile environment policy is considered to have led directly to the subsequent 'Windrush scandal' in 2018 when people of the 'Windrush generation' and other Commonwealth citizens established in the UK for decades were removed to detention centres and/or deported, being unable to prove their right to remain. The 'Windrush generation' refers to around a half a million people who settled in the UK from the Caribbean between 1948 and 1971. The name comes from one particular ship, the HMT *Empire Windrush,* on which some five hundred passengers sailed, most of whom came to fill post-war worker shortages in the UK, but which included many children on board. Many who arrived in the 23 years until the 1971 Immigration Act gave Commonwealth citizens living in the UK indefinite leave to remain came as children travelling on a parent's passport and never had travel documents. Despite being able to provide many forms of evidence of living, being educated, raising families and working in the UK, they were unable to prove their right to remain to the satisfaction of the Home Office and were caught up in the ensuing 'scandal'.

[5] See, for example, Moffat (2016), Müller (2016), and Norris and Inglehart (2019).

When Theresa May became Prime Minister in 2016, her 'Citizens of Nowhere' speech to the Autumn Conservative Party Conference (5 October 2016) was particularly revealing of views towards not only others settled in the UK but also towards UK citizens who came to be considered 'others' in their country of origin: 'if you believe you are a citizen of the world, you are a citizen of nowhere. You don't understand what the very word citizenship means.' The British writer Ali Smith, whose quartet of novels presents a literary meditation on the state of Britain in this period, *Autumn* (2016), *Winter* (2017), *Spring* (2019) and *Summer* (2020), takes Prime Minister May's speech as one of the epigraphs to *Winter*, and it is again used powerfully later in the novel when one of the characters talks about the work she has been doing in Greece with Syrian, Afghan and Iraqi migrants:

> Tell them what it's like to come back here, when you're a citizen of the world who's been working with other citizens of the world, to be told you're a citizen of nowhere, to hear that the world's been equated with nowhere by a British Prime Minister. Ask them what kind of vicar, what kind of church, brings a child up to think that the words *very* and *hostile* and *environment* and *refugees* can ever go together in any response to what happens to people in the real world.
>
> (Smith, 2017: 233; the reference is to Prime Minister May's own upbringing)

Although specifically referencing those in globally focused business who 'behave as though they have more in common with international elites than with the people down the road', as the Prime Minister phrased it targeting a specific group, the speech was more widely interpreted as a jibe at the 'Remain' vote in the 2016 UK Referendum and its pro-European identity. It also supported those interested in further manufacturing the discourse of increasingly hostile 'culture wars' between, on one side, the 'metropolitan [London] liberal elite' and the generally younger, well-educated citizens of the UK's large cities and university towns, and, on the other side, the white working class living in the 'abandoned' satellite towns of the UK's former industrial heartlands, those living in non-urban spaces (including coastal towns) and the 'Little England' of affluent, often rural, older conservative middle-class voters. The ideas on which the speech was based were seemingly a vulgarization of David Goodhart's arguments concerning 'citizens of somewhere' (the local, rooted majority, attached to a place and to the people in that place, considered by him to comprise half of the UK population) and 'citizens of anywhere' (the well-educated socially liberal and socially mobile, attached to their achievements and ideas and less so to a particular place comprising, he believes, 20–25 per cent of the population but whose views, according to him, dominate public life; the rest of the population are characterized by him as 'inbetweeners') (Goodhart, 2017).[6] These two main 'tribes' were more broadly characterized as those who felt themselves to have been left behind and marginalized by globalization and those who had benefited from it, and arguably applicable not only to the 'Brexit' vote in the UK but also, for example, to the election of Donald Trump in the United States, again in 2016. A further, associated narrative maintains that the UK is a 'monolingual society', the subtext often being that it should also be 'monocultural', affirming 'British values', and there is little doubt that linguaphobia, as well as xenophobia, informed voter perceptions at the time of the UK EU Referendum. Similar linguistic and cultural challenges persist in other English-speaking nations, not only the UK, and linguaphobia is evident in a number of contemporary ideological, political, social and cultural contexts across the world, not only the Anglophone world.

As the hospitality offered or withheld by nation states became increasingly problematic during the middle of the second decade of the twenty-first century, what was known as our Small Grants Scheme became an essential, indeed urgent, part of the wider

[6] David Goodhart is a British journalist and author who at the time of writing was Head of the Demographic, Immigration and Integration Unit at the right-leaning Policy Exchange think tank and Director of the Integration Hub website. He was appointed by the Conservative government in 2020 as a commissioner to the Equality and Human Rights Commission which was investigating the Home Office's implementation of its 'hostile environment' immigration policies, after praising May's policy on this.

Language Acts and Worldmaking project. The focus of what follows is based on the development of real-world examples in which our work in and with languages acts to provide possibilities to engage with others hospitably and to establish counter-narratives within the political context outlined above. The original aim of the Small Grants Scheme was to create a community of practice around us that would share, develop and challenge our own work. As part of the UK's Arts and Humanities Research Council's Open World Research Initiative (OWRI) application process, the project research team was asked to demonstrate what it would do with a flexible programme of funding of around £25,000 a year over the lifetime of the four-year funded project (three annual calls were held in 2017, 2018 and 2019). The funding of a series of small 'one-off projects' of the kind for which public funding has become increasingly difficult to obtain in the UK as funding bodies modify and tighten their criteria in the light of their own diminishing funds (often therefore seeking ways to exclude rather than to include applications considered worthy of receiving awards) was proposed. In total, *Language Acts and Worldmaking* funded 109 grants, each one between £500 and £1,500, to a total value of £112,000. Through the Scheme, the research team was able to expand its research community and to bring its own research into the public sphere through, for example, community work, collaborations with artists and writers, and work with a whole range of different schools and the communities around them (Boyle, 2020). This was a genuine exchange. As researchers and teachers, we were able to provide financial support and an intellectual framework. At the same time, we were introduced to truly innovative and consistently thought-provoking work which both challenged us and aided the academic and public objectives of the wider research, helping members of the research team to articulate our own intellectual and political positions (Boyle, 2020). Together, we became linguistic and cultural activists.

The range of the work embodied in these projects often became our own form of 'welcoming the other across languages', demonstrating how such work is conceived and carried out, what happens as it comes into being and is then shared, and the work languages do in the world. Notions of 'being hospitable' were not necessarily explicit in the initial framing of the Small Grants call (although an interest in languages in crisis and endangered languages, in community languages, and in inclusion and integration was explicitly articulated in the later calls for proposals), but it became a compelling theme which emerged organically from a number of the projects which were funded, projects ranging from the more traditionally academic to those from small community groups, and indeed from individuals, often with little access to funding and little experience of applying for grants and, therefore, little experience of delivering projects which crossed the borders between the academy and wider communities. Our practice in assessing and funding the grants was in itself 'hospitable', developing from the inclusive ethos of *Language Acts and Worldmaking,* and one of its most important outcomes was affording legitimacy for the initiatives of individuals and small groups who, as well as normally having little access to funding, were working in areas where access to formal languages teaching and to university is limited or non-existent (Boyle, 2020). We made a commitment to support projects as they took shape, especially if there were changes to the original plan. This approach also developed as we recognized our role in supporting applicants in the development of their ideas and of their work, providing new opportunities and fostering inclusion and diversity. This meant that considerable time and expertise were invested in the Small Grants Scheme in reviewing research questions, helping applicants to articulate aims and objectives and to put together, present and manage a budget. What ensued was effectively the creation of a new community, and of smaller interrelated communities, as we put Small Grants holders in touch with each other, sometimes because of the nature of their research, sometimes because of geographic proximity, through the Small Grants Scheme (Boyle, 2020).

It is an invidious task to select just six projects and the experiences which they produced from the 109 we had the pleasure and privilege of working with, and sometimes participating in. Across a range of some 20 of these, notions of hospitality were immediately apparent, from the more obvious welcoming place of food and music offered as part of a performance to new spaces of digital hospitality, by way of sometimes more unexpected sites of hospitality in museums, archives, schools, universities, poetry, theatre, translation, creative workshops, storytelling, the visual and cinematic arts, psychotherapy and public spaces, and in the naming and sharing of places and of objects. The criteria applied in choosing the six awards outlined below were based not only on the ways in which notions of hospitality were explicitly or implicitly articulated and delivered in the project, but also on who conceived, developed and delivered it, where and how it took place and the kinds of experiences it achieved for a range of people. The principal criterion for selection here was, however, the way in which hospitality was offered and received, how our 'hospes' – in every meaning of the word, our guests, hosts and strangers – exchanged this hospitality, and above all how notions of hospitality were thereby developed and extended in the xenodochial spaces created by this worldmaking and these language acts.

This chapter now takes case studies of language and hospitality in worldmaking as examples of how languages act in the world, thereby highlighting one specific area of our work in community-building and working with diverse communities. These projects demonstrate why and how our work in and with languages is based on, and creates further, possibilities to engage with others hospitably. The six selected projects are presented here principally in the way in which they were described in the words of the award holders (with their consent, of course) in their applications and in their subsequent reports, blogs and archives of materials.

In an act of hospitality that shows the vital, sometimes life-changing and life-saving importance of the work that languages do in the world, 'Safety-nets Reimagined: Domestic Abuse and Migrant Communities' used spoken art forms, co-produced with migrant women, to examine the role of language in migrant survivor journeys towards a 'safety-net', including reflections on the role of language as a barrier and/or facilitator to seeking help. This understanding is key to developing domestic violence and abuse services that need to be more responsive to the cultural and social contexts of racial and ethnic minorities. This creative and public engagement project built on the emerging themes from an ongoing evaluation of Project Safety Net +, a project aimed at supporting migrant victims of domestic abuse across Norfolk and Suffolk (counties in the east region of England which accommodate a range of migrant communities) and including the importance of language in migrant women feeling more able to reach out for help if English is not their first language (Adisa, 2019; www.norfolkcan.org.uk/lisiting/project-safety-net). Meeting the needs of those experiencing domestic violence within migrant communities means practitioners understanding the socio-cultural context of their originating countries. Additionally, immigrant women, particularly those who have arrived recently, may lack the familiarity with the language and public services necessary for seeking help. It is important that immigrant families nurture their cultural identities, but it is not acceptable to use culture as an excuse for violence in families. Addressing questions such as 'In the context of domestic abuse, what does a "safety-net" mean?', 'What role do language and culture play in support and how might we create culturally responsive services to meet the needs of migrant victims'? and 'To what extent is the language of oppression and control used to enforce and monitor female obedience within migrant communities?', an event was organized to invite reflection on the nature and role of language and how its use in migrant communities can foster cultural understandings of domestic violence. To better understand what happens inside migrant communities, this project enabled an examination of the learned language embedded within cultural norms that undermine a woman's autonomy (Adisa, 2019). Using spoken word, storytelling and poetry, a creative exhibition was developed with bilingual community advisors and the women they are working with on Project Safety Net +, providing an outreach opportunity for the whole community. Working with the 'Integration and Inclusion' theme of the Small Grants Scheme, this also provided an opportunity to increase the awareness of those involved concerning how language barriers can create inhospitable conditions for those seeking help. Applying this idea to the context of domestic violence is innovative, as was co-producing the entire project with migrant women, building on the awardee's domestic abuse research examining how domestic abuse is experienced by those on the margins. This event helped to further develop the Domestic Abuse Research Network in the East of England region by including underrepresented groups (Adisa, 2019). The project explicitly and implicitly explored the 'inhospitable', oppressive nature of the 'hostile environment' language and how Project Safety Net + is counteracting this through its bilingual community advisors by drawing on language's 'hospitable', supportive, nurturing uses, as well as providing in itself an hospitable space for migrant women survivors of domestic abuse.

Endangered languages were the focus of a very different cultural act of hospitality. Based in Portree in the Isle of Skye (Scotland), ATLAS Arts organizes collective art projects across Skye, Raasay and Lochalsh, working with artists and local residents to have conversations that are rooted in this place and this time, through a programme of screenings, gatherings, residencies, meals, workshops and sharings. In August 2018, internationally acclaimed artist, writer and performer Caroline Bergvall performed her evolving project *Ragadawn (An t-Eilean Sgitheanach, 57.5°T),* an outdoor sunrise performance, on the rooftop of Sabhal Mòr Ostaig, Scotland's National Centre for Gaelic Language and Culture. A multisensory composition, it featured two voices (spoken and sung), multiple languages, including Scottish Gaelic, and electronic frequencies to accompany and celebrate the new dawn. ATLAS Arts began its collaboration with Caroline Bergvall on this project in 2016, and in 2017 Bergvall embarked on an extensive period of research into the multilinguistic components of the piece. As part of this work, ATLAS Arts hosted a 'Language Station' at Sabhal Mòr Ostaig, one of five Language Stations set up across different European locations (Cameron, 2018, and see below for further information on these). A small group of people who had different relationships with the Gaelic language were invited to attend and share their experiences of the language. The artist met with them, posed questions and recorded the Gaelic speakers, and this recording fed directly into *Ragadawn*. While the whole project is conceived conceptually as an act of hospitality in, with and towards languages, it also incorporated an explicit act of hospitality. Directly following the performance there was a communal breakfast, an integral element of the piece. For this, ATLAS Arts worked directly with local suppliers including Viewfield Garden Collective, a garden project for vulnerable and disadvantaged adults in Skye and Lochalsh, to create a unique breakfast menu offered to the audience. This created an opportunity to participate in collective discussion of the themes raised, to involve and reconnect to time, place and each other. It was designed to deepen the audience's experience of the work, to reflect on the languages and text explored and to strengthen the shared experience of the sunrise (Cameron, 2018). The wider project aims to revitalize connections between languages active in Europe, and during the research and development phase for *Ragadawn* in 2017, contact was made with different linguistic communities, to explore connections between languages from the past and those to come in the future. The languages chosen adhere to one or more of the following: an ancient language which is minoritarian, possibly at risk in the region; a language from a recently settled community, which is developing influence in the region; and/or a specific language that carries with it a renewed perception of the role of poetry and song in a connecting region. In all, the Language Station network (2017–18) focused on the following locations and languages: Santiago de Compostela, Spain – Galician; Aix-en-Provence, France – troubadour conversation and Provençal; Geneva, Switzerland – Romanche; Liverpool, UK – Welsh and Arabic; Isle of Skye, UK – Scottish Gaelic; Copenhagen, Denmark – Greenlandic, Icelandic, Farsi and Korean; London, UK – Anglo-Saxon, Punjabi, Ladino and Sicilian. Bergvall's practice is focused on building an awareness of the histories and cultural politics surrounding linguistic migration and linguistic transformation, and uses this to increase our understanding of, enjoyment of and tolerance for the richness of our multilingual world. Languages like ancient Anglo-Norman, Cumbric, Gaelic, Faroese, Icelandic, New Norwegian and Saami in the northern European regions, as well as nomadic

Berber, Arabic, Galician, revitalized Occitan in the southern regions, and northern French, or new regional UK languages such as Nepalese or Punjabi are all one way or another implicated in the cultural spread and development of new modes of art and literature. In 2018 there were three performances of *Ragadawn*: the premiere was the *Language Acts and Worldmaking*-funded ATLAS Arts performance on the Isle of Skye, followed by two in Marseille, France, in October that year (Cameron, 2018).

In another cultural sphere, the act of hospitality in language took a different form as museums in the West collectively are confronted with the question of how they might 'decolonize' their collections. 'The Waiwai Project' demonstrated how academia and the museum sector can work with an indigenous community. This project brought a member of the Waiwai, an indigenous group from the north-eastern part of the Brazilian Amazon, to London to gain unprecedented access to the collections of his group, some of which are almost 200 years old, and to facilitate knowledge exchange and the 'indigenization' of the Waiwai collections held at the British Museum. The Waiwai inhabit a vast region of tropical forest spread across the south of Guyana (Essequibo River) to the northern part of Brazil across the states of Roraima (Jatapu and Anauá Rivers) and Pará (Nhamundá, Mapuera and Trombetas Rivers). Their language derives from the linguistic family of Karib, and they are historically recognized for training and exchanging and gifting hunting dogs to neighbouring villages and for organizing expeditions to reach non-contacted indigenous groups, known as 'unseen peoples' – *enîhnî komo* (Lana, 2017). One of the aims of the project was to make the collections from ethnographic museums held in European museums more widely known to the indigenous communities in Brazil, allowing them unprecedented access to the objects that are part of their cultural heritage: 'Most indigenous communities from the Amazonian region do not know that European and American museums hold collections of their groups' (Lana, 2017). Furthermore, this project provided a space for an indigenous group to 'indigenize' the collections through the act of translating the names of the objects to Waiwai language and incorporating an indigenous perspective into the museum collection. Such exchanges, if more widely implemented, could help to reshape what is known about historical museum collections, as well as support projects of cultural and political relevance for the indigenous groups themselves. One of the main objectives of the project was not only to give the Waiwai an opportunity to have access to the collections, but also to allow them to question, reinterpret, produce new meanings and actively engage with the collections as 'subjects' of their own culture. This approach also introduces a method of contesting Western curatorial authority within museums, seeking to establish more dialogical and symmetrical ways of engaging with the collections (Lana, 2017). Naming the objects in their own language constituted an important process of 'indigenization' of the understanding of the collection, 'giving insights into the linguistic world in which these objects exist, and also allowing space from which they could construct their own narratives within a museum context. Museum representation, in this sense, can also be conceptualised as worldmaking if it enables indigenous communities to have a say about how they are represented, about the objects, the collections and their history' (Lana, 2017). The project thereby extended the concepts of worldmaking, and of hospitality, this time through widening accessibility to museum collections and renaming, showing another way in which linguistic acts are central to both.

Returning to an act of hospitality concerning a migrant community within the UK, 'Object-Stories' (Kwan, 2017) presented a series of events exploring the stories of objects (owned and/or created) of personal and cultural significance as a way to explore migratory experiences for first- and second-generation British Chinese women in London. The lack of attention generally given to the British Chinese community means that there is a notable lack of research examining the representation of British Chinese women, and of gendered experiences. In order to address this, the project adopted a gendered and material culture perspective to analyse the experiences of both first- and second-generation British Chinese women. The first generation group were 15 women, mostly from Hong Kong, who collectively consider themselves as 'overseas brides' and who are members of a Women's Group in Haringey Chinese Community Centre (north London). The majority of women in the group moved as young women during the 1960s–70s to embark on a new life in the UK and many took up work in the catering industry. Many received a limited education and now, in their retirement years, they attend a weekly English class to improve their language and to socialize with one another. Learning English was an ongoing pursuit, but together they supported and encouraged the education of one another and, as many were grandmothers, they expressed their concern about their ability to communicate with their English-speaking grandchildren (Kwan, 2017). In contrast, the second-generation group of British-born Chinese women were very different. Many of the women held degrees, worked in professional jobs and were fluent in English. Despite their differences of age, class, education and occupation, it is notably their relationship with language that unites the two generations. While the first generation spoke of their difficulty with English, the second generation of British-born Chinese regularly referred to their limited Cantonese and Hakka. These linguistic concerns – viewed from different perspectives – were especially apparent during the second-generation art workshops, as it arose as an organic talking point for the group. This became a lively discussion of language and culture as many of the women talked about a distancing from their family language, whether that was Cantonese or Hakka.[7] The workshops employed creative research methods engaging the participants with art making, collaging and printing. The creative material generated from these workshops and from interview material (one-to-one interviews were also held with participants to discuss their relationship with objects and the work which they created) was publicly documented in an online archive called 'Object-Stories' (available at www.objectstories.co.uk). In addition to this series of art workshops and the creation of the online archive, an opening event celebrating their participation in the workshop and the launch of the online 'Objects-Stories' archive

[7] For much more about the issue of language, see the 'Object-Stories' blog, https://languageacts.org/.

was hosted in central London, at the University of Westminster, for both generations of participants with community leaders and the British Chinese media and press. This project also expanded the concept of worldmaking by examining how the use and movement of objects enable a transnational sense of identity. Objects (whether transported or created) mirror the transitions of the self and enabled both generations to develop a sense of selfhood while they were (re)making their homes and their identity in their new country/country of birth. Simply put, 'when people move, so do objects' (Kwan, 2017). 'Object-Stories', in its exploration of embodied narratives of migration and the counter-narratives they recount, also extended notions of hospitality into the spaces of material culture, of creativity and of the digital archive, as well as in verbal and visual languages.

In the fifth project selected here, an 'International Celebration Evening', a whole range of different communities was welcomed and celebrated. This was ostensibly a single event of the type that is sometimes perceived as being of limited long-term benefit to diversity and inclusion in an institution, but this particular event is distinguished by the depth of experience and engagement with languages and cultures brought to it, highlighting how a school can work within and with its local context. Queen Katharine Academy (QKA) is a very diverse city-centre secondary school (11–16 years old) in one of the most deprived areas of Peterborough, Cambridgeshire (again in the eastern region of England), with 41 different languages spoken by the student body. Newly arrived first-generation migrants, largely from a wide range of European countries, start at the school almost on a weekly basis. The school has above-average numbers of Pupil Premium students (this is funding provided by the government for disadvantaged students which aims to decrease the attainment gap; it is given to schools in addition to free school meals for the child, and is available if a child's parents receive certain social benefits), and it has almost 70 per cent of its cohort with English as an Additional Language (EAL) (Driver, 2019). This ever-changing demographic can be seen as a challenge, but at QKA it is seen as an opportunity to share a common rich identity and global knowledge and to promote sharing identity, culture and language. Within the school, languages are popular and achieve the best results in the school in both home languages and Modern Foreign Languages (Driver, 2019). The 'International Celebration Evening' brought different demographics of students together with their families to celebrate that diversity with music, dance, prose and poetry in a range of languages and an opportunity to try food from different countries. Performances reflected a variety of global art forms, traditional and contemporary, and were delivered in different languages, including Lithuanian, Polish, Spanish, Portuguese, German, Russian, Czech and Romani. The school became a place of hospitality in so many different ways – cultural, linguistic, physical, spiritual and material: 'Providing traditional food gives a clear message to our families that this event is a community event and food is always a good way to break down barriers. By encouraging families to contribute to the food, we are making the school the "kitchen of the community" and bringing students, staff and families together' (Driver, 2019). The school works very hard to understand and engage with all of its families. Notably, QKA has a growing cohort of Eastern European Gypsy-Roma students, many of whom have been subjected to institutionalized racism in their home countries and have not had access to adequate education. As an institution, QKA has carried out (and continues to do) research into Roma history, culture and heritage through links with local Roma charities, regional projects and liaison as well as carrying out a series of visits to Eastern Europe to learn about Roma life and education in their home countries. Since Roma have a mistrust of official institutions due to their previous experiences, the school has actively recruited staff from the Roma community (including a governor) to engage better with this demographic (Driver, 2019). This particular event encouraged the school's Roma families to take their place alongside all of its families in an inclusive cultural, social, political and linguistic act of hospitality based on deep cultural engagement.

Finally, the 'Deptford Community Multilingual Digital Storytelling Project and Film Exhibition' was a collaboration between Goldsmiths, University of London, and Deptford Cinema, leading to a public film exhibition and a multilingual digital storytelling festival at Deptford Cinema celebrating the lives of local people. Run entirely by volunteers, Deptford Cinema is a not-for-profit community-led project, located just off Deptford High Street, in the ethnically diverse London Borough of Lewisham, in the south-east of the capital. This cinema was chosen for the screening and starting point of the workshops due to its shared ethos in working with the local community and location in the heart of Deptford. As a non-hierarchical organization, the cinema operates an open participatory structure, whereby the programming of events and films is open to anyone who wants to get involved. The idea for this project arose through discussions between directors of Goldsmiths' Critical Connections project (an ongoing project, funded by the Paul Hamlyn Foundation [2012–17], which is examining the role that a critical approach to digital storytelling across a range of languages, including Arabic, Chinese, English, French and German, can play in enhancing learning in mainstream and supplementary school contexts; www.gold.ac.uk/clcl/multilingual-learning/criticalconnections) and Deptford Cinema in its aim of providing a platform for community issues and voices through work around film. The project was a novel experience for all those involved, as the organizers moved out of classrooms and schools and set up the project in the centre of the community and opened up the experience to people from many different ages and backgrounds. It was conceived as four workshops under the theme 'Cultural Webs of Deptford: Multilingual Stories of Friendship and Belonging' held on Saturday mornings during January and February 2020. The first workshop brought participants together at the outset of the project, and they saw and discussed a series of multilingual digital stories in the cinema space. Discussions focused on what makes a good digital story and the stories that participants wanted to explore and uncover about their own lives in Deptford and their journeying to Deptford. For the second workshop, held at the Albany (a performing arts centre), participants were asked to bring in personal and cultural objects that mattered to them, photographs of Deptford and other homes, and pictures or poetry or artwork for a planning and storyboarding workshop at the cinema. They engaged in a drama and media workshop interacting with their personal and cultural objects and learned about camera shots, camera angles and video recording. Participants then went on to storyboard and create their bilingual script. The third workshop was a filmmaking workshop at Deptford Lounge (a local library), to which participants took all the footage for their digital story, which could include photographs, artwork and artefacts within the story as well as moving image. The final workshop was a film-editing workshop which took place at Goldsmiths, University of London. Participants learned how to edit their footage and create a short 3–5-minute digital story in a bilingual version. The workshops and public event aimed to position language learning in the community of Deptford and to foster integration and social inclusion through the process of digital storytelling (the films made by the participants are available at: Deptford Storytelling Project 2020, www.goldsmithsmdst.com; and a list of the filmmakers and their films at: https://languageacts.org/). Digital storytelling has its roots in the community, emerging from community arts and oral traditions and often working with disenfranchised and marginalized groups of people. This initiative enabled the awardees of the grant to extend the successful language-and-culture projects they had carried out in the educational sphere over the past seven years, nationally and internationally, to a broader community base (Macleroy, Anderson and Rogers, 2019). Multilingual digital storytelling enables people to gain a better understanding both of others and of themselves, to build confidence and respect, to challenge discriminatory discourses and to be represented for who they are. This resonated strongly with the vision offered by *Language Acts and Worldmaking* because it crosses boundaries between here and there, now and then, real and virtual. It is about encounters in the liminal spaces, transitions and travel. It places language learning in the context of lived experience and personal meaning-making. Importantly it brings an aesthetic dimension drawing on affective experience, memories and imaginings (Macleroy, Anderson and Rogers, 2019).

The project provided an opportunity to explore in a London community context how the creation and sharing of multilingual stories can extend understanding and respect for diversity, leading to greater understanding, empathy and respect in society. The project proved immensely popular, and after filling all the workshop places there was a long waiting list of people interested in becoming part of the multilingual community filmmaking project. The workshops and public event created what the awardees have called 'empathetic engagement and affinity spaces' (Macleroy, Anderson and Rogers, 2019), resonating with our call here to create xenodochial spaces through hospitality and language acts. While it can be argued that, in philosophical terms, empathy is not possible (just like Derrida's 'unconditional hospitality'), it is our belief that we must act as if it is.[8]

None of these projects presented above 'come from nothing', as Catherine Boyle expresses it in her own experience of the final project outlined above (Boyle, April 2020). They come from the experience of the people who conceived and drove them forward, sometimes developing from work carried out over a long time in education, in the community, and in the experiences of multilingualism and multiculturalism, sometimes from much shorter experiences of seeing work that needed to be done and with a will to do something about it. All of this linguistic, cultural, social and activist work is:

> something we need to heed more insistently in education. It needs to come more forcefully into practice in language teaching and learning, into the centre, not the periphery […]. We need to see this experience and knowledge as part of a curriculum and not as add-ons that schools are not able to find the capacity to accommodate, no matter how much good will and desire there is.

(Boyle, April 2020)

[8] With thanks to our colleague Julian Weiss for this intervention on his reading of the chapter in its draft stages.

Conclusion: language acts and hospitality in worldmaking

One of the key aims of *Language Acts and Worldmaking* is to create connected communities of co-researchers that facilitate inclusive access to language learning, teaching and research. Through the Small Grants Scheme we expanded our research community, bringing research into the public sphere and making it a place of genuine mutual exchange. Explicitly or implicitly, hospitality, and specifically hospitality in and through language and languages, informed all of this work. We need powerful counter-narratives in order to challenge and, above all, to shift, and then to change, those dominant narratives outlined in the chapter's introduction. This is a consciously political act on two levels. First, it acts against the growing elitism of formal language learning in educational settings and in the context of multilingual communities whose skills and knowledge do not find a way into closed curricula. This returns us to the opening question here concerning the overlap between the host and the guest, and the need to be vigilant concerning the asymmetrical power relations hidden within 'hospitality'. Second, it is a consciously political act in the current global geopolitical context of exclusion, of manufactured and manipulative 'culture wars' and of the closing of borders of all kinds. It is our own xenodochial call to action.

References

Baker, G.(ed.) (2013) *Hospitality and World Politics*. Basingstoke: Palgrave Macmillan.

Bouda, B. (2017) *Politique de l'hospitalité*. Paris: CNRS Editions.

Boyle, C. (2020) *Small Grants Overview*. Available at: www.languageacts.org

Boyle, C. (April 2020) Blog 'Deptford Storytelling Project 2020'. Available at: www.languageacts.org

Derrida, J. (2000) 'Hostipitality', *Angelaki, Journal of Theoretical Humanities,* 5(3), 3–18.

Goodhart, D. (2017) *The Road to Somewhere: The Populist Revolt and the Future of Politics,* London: C. Hurst and Co.

Le Blanc, G., and Brugère, F. (2017) *La Fin de l'hospitalité. Lampedusa, Lesbos, Calais … jusqu'où irons-nous?* Paris: Flammarion.

Lynch, P., Morrison, A., and Lashley, C. (eds) (2007) *Hospitality: A Social Lens*. London: Routledge.

May, T. (2016), Speech to the Conservative Party Autumn Conference (published in full in *The Daily Telegraph,* 5 October 2016 [Online] [Accessed: 29 October 2020]).

Milne, A.-L. (2020) 'Gendering "hospitality": volunteer labour and (im)mobile men', University of London in Paris Seminar Series, 'The Body at Work: Gender, Labour, Migration', 3 November 2020.

Moffat, B. (2016) *The Global Rise of Populism.* Stanford, CA: Stanford University Press.

Müller, J. W. (2016) *What is Populism?* Philadelphia: University of Pennsylvania Press.

Norris, P., and Inglehart, R. (2019) *Cultural Backlash: Trump, Brexit, and Authoritarian Populism.* Cambridge: Cambridge University Press.

Smith, A. (2017) *Winter*. London: Penguin.

Stan, C. (2018) 'Corina Stan reviews *La Fin de l'hospitalité', Critical Inquiry,* 19 April. Available at: https://criticalinquiry.uchicago_edy/corina_stan_reviews_la_fin_de_lhospitalite (Accessed: 29 October 2020).

Still, J. (2010) *Derrida and Hospitality: Theory and Practice.* Edinburgh: Edinburgh University Press.

Taylor, A., and Lefebvre, A. (2020) 'Three reasons for hospitality: Care for others, care for the world, and care of the self',

Cambridge Core: Perspectives on Politics. Cambridge: Cambridge University Press on behalf on the American Political Science Association, 24 June. Available at: www.cambridge.org/core/journals/perpectives-on-politics/article/three-reasons-for-hospitality-care-for-others-care-for-the world-and-care-of-the-self (Accessed: 29 October 2020).

Small Grants

(Presented in the order discussed in the chapter and referenced by the date of the award of the grant application; reports, blogs and links to other materials created by the award holders available at https://languageacts.org/.)

Adisa, O. (2019) University of Suffolk and Domestic Abuse Research Network, 'Safety-Nets Reimagined: Domestic Abuse and Migrant Communities'.

Cameron, S. (2018) Producer ATLAS Arts, 'Ragadawn. An Outdoor Sunrise Performance by Caroline Bergvall'.

Lana, C. (2017) King's College London Doctoral Student, 'The Waiwai Project'.

Kwan, D. (2017) University of Westminster Doctoral Student, 'Object-Stories'.

Driver, J. (2019) Assistant Principal Queen Katharine Academy Peterborough, 'International Celebration Evening'.

Macleroy, V., Anderson, J., and Rogers, L. (2019) Goldsmiths, University of London, 'Deptford Community Multilingual Digital Storytelling Project and Film Exhibition'.

5

Worlding Iberian Studies and language literature

AbdoolKarim Vakil, Rachel Scott and Julian Weiss

Overview

This contribution reflects on some of the curricular implications of the research conducted by the Travelling Concepts research strand in their work on the reach and significance of the Spanish- and Portuguese-speaking worlds and their global contact zones, from the Middle Ages to the present. Our individual projects and collaborative activities led us on paths winding through Asia, Africa and Europe to the Americas. While these paths decentred the traditional focus on national histories, languages and literatures, our polycentric, transnational approach always returned us to the central goals of the Open World Research Initiative (OWRI): to regenerate, transform and leave a legacy for Modern Languages learning that fully recognizes the work that language does in the world. This chapter, therefore, poses three curricular and disciplinary questions: first, how should we constitute 'Iberian Studies' in the light of the recent 'transnational turn', using as an example the first-year 'Global Iberias' curriculum pioneered at King's College London (Vakil)? Second, and by extension, how might we advocate for the strategic value of Modern Languages as a 'discipline' in relation to associated multi- and interdisciplinary fields such as World and Comparative Literature (Scott)? And third, how might we integrate the study of literature and language both to counter their institutional and disciplinary fragmentation and to encourage students to grasp language as a material, worldmaking force, and not as a mere ancillary skill (Weiss)?

Introduction

Modern Languages departments in the United Kingdom, not unlike (national) literature departments, and their sister disciplines in the humanities and social sciences (Classics, History, Literary Studies, Sociology and Politics, to mention only the most overlapping with Modern Languages concerns), bear in both origins and institutional trajectories the imprints of nation building and empire. Arguably, these still to a large extent inform the curricula and conceptions of programmes in Spanish and Portuguese: the study of the languages, literatures, economies and societies of Spain, Portugal, and of the nations and communities of speakers of Spanish and Portuguese that students are likely to encounter in the course of their degree. Critical engagement with theory, interdisciplinarity, new media, and new social movements and their agendas, no less than the socio-economic and geopolitical impacts of globalization, migrations, diasporas and transnationalisms, have radically altered academic research and writing, and even teaching, but only more incipiently have they impacted the conception of Modern Languages degree programmes, including in Hispanic and Lusophone Studies.

Today's universities are more inclusive institutions, in gender, class and ethnic terms, in staff and student recruitment, and in administration and teaching, though still only partially and very unevenly so across the sector. Importantly, they are (under the UK's Equality Act 2010) statutorily accountable for institutional diversity, and, by and large, explicitly committed to curricular diversity. But 'diversity', especially of 'representation', has also somewhat hollowed out the anti-racist and decolonizing thrust of the changes ambitioned, and the slow progress is manifest in student-led demands and campaigns such as 'decolonize the curriculum' and 'Why is my professor white?'. Modern Languages are in this respect no different, but well positioned to respond.

Present challenges are inside and outside the academy: neoliberal managerialism, early career precarity, and administratively and financially driven restructuring inside; polarization, and post-truth, outside. Ours is an age of populist political narratives, which frame exclusionary senses of national community through both foundational fictions and divisive solidarities of us and them, pitting the 'left behind' victims of globalization against the 'cosmopolitan', liberal elites, on the one hand, and the 'welfare draining' immigrant, refugee and asylum-seeking 'outsiders', on the other. Against the grain of Orwellian Newspeak and fake news, with its debasement of both words and the bonds of social trust, Modern Languages study holds firmly to both the premise and promise of intercultural communication and dialogue, as well as to the recognition of and commitment to critical understanding of the structural and historical inequalities of global relations, exchanges and power.[1]

What we may call a decolonizing minimum in commitments to both curricular inclusiveness (representational, what and who is spoken about, and epistemological, who speaks) and inclusiveness in the classroom (who is heard and valued) has gained ground. But the more robust dimensions of decolonizing, from engaging the histories of the disciplines and how they set the boundaries of what counts as relevant topics of research, valid research methodologies, and especially a corresponding decolonizing of assessments at undergraduate level, rather than postgraduate and faculty research, lag far behind. And in view of mounting institutional pressures to open up modules to meet floor numbers, the asymmetries of global scholarship and publication and their implications for

[1] As the *Language Acts and Worldmaking* project developed, the need for this commitment became increasingly important. See Chapter 4 'Language and hospitality in worldmaking: how languages act in the world' for further discussion.

teaching in translation are perhaps most consequent to meaningful decolonization of the undergraduate education in Modern Languages and the humanities and social sciences.

Studies of the languages, peoples, histories, cultures and societies historically covered in the variously named departments of Spanish and Portuguese, Latin American and Brazilian, or of the Americas, Iberian, Hispanic and Lusophone Studies, have complex histories. These may be local, to individual institutions and countries; conjunctural, to successive waves of administrative and academic restructuring; and ideological or disciplinary, from area studies to epistemologically informed critiques of the names and naming under which we do our work, its ideological loadings, and what they exclude. Several of these are constructively engaged in how to reconceive how students are introduced to their objects of study. Ours is one such, informed by the thrust of the *Language Acts and Worldmaking* project as a whole, but developed under the work of the Travelling Concepts strand in particular. In this chapter we develop three interconnected interventions in the curricular and disciplinary aspects of the strand's work on the reach and significance of the Spanish- and Portuguese-speaking worlds and their global contact zones, from the Middle Ages to the present. These Iberian worlds challenge visions structured by the histories of modern nation states. What we call the 'Iberianate venture', evoked not only by the term 'Iberia' but also by Al-Andalus and Sepharad, constitutes a workshop for interrogating the complex and entangled histories of peoples and places that are both lived and imagined as figures of thought. Our research into the interfaith and intercultural relations between Islamic, Christian and Jewish communities within Europe and beyond interrogates the work done by the language of nationalism and regionalism, orientalism and colonialism, exile and migration.[2] The curricular implications of this approach, and our contribution to the emergent turn to a more transnational Modern Languages, are the issues that underwrite AbdoolKarim Vakil's opening intervention.

[2] A concrete example of our approach is the collaborative volume *Al-Andalus in Motion: Travelling Concepts and Cross-Cultural Contexts* (Scott, Vakil and Weiss, 2021).

Global Iberias: *El Camino Se Hace Caminando*

Global Iberias is our ambitious attempt, at King's College London, to rethink an introductory course for students of Spanish and Portuguese which is informed by and responds frontally to the challenges of our times, in the academy and in society. Its origins lie in the attempt to make a virtue out of a necessity, and creatively respond to three challenges. One was the need to meet the imposed merger of the historically autonomous departments, degrees, students and teaching of 'Spanish and Spanish American Studies' (but in reality also Catalan Studies) and 'Portuguese and Brazilian Studies' (but in reality also Lusophone African Studies) with an intellectually coherent introductory core course spanning the two areas. A second challenge was to balance the imperatives and constraints of an 'introductory' module with the additional challenges of a diversity of combined degree options, and entry-level language: ab initio, post-A level, native speaker and heritage language speakers. This includes: managing the transition from school-based teaching to university-based learning, including the critical skills for independent and critical study in the humanities and Modern Languages; developing both a chronological narrative and a geographical mapping, historical and contemporary, of the relevant contexts, scales, subjects and objects which students will encounter, often to their surprise – and excitement – as part of their studies; and to integrate both linguistic and language learning and so-called 'content' learning as seamless parts of one whole. Third, the challenge of doing justice to both our subjects and objects of study and critical perspectives and approaches, by working against the grain of colonial, Eurocentric and diffusionist narratives of global expansion and of centres and peripheries, and through the nationalizing and partitioning work of states, languages, territories, histories and historiographies.

Global Iberias is decidedly not Iberia globalized, precisely because it critiques the historiographical grand narratives of 'Discoveries' and global expansion along with the ideologies that underpin them; nor is it about the impact of the global in Iberia (a reversal which still leaves Iberia at the centre); rather, it places Iberia within historically shifting networks of trade, conquest, colonization and migration – from words and ideas to technologies, foodstuffs and peoples. For us, therefore, Global Iberias is not so much a narrative as a dynamic, the concatenation of contexts, processes and mutual transformations forged by what we (paraphrasing the pioneering Chicago world historian Marshall Hodgson) call the 'Iberianate venture'. To this end, Global Iberias is of necessity open-ended in its coverage. We shift the contexts, voices and perspectives along the journey, as we move from topic to topic, week by week, in time and geographically. Each year it traces one itinerary among others; there is no one story of the Making of the Worlds of Global Iberias to be told.

No descriptive title satisfactorily names the range of work scholars in our areas do; work which spans the contemporary societies of Spanish- and Portuguese-speaking countries, such as Spain, Portugal, Brazil, and the nations of Central and South America and the Caribbean and of Lusophone Africa, but also other linguistic and indigenous communities of these countries, their languages, cultures, literatures, oral and written, and histories; the minority, diasporic and immigrant communities of Spanish and Portuguese speakers, including significant Latino/a/X communities in the United States; Spanish and Portuguese creole languages, from West Africa to Malaysia; historical linguistic communities of once-colonized regions and port cities, from the Philippines, to Indonesia and China; and the hybrid languages and literatures emerging from novel migratory currents, and their musical and literary expressions, across Portuguese- and Spanish-speaking states.

Divided into 'Histories' (accentuating historical perspectives with a view to unlearning and estranging the categories of the present, from the nation state and its identities, to subjectivities, world views and material cultures)[3] and 'Themes' (adopting a more

[3] This also provides a critical understanding of conventional periodization (when was the Middle Ages? What do we mean by Early Modern? and so on). This is important since they are not just terms of convenience or useful signposts, but are concepts that carry baggage.

thematic and conceptual exploration of cultural production and circulation), any moment, place, object, word, text, individual or event can provide a point of entry which grounds and exemplifies both an aspect of the overall tapestry of stories and the application of a critical skill: from the use of medieval Spanish ballads, samba lyrics, or the tango and the *grotesco criollo* as historical sources for medieval Iberian frontier society, and late nineteenth- and early twentieth-century Brazil and Argentina, respectively; from the *Loas* of the seventeenth-century Mexican nun Sor Juana Inés de la Cruz, to the Latino science fiction of Junot Diaz, and from Portuguese colonial film to postcolonial Lusophone African fiction. Al-Andalus, 1492, or the three, or four, 1492s of the conquest of Granada, the expulsion of the Jews, the Columbus voyage and the publication of Nebrija's grammar; the Atlantic and the Indian Oceans and cross-cultural exchanges; enslavement, resistance and revolution; religion, music, food and art make up the various nexuses, sinews and braidings of its telling. If the meaning is in the usage, Global Iberias is what Modern Languages study *is* in a department of Spanish, Portuguese and Latin American Studies. It is a learning in how to read and map the world anew. Global Iberias builds on lively critical reformulations of our disciplinary and institutional divides, and engages the topical polarizations of contemporary society with a Modern Languages-based commitment to critical literacies. Starting our histories with Al-Andalus and closing it with the contemporary polemics over the memory of Al-Andalus, *convivencia* and Jewish and Muslim heritage in Spain and Portugal, we do three things which bridge research, teaching and public engagement.

First, we draw on a pioneering and diverse range of contemporary contributions from across a range of specialist and institutional divides to expand our disciplinary 'geographies' and subject matter, to comparative and intertextual explorations and conversations bridging Arabic, Islamic and Islamicate Studies, Hebrew, Judeo-Spanish, and Jewish and Judaic Studies, the study of pre-Colombian and indigenous cultures, African Studies and the study of transatlantic exchanges, and Spanish, Portuguese, and Brazilian and Latin American languages, literatures, histories and cultures.

Second, at a time when the discourse of a clash of civilizations has been re-grounded anew in scaremongering and dog-whistle politics over a Hispanic 'challenge' to America and a Muslim 'challenge' to European societies, Al-Andalus and medieval Iberia have gained new and hotly polemic topicality, championed and contested as exemplary models of tolerance or hoodwinking myth. Al-Andalus has been rhetorically weaponized in the context of the War on Terror and migration panics, and its discursive effects are felt by individuals and communities in their everyday lives. We recognize and assume that research and teaching in our areas feed into a broader public discourse, whether we like it or not.

Third, Global Iberias and Travelling Concepts seek to connect the dots from Al-Andalus to the many Andalusias of the imagination, and from research to teaching. *Al-Andalus in Motion: Travelling Concepts and Cross-Cultural Contexts*, our 2018 conference in Istanbul (published as Scott, Vakil and Weiss, 2021), and the opening and closing lectures of Global Iberias, 'Iberian frontiers, or Why Iberia?' and 'Iberia, Europe and Al-Andalus in the age of anxiety', convergently explored the claims and stakes of Sephardic and Andalusi diasporic memories, the legacies of European Romantic and Orientalist exoticizing imagination; cultural appropriations in leisure and heritage tourist commodification; and the citizenship politics of assimilationist backlash and multicultural belonging in conversations between scholars across disciplines from Art History to Anthropology, Literary Studies and Jewish Studies, and among students of Spanish, Portuguese and Latin American Studies in London.

When students arrive at university their understanding can be focused around a very 'instrumental' appreciation of language; Global Iberias fosters a broad understanding of Modern Languages study away from narrower linguistic competence and towards a thicker, more socially and historically grounded conception of language as worldmaking. Through Global Iberias we also seek to build up a shared critical literacy for our discipline: a means of using language as a way of thinking about the world, about the way things are and how they came to be. In this sense, Global Iberias is akin to a way of seeing.

If we were to start the first seminar of the year by asking our students 'Why do you want to study Spanish or Portuguese?', or 'Why do you want to study it at King's?', most would have a ready answer, whether the one carefully crafted for their university application personal statements, or that, perhaps closer to their hearts, of a love and joy of languages and cultures. But what if we were to ask them, instead, '*How* is it that you are able to study Spanish and Portuguese at King's?' This raises two questions that go far beyond any individual interests, enthusiasms, preferences and ambitions which informed their personal choice. What it is asking is two things. One: 'Why is it that *these* languages are taught at King's, or, indeed, in Britain?' After all, not every language is. And two – which is another way of asking the same question – 'Why do people (in sufficient numbers to make it viable to do so) *want* to learn *these* languages?'

Part of the answer lies in the status of these two languages as 'world languages', which in turn is tied to their imperial and global histories. If, as the oft-cited quip goes, the difference between a 'language' and a 'dialect' is that 'a language is a dialect with an army and a navy', then a 'world language' is one in whose making a history of power and empire is never far behind. The larger answer to the *how* question, then, is almost the answer to another question: 'How is the world how it is today, with all its inequalities of power, visibility, voice and agency which characterize it?' And this is precisely what goes to the heart of what Global Iberias is about. Asking students not why they have chosen to study Spanish or Portuguese at King's, but how it is that they are able to study Spanish and Portuguese at King's, begins to raise the kinds of questions of structure and power, in society and in the global order, contemporary and historical, which underlie Global Iberias.

Not so long ago, this relation between language and power was quite transparently, even proudly, worn: the teaching of the languages, culture and literatures of Portugal and Spain was the epic story of Expansion, Discovery and Conquest, its core literature the Golden Age of Empire. It was a narrative of centres and peripheries, in which the making of history flowed outwards, told almost invariably as the heroic story of Iberia unfolding out of Europe to the four corners of the Earth, spreading religion, civilization, and Spanish and Portuguese. In Global Iberias we ask this same question, of how the world we live in was made, but it is interaction that takes centre-stage, and along with this come multiple centres, many peripheries, and a plurality of directions of flow of culture, people, objects, words and knowledge. The languages of Spain and Portugal bear the imprint of their global circulations outwards, and inwards. As importantly, just as the cultures of Spain and Portugal are not the cultures of the Spanish- and Portuguese-speaking worlds, so also are Spanish and Portuguese far from the only – at times and places far even from the main or most important – languages of those worlds.

Part of this involves promoting a greater awareness of the huge range of study being undertaken; the notion that our department simply focuses on Spanish and Portuguese is a misnomer. All kinds of languages are in the mix. Medieval Iberia was Sepharad and Al-Andalus. Hebrew and Arabic, and various combinations of the languages and scripts of Jews, Christians and Muslims, made up the cultural, political, philosophical and literary worlds of what we now call Spain and Portugal, as well as the memories and heritage of the Andalusi and Sephardic diasporas. One Romance language – Castilian – became 'Spanish' and, like Portuguese, served as an imperial language, transformed in the contact zones of trade and conquest, violence and wonder. And the process continues today: the language of migrants and minorities is an important part of how Spanish and Portuguese are developing – in Spain and Portugal, no less than in South America, or in Lusophone Africa, or among Latino/a/X communities in the United States.

We neither aim for nor provide a grand narrative. Our approach to Global Iberias accepts that every curriculum, like every narrative, is a selection: it excludes more than it includes; it backgrounds as it foregrounds; it has an agenda. So we set ours out explicitly. Our agenda is to foreground interconnectedness, the entanglement of histories, the play of power and resistance, and to encourage critical self-reflectiveness – both in our teaching and in our students' learning. We want students to look at the world and ask questions about what they see, what they do not see, and what accounts for these visibilities and invisibilities. Questions about the imbalances of power that have shaped, and unevenly continue to shape, society and culture globally. Questions about what counts as knowledge and who produces it; what counts as cultural authority and who holds it. Questions, finally, about whose voices are heard, whose lives are remembered, and whose deaths are forgotten. Many students who come to the study of Spanish and Portuguese bring with them culturally inherited understanding of the expansion of European civilization around the world and how that shaped global history. But this understanding is shaped by imperial and colonial views built up to justify it. Global Iberias provides an environment to critically challenge these assumptions.

As outlined here, our Global Iberias project clearly intersects with the fields of World and Comparative Literatures. Intellectually productive as it is, the intersection raises questions about the place and contribution of Modern Languages within the institutional and programmatic structures of UK higher education, with its move towards greater interdisciplinarity, motivated in part by academic creativity, in part by the top-down distribution of resources in a marketized higher education. Rachel Scott uses the Iberian Peninsula and the transnational spaces that make up the global Iberian worlds as a 'testing ground' on which to interrogate 'world' as an organizing category, underscoring its multidimensionality and multilingualism, the global and local interrelations and interactions that create it, and its fluidity and its *unfinishedness* ('unfinished' because, like the Global Iberias project described above, we approach it as a dynamic process, open to multiple stories and perspectives). With reference to *Kalila wa-Dimna*, an archetypal work of 'world literature' that forms the basis for her recent research, Scott argues that including transnational texts such as this, which 'belong' to many different languages and cultures, on Modern Languages degree programmes makes visible the heterogeneity of the disciplinary spaces in which we, as Modern Languages practitioners, already naturally work. And furthermore, she demonstrates how as a discipline that builds awareness of what languages *do* as a form of worldmaking and how they function beyond the merely 'communicative', Modern Languages has a fundamentally important role to play in a globally aware pedagogy and curriculum design.

Worlding Iberian Studies: which literature, whose world, and what about language?

> *First*, that we recognise space as the product of interrelations; as constituted through interactions, from the immensity of the global to the intimately tiny [...]. *Second*, that we understand space as the sphere of the possibility of the existence of multiplicity in the sense of contemporaneous plurality; as the sphere in which distinct trajectories coexist; as the sphere therefore of coexisting heterogeneity. Without space, no multiplicity; without multiplicity, no space. If space is indeed the product of interrelations, then it must be predicated upon the existence of plurality. Multiplicity and space as co-constitutive. *Third*, that we recognise space as always under construction. Precisely because space on this reading is a product of relations-between, relations which are necessarily embedded material practices which have to be carried out, it is always in the process of being made. It is never finished; never closed. Perhaps we could imagine space as a simultaneity of stories-so-far.
>
> (Massey, 2005: 9)

Readers may wonder why a chapter about Modern Languages prominently cites the work of the cultural geographer Doreen Massey. However, Massey's opening conceptual propositions to her book *For Space* offer a productive way into some of the issues raised in this part of our chapter. For one, Massey's mention of stories draws attention to the constructed nature of the spaces we inhabit – a proposition that draws some parallels with the idea of worldmaking as a literary activity that has been explored by scholars working in the field of World Literature. Pheng Cheah, for example, describes World Literature as 'a type of world-making activity that enables us to imagine a world' (Cheah, 2008: 26). For Cheah, literature's very openness and ambiguity are what make it so apt for worldmaking, 'as something that is structurally detached from its putative origin and that permits and even solicits an infinite number of interpretations'. He remarks:

> Literature is an exemplary modality of the undecidability that opens a world. It is not merely a product of the human imagination or something that is derived from, represents, or duplicates material reality. Literature is the force of a passage, an experience through which we are given and receive any determinable reality. The issue of receptibility is fundamental here. It does not refer to the reception of a piece of literature but to the structure of opening through which one receives a world and through which another world can appear.
>
> (Cheah, 2008: 35)

In Cheah's view, 'the concept of "world" does not abolish national differences but takes place and is to be found in the intervals, mediations, passages, and crossings between national borders' and is instead 'a form of relating or being-with' (Cheah, 2008: 30). Much like Massey, Cheah therefore emphasizes intersections and interactions as the means by which a particular concept of space – such as 'world' – is created. Like Massey, Cheah also argues for an understanding of 'world' as unbounded and unfinished:

> an ongoing, dynamic process of becoming, something continually made and remade rather than a spatial-geographical entity. Only then can world literature be understood as literature that is of the world, a fundamental force in the ongoing cartography and creation of the world instead of a body of timeless aesthetic objects.
>
> (Cheah, 2008: 30–1)

The concept of storytelling as worldmaking is explored here using examples from research for *Language Acts and Worldmaking* on *Kalila wa-Dimna*, the collection of travelling tales whose centuries of transmission and myriad global trajectories have made it an archetypal work of 'World Literature' – in the sense that it circulated beyond its culture of origin, to use David Damrosch's definition (Damrosch, 2003: 4). As a *textual* space, *Kalila wa-Dimna* embodies the global and local interrelations and interactions, the multiplicity, plurality and heterogeneity, and the unbounded *unfinishedness* that Massey's conceptual propositions point towards and that Cheah also touches on.

These propositions also provide a potentially rich starting point for thinking about some of the thematic concerns of and structural issues facing Modern Languages as a discipline in its own right and in relation (conceptually and institutionally) to associated fields such as World and Comparative Literature. More broadly, in this second part of the chapter there is also further reflection on the challenges facing Modern Languages as the institutional and programmatic structures of the field in UK higher education move towards greater interdisciplinarity. A number of critics have addressed the impact of this move on the future of Modern Languages not only conceptually, as a distinct discipline, but also structurally, institutionally and in human terms (Forsdick, 2010, 2014; Wielander, 2014; Burdett, 2018; Davis, 2018). Charles Forsdick argues that concretizing 'a sense of the disciplinariness' of Modern Languages will 'ensure that the enabling diversity by which our field has been characterized for several decades now does not tip into a disabling, disintegrating fragmentation'

(Forsdick, 2010: 95). As our colleague Chris Pountain rightly suggests, this sense of 'disciplinariness' – to use Forsdick's term – can be found by acknowledging the central place of language alongside linguistics and the study of literature as a language-dependent culture, which Pountain views as 'integral to MFL as an academic discipline' (2017: 262). More than other areas of culture, the 'language-literature link' (Pountain, 2017: 263; quoting Paran, 2006: 8–9) not only ensures that creative literature provides 'wonderful language-learning material', but, Pountain concludes, 'its artistry provokes reflection on the use of language in so many ways' (2017: 265, 268).

To think about the concepts of 'world' and 'global' is to come face to face with language. And yet, as Mary Louise Pratt suggests, this fact has not always been acknowledged:

> If you pick up one of the dozens of anthologies about globalization that have appeared in the last fifteen years, you almost certainly won't find a chapter on language, nor even, in most cases, an entry for language in the index. […] Though some of the people who think about language think about globalization, almost none of the people who think about globalization think about language. Yet globalization has changed the linguistic landscape of the world, and global processes are directed and shaped by language at every turn.
>
> (Pratt, 2014: 274)

Language is also a blind spot that 'readers and advocates of World Literature often appear deliberately or unwittingly to underplay', according to Charles Forsdick (2014: 486). The discipline of 'World Literature' maintains language – usually English – as one of the prerequisites for inclusion: that is, has it been translated into this tongue, or not? This generates partiality and selectivity that shape understanding of the 'world', which is more often than not filtered through an Anglophone lens. Pratt argues that 'world literature seems limited in its ability to explore the linguistic landscapes of globalization, and to grasp linguistic difference as a force in the world' and that 'the very instruments of the worlding [i.e. translation and *lingua franca*] inhibit its ability to enact and explore the new linguistic geographies of our time' (Pratt, 2014: 292–3). Yet this, it can be argued, is precisely where Modern Languages has a role to play, as a discipline that builds awareness of what languages *do* and how they function beyond the merely 'communicative' as a form of worldmaking. As work on the *Language Acts and Worldmaking* project has demonstrated in various ways, language is no passive reflector of an already determined 'reality' but rather it plays an active role in creating how we see and experience that reality. An example of this is the way in which fields of research and teaching are delineated. Labels like 'Hispanic', 'Spanish' and 'Iberian' imply different conceptual, ideological and cultural worlds that do not necessarily map onto the same cartographic spaces (see Dangler, 2006; Menocal, 2006).

In her book *For Space*, Massey acknowledges that her use of the term 'story' 'brings with it connotations of something told, of an interpreted history', but insists that 'what I intend is simply the history, change, movement, of things themselves' (Massey, 2005: 12). But who, we may ask, records, narrates and disseminates these histories, changes and movements? The question of *which* stories get to be told remains, in *For Space*, unconsidered. This is no criticism of Massey's book since this is not the question she seeks to answer or explore. Nevertheless, it echoes that raised by David Damrosch in his introduction to *What Is World Literature?*: 'Which literature, whose world?' (2003: 1) – a question that has also been asked in recent years by historians addressing the global turn in their own discipline. Sebastian Conrad, for example, remarks that Global History

> is about coming to terms with the global past, and thus about *creating the world* for the purposes of the present. These purposes are manifold, and they may be conflicting and contested. [...]. If the 'world' is the subject, who, then, is the 'we' that global historians

write for? And what are the politics of such an approach?

(Conrad, 2016: 205)

Who decides where the boundaries of spaces – cartographic, cultural, literary, disciplinary – lie; what is included and what is excluded? And where does language fit within this issue?

The process by which a text is 'worlded' is never neutral; it is the result of deliberate choices, influenced by political and social interests and ideologies, economic and commercial structures, and technologies (Kadir, 2004). On a broader scale, as already observed above, every curriculum is a selection, based on criteria of exclusion as much as of inclusion. Damrosch's question 'Which literature, whose world?' is thus highly pertinent to the study of languages and their language-dependent cultures in Modern Languages departments. Literature as a language-based activity is rooted in worldmaking, both in the sense of how it creates 'worlds' for readers and also in terms of how it is categorized and taught – something that the creation of curricula for degree programmes forces us to confront. For this process requires that we acknowledge inherent power dynamics, the perspectives that are foreground and those that are not; the blind spots and overlooked voices. It also requires that we take into account which 'stories' – that is, which histories, changes and movements, to use Massey's definition – they include and exclude, and from whose perspectives they are viewed. In short, it requires that we acknowledge that the 'worlds' we are presenting are but one possibility of many. These are questions that the discipline of Modern Languages, like many others, has been grappling with in recent years in particular, as calls to diversify and 'decolonize' curricula have increased, which AbdoolKarim Vakil addresses above. And, as I have discussed elsewhere, a work like *Kalila wa-Dimna* provides an opportunity to address these questions and more.[4]

[4] See Scott (2021).

Karima Laachir, Sara Marzagora and Francesca Orsini argue that questions of language and a recognition of multilingualism are key to the study of 'world literatures'. They question the usefulness of the concepts of 'world' and 'global' (too nebulous, too big, too homogenizing), preferring the idea of 'significant geographies' as an axis upon/through which to consider the wider trajectories of circulation, reception and meaning-making (Laachir, Marzagora and Orsini, 2018: 3). Taking cues from Massey, they 'imagine history/time and space not as linear but as multiple, relational and inevitably fragmentary/discontinuous' (2018: 3). Their concept of significant geographies adopts 'a multilingual approach to archives, texts and genres, and literary tastes' (2018: 3) in recognition of the fact that the world is not singular or fixed or homogenous but formed of multilingual, overlapping and ever-evolving contact zones. The Iberian Peninsula and the transnational spaces that make up the global Iberian worlds provide an excellent example of one such significant geography, one that offers an ideal 'testing ground' on which to interrogate 'world' as an organizing category, underscoring its multidimensionality and multilingualism, the global and local interrelations and interactions that create it, and its fluidity and *unfinishedness*. Including a work like *Kalila wa-Dimna*, which 'belongs' to so many languages and cultures and has been claimed by many different nation states, on a degree programme in Spanish or any other Modern Language makes visible the heterogeneity of the disciplinary spaces in which we, as Modern Languages practitioners, work. It breaks down boundaries between 'national' literary disciplines, demonstrating that our literary/cultural/linguistic 'worlds' are not singular, not unique, not fixed or homogeneous, but porous, malleable and multiple, and that they are constructed through interrelations and interactions on both global and local levels. The book's transmission, crisscrossing from East to West and back again, tells of the complex and entangled histories of peoples and places that are both lived and imagined as figures of thought, of the movement and cross-fertilizations brought about by interactions across boundaries of language, faith and culture.

That *Kalila wa-Dimna* existed in different languages in the Iberian Peninsula during the Middle Ages – Arabic, Hebrew, Latin and Castilian – echoes Massey's idea of space being a 'simultaneity of stories-so-far'. It also underlines how far a 'space' – as an experience of place, a concept or an intellectual discipline – is created by 'stories' in the sense of language and literature. The synchronicity of the book's presence in Iberia reveals a need to appropriate the fables into markedly different religious, cultural, linguistic and political 'worlds'. And while some medieval readers may have been able to access the book in more than one language, the perspective they would gain on the stories' morals and meanings in each case would not necessarily overlap, in part due to the different 'baggage' carried and work done by each language. *Kalila wa-Dimna* enables its readers to test particular moral and practical challenges by placing themselves in the centre of the action or issue through the act of reading and storytelling. It does so through a many-layered, emboxed structure: the tales within tales within tales create micro 'worlds' within the internal narrative, foregrounding differing perspectives and voices at each turn in a dizzying array of protagonists and points of view. This structure allows for the addition of new stories, or the removal of others, providing an open work that encourages interventions – recalling Cheah's comment about receptibility, about literature as the 'structure of opening through which one receives a world and through which another world can appear' (Cheah, 2008: 35). *Kalila wa-Dimna* also provides an early (i.e. non-contemporary) example of Rebecca Walkowitz's theory that some texts are 'born translated' in the sense that translation is not secondary or incidental to it, but rather a condition of its very production (2015: 4). In such texts:

> translation functions as a thematic, structural, conceptual, and sometimes even typographical device.

> These works are *written for translation*, in the hope of being translated, but they are also often *written as translations*, pretending to take place in a language other than the one in which they have, in fact, been composed.
>
> (Walkowitz, 2015: 4; author's own emphasis)

It is no coincidence that the paratexts of many medieval and early modern versions of the fables address (assumed) linguistic hierarchies, the relationships between languages and their dependent cultures, and the ethics of translation as not only a linguistic or cultural act but a political one. Nor that the book is claimed as a means of fashioning a particular national or imperial identity – an act of worldmaking through translation (e.g. Alfonso X's appropriation of the fables into Castilian as part of his imperial ambitions, or Vincente Bratutti's translation into Spanish for Philip IV in the context of the reorientation of Spain's global position in the seventeenth century). A text without a fixed 'original', *Kalila wa-Dimna* lives through translation, through the adaptations and rewritings it has undergone throughout its many 'afterlives'. As such, its transmission not only exemplifies how storytelling functions as an act of worldmaking but reveals the centrality of language to the study of world literary cultures in general.

In her introduction to *Modern Languages Open* Comparative Literature Launch Issue (2018), Emma Bond talks about the necessity of situating discussions about Comparative Literature within and alongside Modern Languages. Not only do the majority of Comparative Literature courses in the UK tend to be 'housed' within departments of Modern Languages, she argues, but there are parallels between the two disciplines in terms of anxieties around the respective status and direction of each field. Bond argues that Modern Languages and Comparative Literature represent a 'disciplinary interface' that can provide a challenge to 'the monolithic presence of what Gayatri Chakravorty Spivak has termed a "canonical World Literature" – often practically in translation – that is being propagated, generally from the old metropole' (Bond, 2018: 1–2; quoting Spivak, 2014), predominantly in English. Bond continues by noting that:

> This opportunity – indeed, necessity – to redefine the parameters of the field of study, and to 'disturb the reigning order of priorities', is an equally pressing matter for modern languages, and I would argue that it is precisely by thinking each field through the other that we might find just cause for optimism and mutual renewal of purpose.
>
> (Bond, 2018: 1–2; quoting Saussy, 2014)

Rather than thinking about World and Comparative Literatures as a threat to Modern Languages' 'disciplinariness', could it not be productive to instead ask what Modern Languages can do for other related fields such as World and Comparative Literatures?

This is perhaps best given expression in my own recent languages journey and professional life, having recently moved from a role within the more 'traditional' structure of a Modern Languages department of Spanish, Portuguese and Latin American Studies to an interdisciplinary department of Languages, Literatures and Cultures in which Modern Languages and Translation Studies sit alongside Comparative and World Literatures and Cultures, History of Art and Visual Culture, Film Studies and Liberal Arts. As my research interests in the transnational and global circulation of literature have been put to exciting new pedagogic uses in the development of new programmes in World and Comparative Literatures and Cultures, I have striven to address not only the fundamental question of curriculum creation – 'Which literature, whose world?' – but how in 'worlding' literatures and cultures we come face to face with language, and how to embed this into curricula that are necessarily increasingly taught in translation. I have no concrete answers to this situation, only an awareness that such issues need to be contended with and that, to employ Massey's propositions once again, the disciplinary areas in which we work are not fixed entities but plural and heterogeneous spaces in constant flux.[5] The unceasing process of making and remaking the boundaries of our intellectual and professional worlds is not, I suggest, therefore necessarily negative: indeed, considering what Modern Languages *is* and what languages *do* within broader intellectual and disciplinary structures – seeing them 'not as an enclosed area of a strictly bounded discipline but as a contested site on which important issues – literary, cultural, historical and other [...] – may be explored' (LaCapra, 2000: 226; quoted in Forsdick, 2010: 105) – should be a positive catalyst for the field's evolution above and beyond the fight for its ongoing survival. In practical terms, what might this mean for the development of specific modules within a Modern Languages programme of study? Julian Weiss sketches out one possible answer below.

Language literature, lost and found

Rebecca Solnit begins her invaluable *Field Guide to Getting Lost* with a simple premise: before you can be found, you must first be lost. In a creative life, of course, being lost and found is never a single operation, but a continuous willingness to 'leave the door open for the unknown, the door into the dark' (Solnit, 2006: 4). As in a creative life, so in that creative thing called 'literature'. There have been countless attempts to pin down that elusive category and trace how and when it emerged to wander its way through the cultural taxonomies of Western thought, and this elusiveness returns in the final pages of this chapter. The currently precarious academic status of 'literature' has led to a thriving market for such books as *Why Literature Matters in the 21st Century* (Roche, 2004), *Literature: Why It Matters* (Eaglestone, 2019), *The Written World: How Literature Shaped History* (Puchner, 2017) or *How to*

[5] This unfinishedness is something that my colleagues on the Diasporic Identities and the Politics of Language Teaching research strand address in their chapter here on the complex, multi layered and non-linear process of becoming experienced by language teachers and researchers, which they describe as 'an embodied, lived and unstable experience that unfolds itself within many territories, across different languages, and that is rooted in personal experiences. Never finished, always in progress. It is an 'assemblage' of doing, being and becoming within a nomadic, inter- and cross-cultural framework of reference.' (p. 6; emphasis is my own).

Read Literature (Eagleton, 2013). Eagleton prefaces his book with the assertion that, 'like clog dancing, the art of analysing works of literature is almost dead on its feet. A whole tradition of what Nietzsche called "slow reading" is in danger of sinking without trace' (Eagleton, 2013: ix).

Similarly, Modern Languages researchers, teachers and students may be forgiven for thinking that their interest in language is currently lost within not one but several disciplinary fields. Take the current definition of Modern Languages Research as a unit of assessment (UOA) within the British Research Excellence Framework (REF), a peer-review process that assesses research quality in UK higher education. Modern Languages research is located within assessment panel D (Humanities), subpanel 26: 'Modern Languages and Linguistics'. Having mapped out its geographic and linguistic terrain (Europe, Latin America and Europe's cultural and linguistic contact zones, past and present), the sub-panel explains that, for the purposes of quality assessment, it will take 'a broad view of what constitutes modern language studies'. Though an entirely conventional academic term, the plural 'studies' acquires a special resonance when we read that the 'unit' – straining against its etymology – embraces 'all areas of general, historical, theoretical, descriptive and applied linguistics, phonetics, and translation and interpreting studies, regardless of the methodology used or the language to which the studies are applied'. For those trying to puzzle out where their interests fit, the REF provides some helpful signposts:

> literature and thought; cultural studies; theatre studies; film and media studies; visual cultures; language studies; translation and interpreting studies; political, social and historical studies; editorial scholarship, bibliography, textual criticism and theory and history of the book; philosophy and critical theory; world literature and comparative literature; literature in relation to the other arts; and applied, practice-based and pedagogical research, including translation and creative writing.

Into this mixed and hospitable neighbourhood, the sub-panel also welcomes 'interdisciplinary research', because language and literature have recently struck up conversations with 'science, medicine and technology, digital humanities, or creative technologies'. And the intellectual horizons of Modern Languages and Linguistics stretch even further when one considers that the REF also anticipates 'significant overlap with Area Studies'.

In disciplinary terms, it has to be said, the REF is not intended as a prescriptive blueprint but as a responsive and dynamic peer-review process, sensitive to academic developments within the specific institutional contexts of UK higher education. It simultaneously reflects and supports the research and teaching of Modern Languages and Linguistics as a multidisciplinary field, whose practitioners are located within and across multiple institutional settings. In principle, this multilocational setting is positive. Potentially, it broadens the role of language and linguistics within the humanities, social sciences and sciences (e.g. Medicine); potentially, it widens the appeal of learning another language; potentially, it poses questions about how language choice shapes the way research is conducted: put differently, is language knowledge simply an ancillary skill, of instrumental value, or does working and thinking in another language change your approach and open doors into other cultures, in creative engagement with difference and strangeness? Through language we not only find our identities or acquire them as we are born into language; through language we also are able to challenge, shed or change given identities as we learn a way of being in the world deemed to be 'foreign'; heritage learners will find a sense of belonging, once felt to be lost, now available to be found. Learning another language will not guarantee it, but it will create the conditions for becoming, as Julia Kristeva puts it, 'strangers to ourselves' and through a critically aware cosmopolitanism live with others (Kristeva, 1991).[6]

[6] For more on language learning as a form of hospitality, see Chapter 4: 'Language and hospitality in worldmaking: how languages act in the world'.

The capacity of Modern Languages study to operate within and across so many fields is an undoubted strength. From an institutional viewpoint it is also a weakness, when multi- and interdisciplinarity stray into uncritical diffuseness, a pervasive vagueness (tolerated, if not exactly shared, by university managers, staff and students) about the actual practice of Modern Languages and Linguistics (as already pointed out above, referring to the arguments of Forsdick and others). Whether one thinks of these areas as a multidisciplinary field or a discipline that makes interdisciplinarity possible is a fundamental topic for debate. But the debate will remain 'academic' (in that peculiarly English sense of possessing only theoretical interest) so long as it is separated from the actual practice and management of the discipline(s) within the institutional structures of higher education and their related divisions of labour and resources. The asymmetrical relations between these contiguous and overlapping fields require one to be adept in what Mary Louise Pratt called the 'arts of the contact zone' (Pratt, 1991). One institutional and intellectual contact zone that cries out for these arts is the one that theoretically connects but so often separates the teaching of 'language' and (to use a widespread but highly problematic term) 'content' (modules on literature, visual arts, history offered by language departments, individually or cross-listed). To broaden access to modules that budget-conscious university administrators in a heavily marketized system may regard as undersubscribed, these 'content' modules can be offered using either original texts with supporting translations or mainly using translations with (where possible) original texts for reference or further study.

Translation of materials into English sifts out or skews ideas, modes of thought, histories. This is not an attack on translation, either in the classroom or in research. Quite the opposite. It is an attack on its uncritical instrumental use, and an argument to further integrate the study of translation as historical theory and as reflective practice, a way of knowing and speaking across boundaries of time and culture. The focus here is not the pedagogical and intellectual issues related to teaching in or through translation (reading in translation is better than not reading at all). The creative opportunities it offers will return later in the discussion of the core question here, namely, how to reconnect language and 'content', which in this case is 'literature', another highly elastic and historically contentious term.

As noted above, in his manifesto for 'The three Ls of Modern Foreign Languages', Chris Pountain called for closer and, above all, more meaningful connection between the three areas of study – language, linguistics and literature – that he argues should constitute the 'cornerstones of Modern Foreign Languages as an academic discipline' (Pountain, 2017: 257). Commenting on literature's contribution, he points to its historical role in determining (and subverting) the linguistic standard; to its motivational power, challenging students with complex ideas; to its artistry that 'provokes reflection on the use of language in so many ways' (2017: 262–8). Wisely avoiding any single definition of 'literature', Pountain wraps the term in quotation marks, recognizing that, as a 'cultural discourse', it has lent itself to multiple definitions (262). For present purposes, as I reflect on what Pountain calls the 'language-literature link', I want simply to remove the hyphen and talk about 'language literature'.

By 'language literature' I am referring to one of the defining forces at work in the historical emergence of 'literature' as a socially constructed discourse: namely, the struggle to access the cultural capital of literacy. The term in its modern romance forms – *literatura, littérature, letteratura* – did not exist before the late seventeenth and eighteenth centuries, when a more specialized term was required to replace the earlier, more amorphous category of 'letters'. As Raymond Williams, among others, has observed, until the eighteenth century, the writings now gathered under the term 'literature' related primarily to 'a generalized social concept, expressing a certain (minority) level of educational experience' (Williams, 1977: 47). Etymologically, the origins of 'literature' lie in 'letters', the written, visible word, accessed through that (minority) educational experience. Culturally, its history is inextricably tied to other categories and terms: the author, the reader, the book (manuscript and printed), canon formation, among others. Ideologically, the history of literature is the history of a two-way exchange between an object ('letters') and its users (those who are 'lettered'). The qualities and status perceived in one are transferred on to the other, as if in a mutually reinforcing contract. As Terry Eagleton observed: 'Some texts are born literary, some achieve literariness, and some have literariness thrust upon them. Breeding in this respect may count for a good deal more than birth' (Eagleton, 1983: 8–9).

What I call 'language literature' are the works that either expressly or tacitly examine that breeding. They are works that are born in the struggle over the expressive power of language, which is at the same time a struggle over social status and intersecting genealogies of power, be it based on hierarchies of class, caste, gender, nation, race or the intersections between them. They are works that consciously engage with language understood not as a transparent medium of expression but as a material force in the world that conditions, though never determines, our individual and collective identities. They are works that foreground how meaning is never simply given or passively received but co-created by writers and readers: or speakers and listeners, because even in the most 'lettered' texts, the voice is always there, as what John Dagenais once called that 'bothersome residue' (Dagenais, 1991). In short, language literature is the literature about searching for a voice, finding it, only to realize that that voice is never entirely your own, because other voices are already hidden in it. That drama lies at the heart of Italo Calvino's definition of literature:

> The ideal library that I would like to see is one that gravitates toward the outside, toward the 'apocryphal' books, in the etymological sense of the word: that is, 'hidden' books. Literature is a search for the book hidden in the distance that alters the value and meaning of the known books; it is the pull toward the new apocryphal text still to be rediscovered or invented.
>
> (Calvino, 1987: 50)

The desire to place language at the heart of the category 'literature' shaped my attempt to combine, within the confines of a single undergraduate module, the three Ls that Pountain proposed for a Modern Languages curriculum. 'Language Acts and Worldmaking in Premodern Spain', first taught in 2017, is a second-year module based on a selection of now canonical Castilian texts composed roughly between 1300 and 1700. From the perspective of language and linguistics, it provides a basic introduction to the phonology and morphology of Old Spanish (sufficient for students to navigate their way through a modern critical edition of a medieval or early modern text, editions which are in an important sense forms of translation); it consolidates competency in the analytic use of grammatical terms and in syntactic structures shaped by oral and textual modes of communication; and it draws on sociolinguistic approaches to understand how particular texts construct their speech communities. As far as the literary element is concerned, the module is based on works that share a preoccupation with the way language shapes our perceptions of the world and how we live in it (similar to the approach of Pheng Cheah, mentioned above in the second part of this chapter). The choice of texts was also determined by practical and programmatic considerations: fitting a rather dense set of objectives into ten weeks; integrating the module into a progressive programme, which provides a platform for advanced courses and avoids duplication; introducing a range of literary forms; building on student awareness of the social and ideological concerns of humanities research. In its current iteration, the chosen works are: extracts from the *romancero viejo* (traditional ballads, from sixteenth-century printed anthologies); exemplary tales and fables from Eastern and Western traditions (*Conde Lucanor* by Juan Manuel and Juan Ruiz's *Libro de buen amor*, both first half of the fourteenth century), the proto-novel in dialogue (*Celestina* by Fernando de Rojas, 1499 – a sixteenth-century European bestseller), and lyric verse by seventeenth-century female poets from Spain and Mexico.

There is no space here to do anything more than sketch out some of the pedagogic features of the module and its learning outcomes (see https://languageacts.org/travelling-concepts/curriculum-development/). Selected phonological and morphological features of Old Castilian are taught through in-class practice, backed up with extracts from Pountain (2001) and others. Progress is monitored through formative assignments, testing linguistic and literary comprehension. Translation plays an important role here: not simply into English but also into modern Spanish. Modernized versions of, for example, Juan Manuel's prose significantly alter his syntax, turning his paratactic structures into hypotactic ones more familiar to the modern eye and ear. Translation offers the opportunity for creative rewritings of passages, as do exercises asking students to reimagine a scene from a different perspective, written in Spanish. Memorizing a ballad is a powerful tool: one cannot 'teach' what it feels like to know something 'by heart', to experience the sounds embodied, and to appreciate the cultural role of language memory, and have the freedom to improvise. The main concern, however, is to explain why language is the protagonist of the story these texts tell about the prehistory of 'literature' – whether it be understood as Solnit's 'door into the dark' or Calvino's 'new apocryphal text still to be rediscovered or invented'. We begin by taking students back to the word, positioned between sound and sight. One of the module's fundamental themes is orality and textuality, and the constant interplay between them. Students first encountering premodern texts read them as texts, rather than hear them as sound. Their condition as spoken words, heard not seen, is the first obstacle to be overcome as well as being an opportunity to explore the historical desire to control the graphic representation of sound. The practical benefit of helping students recognize words on the pages of modern critical editions, and to understand what modern editors do to regularize orthographic variation, raises awareness of the historical and social implications of standardization: we examine passages from the orthographic sections of the first *Diccionario de Autoridades* (1726–39) and the latest orthographic manual produced by the Real Academia Española (2010). In the process, we learn how orthographies are presented as forms of social cohesion, cementing a common pan-Hispanic identity, as a way into the broader idea of spelling as 'social action' (Sebba, 2012).

For this module's period and cultures, there is no such thing as pure orality, but it is important to understand what Walter Ong (1982) called the 'psychodynamics of orality' and its conditioning effect on syntax, expression, and the implied relations between speaker/author, work and audience/reader. For this, the traditional Spanish ballad (*romancero viejo*) is ideal. The ballads are late medieval and early modern versions of Homeric 'winged words': they constitute a language all of their own (Gilman, 1972), which is participatory and collective. The first printed compilations of the ballads illustrate their contribution to the development of the Renaissance idea of a national canon, a heritage that defines a collective identity. Some ballads thematize the operation of language itself. The most famous example is the ballad about Count Arnaldos who, while hunting by the seashore, sees a magical boat approach. The world stands still while the sailor sings a song. The only way to learn the song is to enter the boat and sail away; such is the power of the performed and embodied word to take you to new worlds. In the oral ballad, the modern concept of 'author' does not apply. But the authority of the word and those who write is the shared concern of two early fourteenth-century men, the powerful magnate Juan Manuel and the cleric Juan Ruiz. Read side by side, their collections of exemplary tales, *Conde Lucanor* and *Libro de buen amor* (both 1330s), illustrate the emergence in the vernacular of the idea of the 'author', the first in simple but artful paratactic prose, the second in highly complex monorhymed alexandrines (Weiss, 2005). In different ways, conditioned by their respective social estates (Juan Manuel as a layman was not expected to be literate; Juan Ruiz is supremely confident in his professional mastery of the written word), they explore the problem of where authority for meaning lies and of the efficacy of human language itself: language being the sign of humankind's fallen nature (Jager, 1993). And since it is inherently fallen, language is a form of desire. Juan Manuel, evoking conventional rhetorical concepts of language as an art of persuasion, boasts of his 'flattering words' that will bend his readers to his will; Juan Ruiz recreates the Ovidian *vetula* (old woman) employed by youths to seduce the object of their desire and uses her to symbolize language itself as 'the meretricious word' (Brown, 1997).

Towards the end of the Middle Ages, after the spread of lay literacy among non-professional readers – mainly aristocratic men and women, but also the burgeoning urban middle classes – and when Castilian is being redefined as the companion to empire (according to Antonio de Nebrija's ground-breaking *Gramática castellana*, 1492), Fernando de Rojas, a young law student at the university of Salamanca, finds a fragment of a humanist comedy about two young lovers and grafts on to it Spanish literature's most corrosive depiction of language at work in the world. Originally entitled *Comedia de Calisto y Melibea*, then, in an expanded second edition, *Tragicomedia*, it soon became known after one of its protagonists, Celestina, a former prostitute, now brothelkeeper, go-between and practitioner of black magic – a darker version of Juan Ruiz's Trotaconventos ('Convent-Trotter'). Rojas also turns her into the embodiment of the magical power of language to create and transform identities (see, for example, Gifford, 1981; Scott, 2017). But our focus is principally on Melibea, the young woman, trapped in a patriarchal world, who lives her life through the books she has read – classical and romance fictions – and yearns for erotic freedom. Rojas's novel is a book about books, and we see the two lovers strive to inhabit, awkwardly, deceptively, tragically, roles prescribed by the works they have read. Its textuality is rich with linguistic and literary registers; but it remains a novel in dialogue: to be understood, according to its first Renaissance editor, Alonso de Proaza, it needs to be voiced. Melibea's suicide speech illustrates how Rojas depicts language operating both to empower agency and to limit communication and self-understanding: Melibea is highly articulate; she commands language, though she is also at the mercy of courtly literature's tragic conventions, as she imagines being reunited with her dead lover in an erotic hell.

Melibea throws herself to her death, accusingly, at her father's feet. As she finds her voice, she dies. Her gesture of refusal would acquire more liberating and positive effect as Hispanic women, often nuns, found the space and resources to speak and write (Olivares and Boyce, 2012). When they did so, they often challenged the patriarchal order on the grounds of the disfiguring misrepresentation of women in language and literature. To illustrate this, we examine, among other works, poems by Sor Juana Inés de la Cruz (1648–95) and the Spanish noblewoman Catalina Clara Ramírez de Guzmán (1611–84), who subvert the masculine literary convention of 'portrait poems', usually male-authored sonnets idealizing female beauty. They look in the mirror of these word pictures and refuse to recognize themselves. They reinvent, re-find, voices that have not been lost so much as suppressed and overwritten. The greatest example is Sor Juana's sonnet 145, 'Este, que ves, engaño colorido' ('This thing that you see, colourful deceit'; Clamurro, 1986; Prendergast, 2007). Teaching this brilliant rhetorical artifice that unmasks the artifice of language itself throws into relief the concept of language literature: literature not simply as artistry (though it is certainly that) but the power relations embedded in words, individually as well as when combined into conventions and motifs; it taxes students' grammatical and linguistic capacity; their appreciation of metrics; and their ability to move between Spanish then and now. Sor Juana realized, long before Robert Eaglestone, that 'Literature can change who you are, turning you from a "reader" into a "critic": someone attuned to the ways we make meaning in our world' (Eaglestone, 2019). Sor Juana's fascination with language also demonstrates her awareness of literature as 'a living conversation which provides endless opportunities to rethink and reinterpret our societies and ourselves'.

An afterword: map!

Eaglestone's literature as 'a living conversation' might sound a little too chummy for some – cosy senior common rooms with a glass of amontillado – for it overlooks the situatedness of the exchange, the way the 'conversation' always takes place within particular historical conditions and relations of power. This is true of literature as an object of academic study as well as an evolving historical practice and discourse. It is also true of the academic study of another language. As we indicated in our introduction, and as AbdoolKarim Vakil emphasized in his contribution, critical awareness of the asymmetries, exclusions and selectiveness embedded in our curricula and degree programmes is paramount. We recognize that the kinds of module we describe here are possible only because of the particular institutional frameworks within which we currently work. We do not offer a prescriptive curricular template so much as a set of concerns and approaches that could be adapted according to various institutional settings, needs and resources. Modern Languages constitute a multidisciplinary field, but also a multilocational practice.

Wherever that practice is situated institutionally – within university schools or departments of one or more languages, programmes within larger units of, say, World or Comparative Literature, History, Modern Languages centres, and so forth – and however the balance is struck between teaching in and through the target language or in and through English translations, there will remain one central concern: namely, to understand how 'a definition of language is always, implicitly or explicitly, a definition of human beings in the world' (Williams, 1977: 21). Our place in the world will vary according to the language(s) we use (and which use us). Our aim as advocates for the study of another language that is our own not by birth but by willed affiliation is to investigate the role of language in what Cheah (speaking of literature) called 'the ongoing cartography and creation of the world' (Cheah, 2008: 31). As there are many languages, and many ways of speaking and writing them, so there is no single objective way of perceiving, defining and mapping the world and the ways we lay claim to it, live in it and belong to it. The Jamaican poet Kei Miller expresses this powerfully in his collection *The Cartographer Tries to Map a Way to Zion* (2014). This poetic sequence begins with an exchange (Eaglestone's literature as a 'living conversation') between a cartographer and a rastaman. The cartographer says that his worldmapping is 'science', which displays the earth 'as it is, without bias [...] to show the full / of a place in just a glance'. And in reply:

> The rastaman thinks, draw me a map of what you see
> then I will draw a map of what you never see
> and guess me whose map will be bigger than whose?
> Guess me whose map will tell the larger truth?

Our research in the Travelling Concepts strand of the *Language Acts and Worldmaking* project underscores the urgency of working in the gap opened up between the cartographer's and rastaman's perspectives, of understanding its conditions of possibility and of acquiring the critical literacies necessary to articulate and debate the terms and concepts that join and separate the scientific and the experiential, be they 'world', 'literature', 'Iberia', 'Spain', 'Portugal' or, of course, 'language' itself. Just as the word 'acts' in 'Language Acts' is both object of study and lived action, so our 'after' but never 'final' word is 'map!', as both noun and verb (here in imperative mode).

References

Bond, E. (2018) '*Modern Languages Open* Comparative Literature Launch Issue', *Modern Languages Open*, 1(17), 1–5. DOI: 10.3828/mlo.v0i0.234

Brown, C. (1997) 'The meretricious letter of the *Libro de buen amor*', *Exemplaria*, 9(1), 63–90.

Burdett, C. (2018) 'Moving from a National to a Transnational Curriculum', Languages, *Society & Policy*. Available from: www.meits.org/policy-papers/paper/moving-from-a-national-to-a-transnational-curriculum-the-case-of-italian-st (Accessed: 8 September 2020).

Calvino, I. (1987) *The Literature Machine: Essays*, trans. Patrick Creagh. London: Secker & Warburg.

Cheah, P. (2008) 'What is a world? On world literature as world-making activity', *Daedalus*, 137(3), 26–38.

Clamurro, W. H. (1986) 'Sor Juana Inés de la Cruz reads her portrait', *Revista de Estudios Hispánicos*, 20(1), 27–43.

Conrad, S. (2016) *What Is Global History?* Princeton, NJ: Princeton University Press.

Dagenais, J. (1991) 'That bothersome residue: Toward a theory of the physical text', in Doan, A. B. and Pasternack, C. B.(Eds), *Vox Intexta: Orality and Textuality in the Middle Ages*. Madison, WI: University of Wisconsin Press, pp. 246–59.

Damrosch, D. (2003) *What Is World Literature?* Princeton, NJ: Princeton University Press.

Dangler, J. (2006) 'Edging toward Iberia', *Diacritics*, 36(3–4), 12–26.

Davis, S. (2018) 'The state of the discipline: Hispanic literature and film in U.K. Spanish degrees', *Journal of Romance Studies*, 18, 25–44.

Eaglestone, R. (2019) *Literature: Why It Matters*. Cambridge: Polity.

Eagleton, T. (1983) *Literary Theory: An Introduction*. Oxford: Basil Blackwell.

Eagleton, T. (2013) *How to Read Literature*. New Haven, CT: Yale University Press.

Forsdick, C. (2010) '"On the abolition of the French Department"? Exploring the disciplinary contexts of *Littérature-monde*', in Hargreaves, A. G. Forsdick, C. and Murphy, D. (Eds), *Transnational French Studies: Postcolonialism and Littérature-monde*. Liverpool: Liverpool University Press, pp. 89–108.

Forsdick, C. (2014) 'Worlds in collision: The languages and locations of world literature', in A. Behdad and D. Thomas (eds) *A Companion to Comparative Literature*. Chichester: Blackwell, pp. 473–89.

Gifford, D. J. (1981) 'Magical patter: The place of verbal fascination in *La Celestina*', in Hodcroft, F. et al. (eds), *Medieval and Renaissance Studies on Spain and Portugal in Honour of P. E. Russell*. Oxford: The Society for the Study of Mediaeval Languages and Literature, pp. 30–7.

Gilman, S. (1972). 'On *Romancero* as poetic language', in Pincus Sigele, R. and Sobejano, G. (eds), *Homenaje a Casalduero*. Madrid: Gredos, pp. 151–60.

Hayot, E. (2012) *On Literary Worlds*. Oxford: Oxford University Press.

Jager, E. (1993) *The Tempter's Voice: Language and the Fall in Medieval Literature*. Ithaca, NY: Cornell University Press.

Kadir, D. (2004) 'To world, to globalize – Comparative Literature's crossroads', *Comparative Literature Studies*, 41(1), 1–9.

Kristeva, J. (1991) *Strangers to Ourselves*, trans. Leon S. Roudiez. New York: Columbia University Press.

Laachir, K., Marzagora, S., and Orsini, F. (2018) 'Multilingual locals and significant geographies: For a ground-up and located approach to World Literature', *Modern Languages Open*, 1(19), 1–8. https://doi.org/10.3828/mlo.v0i0.190.

LaCapra, D. (2000) *History and Reading: Toqueville, Foucault, French Studies*. Toronto: University of Toronto Press.

Massey, D. (2005) *For Space*. London: Sage.

Menocal, M. R. (2006) 'Why Iberia?', *Diacritics*, 36(3–4), 7–11.

Miller, K. (2014) *The Cartographer Tries to Map a Way to Zion*. Manchester: Carcanet.

Olivares, J., and Boyce, E. S. (eds) (2012) *Tras el espejo la musa escribe*, 2nd edn. Madrid: Siglo Veintiuno.

Ong, W. J. (1982) *Orality and Literacy: The Technologizing of the Word*. London: Methuen.

Paran, A. (2006) *Literature in Language Teaching and Learning*. Alexandria, VA: Teachers of English to Speakers of Other Languages Inc.

Pountain, C. J. (2001) *A History of the Spanish Language through Texts*. London: Routledge.

Pountain, C. J. (2017) 'The three Ls of Modern Foreign Languages: Language, linguistics, literature', *Hispanic Research Journal*, 18(3), 253–71.

Pratt, M. L. (1991) 'Arts of the contact zone', *Profession*, 33–40. Available from: http://www.jstor.org/stable/25595469 (Accessed: 20 November 2020).

Pratt, M. L. (2014) 'Comparative Literature and the global languagescape', in A. Behdad and D. Thomas (eds), *A Companion to Comparative Literature*. Chichester: Blackwell, pp. 273–95.

Prendergast, R. (2007) 'Constructing an icon: The self-referentiality and framing of Sor Juana Inés de la Cruz', *Journal for Early Modern Cultural Studies*, 7: 28–56.

Puchner, M. (2017) *The Written World: How Literature Shaped History*. London: Granta.

Roche, M. W. (2004) *Why Literature Matters in the 21st Century*. New Haven, CT: Yale University Press.

Saussy, H. (2014) 'Comparative Literature: The next ten years', 9 March. Available from: https://stateofthediscipline.acla.org/entry/comparative-literature-next-ten-years (Accessed: 5 October 2020).

Scott, R. (2017) *'Celestina' and the Human Condition in Early Modern Spain and Italy*. Woodbridge: Tamesis.

Scott, R. (2021) 'Ethics', in Burns, J. and Duncan, D. (eds), *Transnational Modern Languages: A Handbook*. Liverpool: Liverpool University Press

Scott, R., Vakil, A., and Weiss, J.(eds) (2021) *Al-Andalus in Motion: Travelling Concepts and Cross-Cultural Contexts*, King's College London Medieval Studies, 28. London: Centre for Late Antique and Medieval Studies, King's College London.

Sebba, M. (2012) 'Orthography as social action: Scripts, spelling, identity and power', in Jaffe, A. et al. (eds), *Orthography as Social Action: Scripts, Spelling, Identity and Power*,. Berlin: De Gruyter Mouton, pp. 1–20.

Solnit, R. (2006) *A Field Guide to Getting Lost.* Edinburgh: Canongate.

Spivak, G. C. (2014) 'The end of languages?', 3 March. Available from: https://stateofthediscipline.acla.org/entry/end-languages (Accessed: 5 October 2020).

Walkowitz, R. (2015) *Born Translated: The Contemporary Novel in an Age of World Literature.* New York: Columbia University Press.

Weiss, J. (2005) 'Literary theory and polemic in Castile, c. 1200–1500', in A. Minnis and I. Johnston (eds), *The Cambridge History of Literary Criticism, 2: The Middle Ages.* Cambridge: Cambridge University Press, pp. 496–532.

Wielander, G. (2014) 'In defence of Modern Languages', *Modern Languages Open*, 1, n.p. http://doi.org/10.3828/mlo.v0i1.40.

Williams, R. (1977) *Marxism and Literature.* Oxford: Oxford University Press.

6

How old words become new (and then old again)

Christopher Pountain, Bozena Wislocka Breit, Rocío Díaz-Bravo and Isabel García Ortiz

Overview

What we call 'cultured borrowings', that is to say, borrowings into modern languages from Latin or Greek, or from Greek via Latin, are an important source of loanwords in Western European languages, especially the Romance languages and English. In the case of the Romance languages, many may be viewed as 'old' words which did not survive in the evolution of Latin to Romance, but which as borrowings were taken over as 'new' words. Some of these have over the years (and sometimes many centuries) come to number among the commonest words in their host languages, even to the extent of replacing existing words and making a structural impact on the language, and so have become well established and relatively 'old' again. Using Spanish case studies and the evidence of large corpora, we have been able to identify the characteristic features which accompany successful linguistic and social embedding. We also call attention to the role of transnational contact in this process, which has brought about a remarkable degree of commonality and convergence among the Western European languages. Cultured borrowings are an interesting instance of how the language act of borrowing contributes to the linguistic representation of perceived reality and hence 'makes worlds'.

Introduction

The subject of research in the Loaded Meanings strand of the *Language Acts and Worldmaking* project is the incorporation of what have traditionally been labelled in English 'learnèd words' into Spanish and other languages of Western Europe. The term 'learnèd word', and its equivalents in the Romance languages (Sp. *palabra culta* or *cultismo*, Fr. *mot savant*, It. *parola dotta*), has been given varying definitions by historical linguists, some of which are reviewed briefly in the second section here, 'More specific considerations'. We instead use the term 'cultured borrowing' (henceforward this term will be used without inverted commas), and delimit the meaning of this term as a word of Latin or Greek derivation which appears to have been borrowed directly into these languages with only minimal phonetic and morphological adaptation. We will not, in general, mean a Latin term which is used unmodified and may more appropriately be regarded as a 'Latinism', such as Eng. *et cetera, inter alia, anno domini,* even though some such expressions have become very common.
As a clear example of a cultured borrowing, we may think of Greek σύμπτωμα, which was borrowed into Late Latin as *symptoma* and is today evident in Eng. *symptom*, Fr. *symptôme*, Sp. *síntoma*, Pg. *sintoma*, It. *sintomo* (English translations of words in other languages where these have an obvious cognate with similar meaning in English are not given, as is the case for most cultured borrowings). It seems clear that the route by which cultured borrowings entered their vernacular host languages was their use by educated writers for cultural or technical purposes as the language became elaborated for such kinds of expression; but a remarkable number of them have now come into everyday usage in their host languages and label concepts which present-day speakers would judge to be basic. An example of that process is

Eng. *difficult* (Sp. *difícil*, Fr. *difficile*, It. *difficile*; Lat. *difficilis*), which first appears in texts written in the Western European vernaculars in the fourteenth century and thereafter steadily gains in frequency. (Eng. *difficult* is probably a back-formation from *difficulty*, which in turn may be primarily a borrowing from French (the *OED* characterizes it as: 'Of multiple origins. Partly a borrowing from French. Partly a borrowing from Latin'). While the standard Western Romance languages have also adopted a cultured borrowing from Lat. *facilis* (Fr. *facile*, Sp. *fácil*, It. *facile*) as the default antonym, English uses *facile* only in a more restricted sense, and it has not diffused as readily; Eng. *easy* is borrowed from Fr. *aisé*.)

It is this process of diffusion which we are particularly interested in, since cultured borrowings play a crucial part in the linguistic representation of perceived reality (worldmaking) that is at the heart of our overall project. Lexical borrowing is in fact one of the most obvious language acts performed by speakers, and is particularly interesting because, unlike some of the other ways in which speakers bring about change (which is a universal characteristic of living languages), it is in the case of cultured borrowing in the first place done quite consciously, sometimes to label a new concept and sometimes for what we may take to be the creation of an expressive effect. Its motivation is speakers' admiration for a foreign culture and an acknowledgement of its prestige. The act of borrowing therefore leads in principle to an enhancement of the worldmaking potential of a language. However, the adoption of borrowings into everyday usage raises the question as to how much they may change speakers' 'normal' perception of the world.

More specific considerations

We have already pointed to the fact that the traditional terms ('learnèd word' etc.) for the phenomenon with which we are concerned have been used in different ways, and although we have distanced ourselves from such controversies, it is worth clarifying the basis of them. We have already separated cultured borrowings, which are incorporated into the structure of their host languages, from Latinisms, which remain in their original form. Such a clear distinction is, however, not always easy to sustain. The Spanish cultured borrowing *crisis*, for example, has come from Gk *κρίσις* via Lat. *crisis* intact, with the somewhat unusual ending *-is* (contrast the cognate Fr. *crise*, which has been shorn of its anomalous ending) which also poses a challenge for the formation of the plural (the plural is in fact invariable; compare Eng. *crises*, which once again copies Latin). On the other hand, the apparent Latinism *statu quo* in Spanish, which is so Latinate as usually to be written in italics and has failed to be adapted even minimally to the phonological pattern of its host by the addition of *e* before the *st-* group (compare the modern borrowing *estatus*, from Eng. *status*), does not have the final *-s* which the Latin citation form had (again compare Eng. *status quo*).

The terms Eng. 'learnèd', Sp. 'culto' and so forth also imply association with a cultured, élite, level of language which linguists have characterized as 'high register'. Thus it is sometimes assumed either that this association has continued, or that all words which appear in high register usage are 'learnèd'. The correlation between words borrowed from Latin and high register has a certain justification in English, where we have such pairs as *ignite/light, luminosity/shine;* it is also true that many Latin borrowings in the Romance languages are still associated with high register, such as Sp. *filantrópico* as against *generoso, certamen,* competition as against *concurso* (though *generoso* and *concurso* are also cultured borrowings in our sense). But, as we will stress repeatedly, cultured borrowings are not limited to high register in the modern host languages: one striking instance of this are words of general approbation which appear in everyday speech, such as Eng. *phenomenal*, Fr. *magnifique*, Sp. *estupendo*, Pg. *legal*, It. *fantastico* (see 'Hyperbolic usage', a subsection in the third part of the chapter, 'Embedding', below).

Cultured borrowings are a particularly intriguing feature of the Romance languages because it is from Latin that these languages also derive, and a cultured borrowing may be a doublet development of the 'same' inherited word, such as Fr. *fragile*, fragile (learnèd), as against *frêle*, thin, frail (inherited). The differentiation of such doublets is possible because, while the borrowing is assimilated into the host language with minimal adaptation, the inherited word (sometimes referred to as 'popular') will have undergone sound changes which have moved it away significantly from its Latin form, as in this case, where Lat. *fragilem* (the accusative form of *fragilis* which was in fact the origin of the derived Romance forms) has lost its final *-m* and undergone a palatalization and weakening of the *-g-* which has removed the consonant altogether: this palatalization has also resulted in the change of the stressed vowel *a* to *ê*, probably via an intermediate *ai*. There is thus a very clear association between apparent irregularity in sound change and cultured borrowing, and this was important in working out the regular sound changes in the evolution of Latin to the various forms of Romance, which was the major concern of language historians working in the Neogrammarian tradition. The Neogrammarians, *Junggrammatiker*, were a group of late nineteenth-century German philologists who advanced the hypothesis that sound changes were regular and therefore permitted the reconstruction of ancestral languages on the basis of the comparison of their descendants. Indeed, the failure of a given word of Latin origin to display all expected sound changes was enough to lead to its characterization as 'learnèd', quite separately from its possibly elitist use. Unfortunately, however, the simple dichotomy between 'learnèd' and 'popular' is not always possible to sustain, since there are a number of words which appear to have undergone only some of the expected changes and do not obviously pertain to high register. A well-known example from Spanish is the word *iglesia*, church, from Gr. *ἐκκλησία*, borrowed into Late Latin as *ecclesia*. While the *c* has become *g* as a result of assimilation to the following *l*, the sequence *si* has remained intact, whereas in clearly inherited words the *i* was lost (and could change the vowel preceding the *s*, so that, for example, Lat. *basium*, kiss, became Sp. *beso*). Such words have been characterized as 'semilearnèd' (Sp. *semiculto*) as a result and have attracted much controversy. We have not entered into this matter in our investigations but have concentrated instead on words which appear on the basis of the date of their first textual attestation clearly to have been taken into their host language in the course of the Middle Ages or later, and have not undergone any of the expected sound changes. They may, of course, have undergone later sound changes as they are adapted to the structure of the host, some of which have actually produced doublet developments of the cultured borrowing, such as Sp. *afección* and *afición*, love, liking, from Lat. *affectionem*; they may, less obviously, have been modified to suit existing morphological patterns, such as Sp. *transmitir*, to transmit, from Lat. *transmittĕre* (cf. *remitir*, *dimitir* and see also 'Structural impact', the penultimate section of this chapter); they may be neologisms created from Latin words, such as the intriguing paradigm Sp. *interés, interesar, interesante* (the corresponding Latin source is the irregular verb *interesse*; the nouns Fr. *intérêt* and Eng. *interest*, and hence also Sp. *interés*, appear to be based on the third-person singular of this verb, Lat. *interest*, while the verb and adjective are coined on the basis of the new noun).

Ideally, then, a cultured borrowing is identifiable on the basis of a number of features. First, the absence of expected sound changes; second, a relatively late date of first textual attestation; third, an initial meaning which suggests a specialized or technical use. In the course of this chapter we will show how these criteria can be refined as we strive to understand the factors which favoured the diffusion into everyday usage of a good number of them.

Embedding

Not all such cultured borrowings enjoyed what might be regarded as equal 'success', by which is meant successful embedding (in the sense of Weinreich, Labov and Herzog, 1968: 183–7), or integration, into their host language. Some words were purely ephemeral and are preserved in dictionaries only because the modern notion of what constitutes a language has a diachronic dimension: the Spanish word *longincuo*, distant, which still appears in the *DLE*, has just one attestation in the massive CORPESXXI corpus of present-day Spanish (Pountain and García Ortiz, 2019). Others remained infrequent, or limited to specialized linguistic registers: the Spanish word *receptáculo* (from Lat. *receptaculum*), first encountered in the first half of the sixteenth century both in the general sense of 'receptacle, reservoir' and the more specialized meaning observable in Latin of 'hiding place, refuge', is not present at all in CORPESXXI, although it is still used as a technical botanical term (the Spanish term corresponding to Eng. *receptacle* in its general meaning is *recipiente*). But, as we have already seen in the 'More specific considerations' section above, some now figure among the commonest words today. many words of general approbation appear in everyday speech, such as Eng. *phenomenal*, Fr. *magnifique*, Sp. *estupendo*, Pg. *legal*, It. *fantastico* (again, see 'Hyperbolic usage' in the section below). Even words which initially had a very limited, abstract, sense have proved capable of such diffusion: Gk. πρόβλημα (Lat. *problema*), borrowed as Eng. *problem*, Fr. *problème*, Sp./Pg./It. *problema*, originally denoting a difficult philosophical, later mathematical, problem, or a riddle, has come to be a very general word for 'difficulty' (see the fourth section below, 'Contact and convergence'). We are particularly interested in this last kind of change because it can be regarded as a manifestation of what is sometimes known as 'change from above' (Labov, 1994: 78): in this case, a feature of elitist, typically written, language which diffuses into ordinary usage by all speakers.

The metrics of embedding

The first question to be answered is that of how such embedding can be diagnosed. Since our investigations have focused on Spanish, we shall use examples from that language unless otherwise stated, but the techniques described are universally applicable.

Frequency

The most obvious metric is that of simple frequency. We are fortunate in having at our disposal various large historical corpora of

Spanish; of these, the one which offers the most straightforward means of calculating lexical frequency, on a century-by-century basis, is that of the *Corpus del español* (henceforward CDE). Extracting this data is not altogether automatic, and a good deal of manual post-processing, alias philological mediation, is needed to exclude inadmissible tokens. Searches in the CDE will typically return some purely Latin instances, because quotations and more extensive passages in Latin are often contained in written Romance texts, and there are sometimes modern editorial additions in older works which have not been excluded. Some texts are incorrectly dated. We must be vigilant in identifying homonyms: *tema*, which of course is also a subjunctive form of the verb *temer*, to fear, is particularly problematic in this regard, and in the end we have considered only the data for *tema* preceded by an article: this is why it has a rather lower apparent frequency than the other nine words in Figure 1. We must also try to identify as many variant spellings as possible (the frequency of *idea* can be radically misjudged for the fifteenth century if it is not recognized that it can also be spelled *ydea*). Singular and plural forms must be recorded for nouns and adjectives, masculine and feminine for adjectives, and the many person/number forms of verbs.

With all these caveats in mind, Figure 1 shows frequency data from the CDE of ten of the most common cultured borrowings in Spanish (all among the 300 commonest words in the language according to Davies and Davies, 2017), which makes an immediate point: while their first attestation dates from up to five or six centuries ago, or even before, their gaining of a significant frequency in the language, which can be taken as indicating their social embedding, really only takes place from the eighteenth century to the present time. This conclusion is of great importance, since research on cultured borrowings has most often focused on establishing a date of first attestation as evidence of when the word 'enters the language'. However, nothing could be further from the case: these words only truly 'enter the language' of most speakers when they become frequently used and hence familiar, and that is shown in all cases to be a relatively recent process after a period of steady growth.

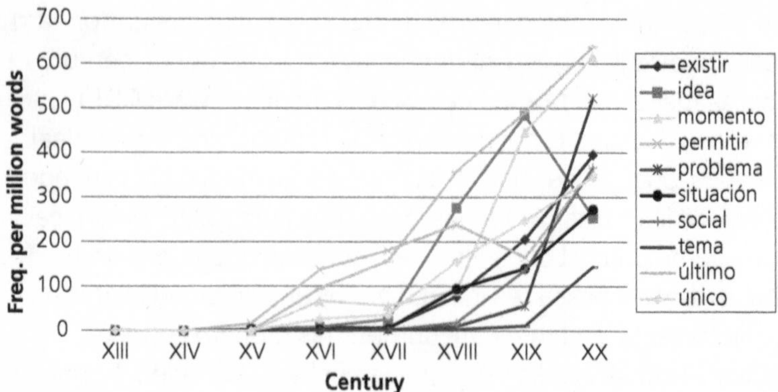

Figure 1. Growth in frequency of ten of the commonest cultured borrowings (CDE).[1]

Yet growth in frequency can also be relatively sudden. Research we have completed on adjectives of positive evaluation in Spanish (Pountain, forthcoming (a)) shows that one which is today very common, *espectacular* (derived from the earlier *espectáculo* from Lat. *spectaculum*: there is no form corresponding to *espectacular* in Latin which dates back to the sixteenth century), is first attested only in the early twentieth century but immediately achieves an impressive frequency.

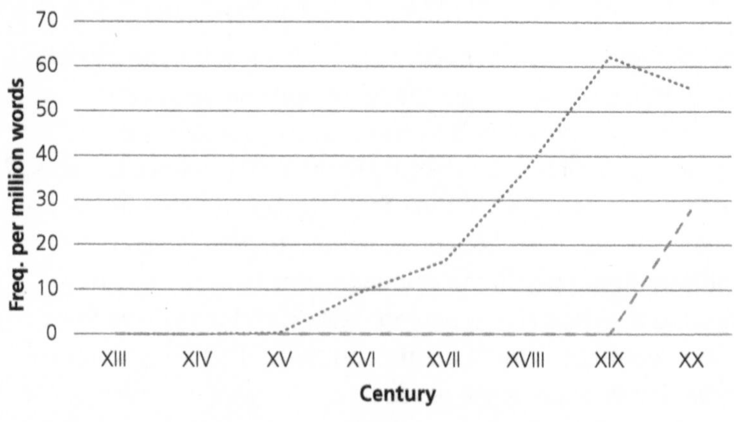

Figure 2. Appearance and growth in frequency of *espectacular* in Spanish; the statistics for es*pectáculo* are also shown (CDE).

[1] In the majority of the statistical graphs, centuries lie along the *x* axis and are not further subdivided; the *y* axis shows frequency per million words, since anything less would make the trends represented difficult to appreciate.

Genre/register

While simple frequency is probably indicative of the success of the embedding process, it does not tell us a great deal about the stages by which embedding actually takes place, or the mechanisms by which embedding is achieved. As we have said, the most obvious assumption concerning the embedding of cultured borrowings is that they diffuse from an originally restricted use in technical or cultural registers into wider usage. However, evidence of such progress is difficult to establish, since our knowledge of former states of present-day languages prior to the twentieth century is based entirely on written texts. However, for the twentieth century we can be more discriminating. The CDE distinguishes four linguistic registers for its twentieth-century data: Acad[emic], News, Fict[ion] and Oral, the latter having the advantage of consisting mainly of authentic transcribed speech from the *Habla culta* project (e.g. Esgueva and Cantarero, 1981). In Table 1 we see the distribution of five cultured borrowings in this corpus. We have already met the first two, *problema* and *momento*, in Figure 1: these are what might be called 'successful' cultured borrowings simply in terms of gross frequency, but these figures show that their success is today in no small measure due to their adoption in oral register, in which they are in fact most frequent (the size of each of these four categories is roughly 25 per cent of the total, so raw occurrences can be taken as an indication of relative frequency, too). Rather lower in overall frequency, but also with a significantly higher occurrence in oral register, are three 'everyday' cultured borrowings (see Pountain forthcoming (a)), *fabuloso, estupendo* and *fenomenal*, the frequency of which may be seen to have been boosted by their hyperbolic adoption in speech as expressions of general approval. Recourse to hyperbole, long recognized as a powerful cause of semantic change (see, specifically, Ullmann, 1970: 137), also gives us an explanation of why such diffusion might have taken place (again see also 'Hyperbolic usage' below).

Table 1. Occurrences of five cultured borrowings in twentieth-century registers of Spanish (CDE).

	ACAD	NEWS	FICT	ORAL
problema(s)	1737	2957	943	5109
momento(s)	1424	2895	3921	4403
fabuloso, etc.	11	33	86	150
estupendo, etc.	2	78	75	206
fenomenal(es)	0	6	47	53

However, a broader historical dimension for such register-based analysis is more difficult to achieve (Díaz-Bravo, 2018; 2015: 381–3). Although literary plays and dialogued novels (represented and searchable by genre in large diachronic reference corpora like *CORDE* as 'Prosa dramática' and 'Prosa narrativa', respectively) might be considered to be appropriate sources for the study of spontaneous conversation in the history of Spanish, conclusions must be taken cautiously. Ascribing one literary text to one single genre and register is problematic, since there are complex literary texts where different discourse types and registers can be found (Pountain, 2006). This is the case of the literary work *Retrato de la Loçana andaluza,* a dialogued novel with a great structural and discourse complexity in which the author (Delicado) aims to portray his characters from a linguistic point of view (Díaz-Bravo, 2019a; 2019b). In order to study cultured borrowings in this text, Díaz-Bravo and Vaamonde (2020) take into account different discourse types and the educational level of the character, proving that both variables are statistically significant: cultured borrowings are more frequent in registers closer to communicative distance (e.g. letters, narrative writing and epilogues); furthermore, Delicado used a striking number of cultured borrowings to portray his learnèd characters. A quantitative study of cultured borrowings using different variables (discourse type and educational level of characters) has been possible thanks to *Digital Lozana* (Díaz-Bravo and Vaamonde, 2019–), a digital edition that allows corpus-based and automatic linguistic analysis of this literary work.

Occasionally, we are fortunate enough to have valuable secondary evidence of the familiarity of a word or attitudes towards it (for a fuller discussion and more examples, see Pountain and García Ortiz , 2019). Example (1) below is a most important piece of such evidence. Enrique de Villena (1384–1434), to whose work is due the early attestations of many cultured borrowings, here explains his policy in translating the *Aeneid* into Castilian: his practice is to explain unfamiliar words for the convenience of readers, from which we may deduce that such words (here *subintellectas, tractable* and *latente*) were not general at this stage, and were by no means assimilated (we can imagine that in modern typography they would have appeared in italics, as they do in our translation, or quotation marks); in fact some, like *subintellecto,* were not, while others, like *latente,* remained relatively restricted. *Latente* in fact seems not to have been used again in Spanish until the eighteenth century, when it has a pejorative meaning: *Sólo un escribano, hombre advertido y sagaz, sospechó algún latente engaño en el que todos los demás juzgaban indubitable prodigio* (CORDE: Benito Jerónimo Feijoo, *Teatro crítico universal,* 1729) 'Only a scribe, a sharp and astute man, suspected some hidden deception in what everyone else judged to be an indubitable wonder'.

(1) A vós, señor muy exclaresçido, e a los otros leedores sea manifiesto que en la presente traslaçión tove tal, manera que non de palabra a palabra, ne por la orden de palabras que está en el original latino, mas de palabra a palabra según el entendimiento e por la orden que mejor suena, siquiere paresçe en la vulgar lengua. En tal guisa que alguna cosa non es dexada ho pospuesta, siquiere obmetida, de lo contenido en su original, antes aquí es mejor declarada e será mejor entendido por algunas expresiones que pongo acullá **subintellectas,** siquiere implíçitas ho escuro puestas, según claramente verá el que ambas las lenguas latina e vulgar sopiere e viere el original con esta traslaçión comparado. Esto fize porque sea más **tractable** e mejor entendido e con menos estudio e trabajo vós, señor, e aquéllos poderes sentir, siquiere mentalmente gustar, el fructo de la doctrina **latente,** siquiere cubierta, en el artifiçioso dezir. (CORDE: Enrique de Villena, *Traducción y glosas de la Eneida. Libros I–III,* 1427–8)

> Let it be clear to you, my most illustrious lord, and to other readers that in the present translation I adopted a method which proceeds not word by word according to the order of the original Latin, but word by word according to the meaning and the order which sounds or appears better in the vulgar tongue. So nothing of the content in the original is left, deferred or omitted, but rather is expressed better and will be understood better through the use of some expressions which I place *subintellectas* (that is, implicit or obscurely expressed) from time to time, as anyone who knows both languages, Latin and the vernacular, and views the original compared with this translation, will see. I have done this so that it will be more *tractable* (more easily understood, with less work and study), by you, my lord, and so that you can appreciate and mentally enjoy the fruit of the *latente* (that is, hidden) teaching which is in the artful manner of expression.

The characteristics of embedding

We notice that the historical trajectory of successfully embedded cultured borrowings is characterized by a number of linguistic, social and cultural features, which we will now introduce and discuss. We cannot go so far as to say that such features are the factors responsible for embedding of these words, though they appear to be recurrent characteristics. Furthermore, we must bear in mind the well-known principle that every word has its own semantic history, and cultured borrowings are no exception to this. But just as it is possible to identify some recurrent types of lexical change, so it is possible to observe typical scenarios which favour the incorporation and diffusion of cultured borrowings.

Widening of meaning

The history of all the successful cultured borrowings we have so far examined is characterized by a broadening of meaning from a specialized to more general field of discourse, to such an extent that this may be seen as an essential requirement for their popularization.

Case study: *idea*

The evolution of *idea* (Gr. *ἰδέα*, borrowed into Latin as *idea*) illustrates this kind of movement very clearly. The congeners of this word are widely attested in medieval Romance with the very specific meaning of a Platonic archetype. But by the time of one of the earliest examples in Spanish (2) (strictly speaking, it is inappropriate to use the term 'Spanish' as a designation for the language prior to the late fifteenth century – 'Castilian' is to be preferred – but we will do so consistently in this chapter to avoid any confusion), it is used with the meaning of 'image, form, similarity', the sense it had also come to have in post-classical Latin (Du Cange et al., 1883–7, t.4, col. 283c), although the context suggests that the word was still not really familiar and needed explanation, here achieved by glossing with *semblança*.

(2) Otros los átomos, ynfinitos en nilmero, e otros las **ydeas** o senblanças que eran en la cabsa primera. (CORDE: Alfonso de la Torre, *Visión deleytable,* c.1430–40)

Other people [said] it was atoms, infinite in number, and others [said] it was ideas or images which were in the prime cause.[2]

But as we move through definitions given in Covarrubias Orozco (3a), *Aut.* (3a) and ultimately the present-day *DLE* (3c), the meaning becomes steadily more general. Covarrubias Orozco (3a) records the meanings of 'preliminary plan', *Aut.* (3b) those of 'intention', which presumably evolved from the meaning of 'image' (something not yet realized), and 'belief', 'mania', 'obsession' and, widest of all, the modern meaning of 'concept, opinion', which in the current *DLE* (3c) is the primary meaning listed.

(3) a. Tambien llamamos **idea** la imaginacion que traçamos en nuestro entendimiento, co mo el arquitecto, que traça vna casa, o otro edificio, le fabrica primero en su entendimiento [...]. (Covarrubias Orozco, 1611).

[2] The translations of examples given here aim to reveal the word-by-word structure and meaning of the original, and are therefore as literal as possible.

We also call an idea the imagination we draw in our understanding, just as the architect who draws a house or other building makes it first of all in his understanding [...].

b. [Idea] [...] Vale tambien el fin o objeto que se aprehende para alguna operación, encaminada a lo futúro. [...] Se toma muchas veces por falsa imaginación, o opinión: y en este sentido se dice de alguno que tiene **idéas**. *(Aut.*, 1734)

Also means the end or object which is in mind for any operation directed towards the future. It is often taken as meaning false imagination or opinion, and in this sense it is said of someone that they 'have ideas'.

c. [Idea] Primero y más obvio de los actos del entendimiento, que se limita al simple conocimiento de algo. *(DLE,* http://dle.rae.es/?id=KtN78ZO, accessed 6 March 2017)

The first and most obvious of the acts of understanding, which is limited to simple awareness of something.

We see, then, how *idea* has steadily become so generalized in meaning as actually to become today a hypernymic, or generic, term.

Particular kinds of extension of meaning

We can identify a number of ways in which the meaning of cultured borrowings is extended: these processes are, of course, not specific to cultured borrowings but are frequently encountered in the semantic histories of other words, too.

Metaphorical extension

A clear example of metaphorical extension of the meaning of a word can be seen in Sp./Pg. *célula* / Fr. *cellule* / It. *cellula* from Lat. *cellula*, a diminutive form of *cella* 'store room, chamber' (Lat. *cella* itself develops into the inherited words Sp. *celda* / Pg. *cela* / It. *cella* and also older French *celle*, from which Eng. *cell*; Fr. *celle* is replaced by the Latinism *cella* and, more commonly, its meanings are taken over by *cellule*, perhaps because of the clash with the demonstrative pronoun *celle*).

If we follow the semantic trajectory of Sp. *célula*, we find it first attested in the fourteenth century with the meaning of 'small chamber, particularly of a monastery', following one of its late Latin meanings (Du Cange et al., 1883–7: 250), which is now rendered exclusively by *celda*. It is also used, as was *cellula* in Medieval Latin, to denote a bodily cavity (we also find an imitative neologistic coining *celdilla* used preferentially in this sense as late as the nineteenth century and even today in such expressions as *celdilla etmoidal, celdilla mastoidea*: see *DTM*), and in the nineteenth century it is established as the technical term for the smallest structural and functional unit of an organism. Since this is a key biological concept, it is not surprising to find it significantly increasing in frequency from that time; but it also came to be used not only in other technical contexts, for example *célula fotoeléctrica,* but much more broadly:

(4) Perezoso, ignorante, sensual, sin energía ni vigor, juguete de las pasiones, incapaz de trabajar y de servir a su patria, mujeriego, pendenciero, escéptico a fuerza de indolencia y egoísmo, inútil para fundar una familia, **célula** ociosa en el organismo social … ¡Hay tantos así! (CORDE: Emilia Pardo Bazán, *Insolación*, 1889)

Lazy, ignorant, sensual, without energy or vigour, a plaything of the passions, incapable of working and serving his country, womanising, quarrelsome, sceptical through indolence and selfishness, useless for founding a family, an idle cell in the social organism … There are so many like that!

Such literary examples are, however, atypical of their time: the overwhelming majority of the 464 nineteenth-century instances of *célula* in CORDE are from scientific works.

We in fact have valuable secondary evidence of this process of the adoption of the metaphorical extension of this and other scientific terms in an observation by Leopoldo Alas (Clarín), also from the end of the nineteenth century:

(5) Caballeros que nunca habían visto un cadáver hablaban de anatomía y de fisiología, y cualquiera podría pensar que pasaban la vida en el anfiteatro rompiendo huesos, metidos en entrañas humanas, calientes y sangrando, hasta las rodillas. Había allí una carnicería teórica. Las mismas palabras del tecnicismo fisiológico iban y venían mil veces, sin que las comprendiera casi nadie; el individuo era el protoplasma, la familia la **célula**, y la sociedad un tejido ... un tejido de disparates. (CORDE: Leopoldo Alas (Clarín), *Sinfonía de dos novelas*, 1889)

Gentlemen who had never seen a body talked about anatomy and physiology, and anyone would think they spent their lives in the theatre breaking bones, up to their knees in hot and bleeding human entrails. There was a theoretical butchery. The same words used in physiological technology came and went a thousand times, without anyone understanding them; the individual was protoplasm, the family the cell, and society a tissue ... a tissue of stupidities.

A later, more specific, usage of the word is that of a political or religious group, especially *célula terrorista*, a collocation actually attested in CORPESXXI only in 2004, though it must have been in existence earlier.

Hyperbolic usage

Of particular interest in accounting for the growing use of cultured borrowings as expressions of approval in everyday speech is hyperbole, or exaggeration (already referred to in the subsection 'Genre/register' above). In Pountain (forthcoming (a)) we trace the evolution of Sp. *estupendo*, from Lat. *stupendus*, a participle of the verb *stupeo*, 'to be struck senseless, to be astonished'. Even though *estupendo* has always been used in a positive sense, its literal Latin meaning was maintained until at least the eighteenth century:

(6) por aver oído de noche él y todos sus soldados los **estupendos** bramidos que daba aquella fiera dentro del agua. (CORDE: José Oviedo y Baños, *Historia de la conquista y población de la provincia de Venezuela*, 1ª parte, 1723)

because he and all his soldiers had heard at night the astonishing bellowing which that wild beast was giving in the water.

But from the eighteenth century onwards the positive use predominates; it is also from this century that we have the first documented evidence of its use in an exclamative context:

(7) ¡Qué sillas tan bellas! ¡Qué mesas de oro! ¡Qué **estupendos** cristales! (CORDE: Ramón de la Cruz, *Las segadoras. Zarzuela,* 1768)

What beautiful chairs! What golden tables! What admirable glasses!

Today it can be used as a freestanding expression of approval (8a) and even with an adverbial function (8b); these are characteristic features of such expressions:

(8) a. ¡Ah, **estupendo,** pues salid! (CORPESXXI: *El club de la Comedia Presenta Ventajas de ser incompetente y otros monólogos de humor.* Madrid: Aguilar, 2001)

Oh, great, so go!

b. 'En el Monumental, por ejemplo, nos hemos presentado por 30 minutos durante un concierto y la gente lo ha recibido **estupendo** … eso es importante', resalta Bunster orgulloso. (CORPESXXI: *Impulsos.* Santiago de Chile: Área de Danza, División de Cultura, Ministerio de Educación, 2001)

'In the [Teatro] Monumental, for example, we performed for 30 minutes during a concert and people received it fantastically … that's important,' emphasized Bunster proudly.

Competition with existing words

The prime initial motivation for the use of cultured borrowings must be communicative factors such as the need to label a new artefact or concept or to provide a more economical, or structurally more advantageous, way of expression. Yet in common with other borrowings they sometimes enter into competition with existing words; and another indication of the process of embedding is that such competition is successful. *Idea* and *problema* illustrate the first of these processes: they are in the first place precise terminological labels for philosophical concepts. The achievement of greater semantic discrimination, which may be seen as another advantage of borrowing, may also be a reason for popularization of cultured borrowings, which in this respect behave exactly like other loanwords.

Case study: *único*

Único has been successfully incorporated into Spanish perhaps because it discriminates the notion of 'no other' from that of 'alone' (*un hombre solo,* a man alone / un *hombre único,* a unique man, a man like no other), meanings which were part of the very general referential area covered by the inherited word *solo.* Figure 3 shows very clearly the rise of *único* at the expense of *solo* in the environment *el* – N[oun], the context in which it typically bears the meaning of 'no other' (*la única razón,* the only reason; there is no other).

Such cases of competition are particularly interesting[3] because, despite the high degree of commonality of cultured borrowing among the Western European languages, they do not resolve in the same way in different languages. In French, *seul* was much more tenacious than Sp. *solo,* and can still be used in the sense of 'no other' (Fr. *la seule raison* / Sp. *la única razón,* the only reason); in English, *unique* was still regarded as an oddity until the second half of the nineteenth century and is similarly more restricted than Sp. *único.* (The adjective was not fully naturalized until the second half of the nineteenth century, and its use was sometimes deprecated; it was entered in H.J. Todd Johnson's *Dict[ionary of the Eng[lish] Lang[uage]* (1818) as a foreign word

[3] Competing variants (e.g. *único/solo, agricultor/campesino, homosexual/gay, lesbiana/tortillera, invidente/ciego, clave/contraseña, congratular/felicitar, insípido/desaborido, minusválido/discapacitado* ...) are particularly useful to engage undergraduates in lexical-semantic studies and in the use of different sources for lexical analysis (dictionaries, online corpora and other digital resources such as Google Trends and N-gram viewer). In particular, a successful experiment conducted at the University of Granada showed that the students were able to become language researchers and teachers by conducting their own linguistic research and presenting it with self-designed activities to their peers.

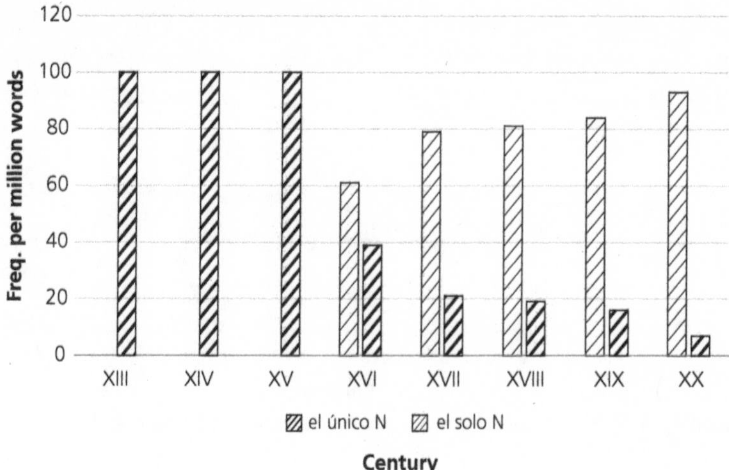

Figure 3. Competition between *único* and *solo* in Spanish (CDE).

and characterized as 'an affected and useless term of modern times' (*OED*).)

Participation in idioms and syntagms

Another factor likely to be associated with embedding is the participation of cultured borrowings in set phrases and idioms, which has the effect of increasing their frequency.

Case study: *momento*

Momento, for example, became especially frequent in periphrastic time expressions. Figure 4 shows statistics taken from CDE for Sp. *en (aqu)este/(aqu)ese/aquel momento*, at this/that moment, and although this is likely to be an incomplete picture, the results are nonetheless very suggestive (CORDE actually has instances from centuries prior to the nineteenth century, but it is impossible to project comparable century-by-century statistics from CORDE).

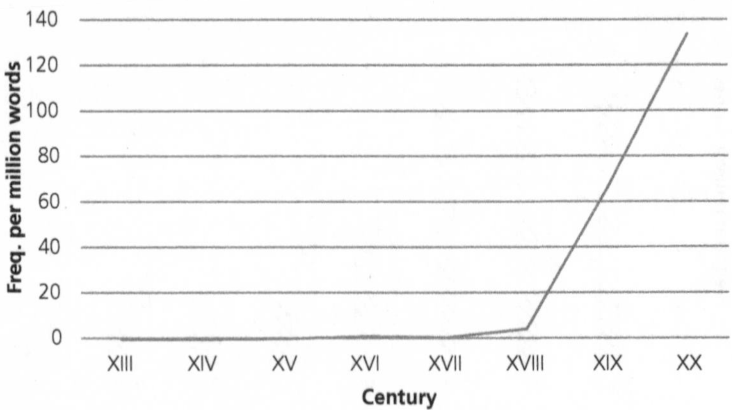

Figure 4. Rise in frequency of time expressions with Sp. *momento*.

Derivational paradigms

In addition to the syntagmatic relations referred to in the preceding section, the paradigmatic relations developed by cultured borrowings may be an important factor in their success, since the use of the same lexical stem in a range of semantically related parts of speech not only increases the frequency of that stem but embeds it structurally in the host language.

Case study: *situación*

This may even extend to the coining of new members of a derivational paradigm. We have already noted in the 'More specific considerations' section above how a set of related words based on Lat. *interest* effectively creates a new regular verb (Sp. *interesar*, Fr. *intéresser*, It. *interessare*) and associated derived forms (just to cite the Spanish forms: *interesarse, interesado, interesante, desinterés, desinteresarse, desinteresado*). We see something of the same kind of process with *situación*. While the form *situatus* existed in Late Latin (Lewis and Short, 1879: 1713), there was no verb *situo* or nominalization *situatio*, the Classical equivalent of the latter being *situs*, formally the supine (past participle) of *sino*, to be situated. *Situatio* is recorded in Du Cange et al. (1883–7) in a French royal document from 1380, and the first examples of *situación* and its congeners in Romance (a Spanish example is given in (9)) are roughly contemporaneous.

(9) Capitulo xlvii, de la çerca de Çesarea la grande & [...] de la **situaçion** de Iturea & de la region de Traconitida. (CORDE: Anon., translation of *Historia de Jerusalem abreviada* by Jacobo de Vitriaco: 1350)

Chapter 47: on the siege of Caesarea the Great and [...] on the situation of Iturea and the region of Traconitide.

There was in fact an earlier derivational experiment in both Spanish and Portuguese (Sp. *situamiento* and Pg. *situamento*), which did not survive:

(10) Dela elecçion & **situamjento** del campo (CDE: Anon., translation of Palladius, *De re rustica* (*Tratado de Agricultura*), 14th cent.)

On the choice and siting of the field.

The initial motivation for the introduction of *situación* would therefore seem to be morphological, and its embedding encouraged by the creation of a derivational paradigm widely shared among verb stems of the majority conjugation-type.

Case study: *social*

Another dimension of integration into the morphological system is shown by the adjective *social*, a word which begins its existence in Romance with a very restricted meaning indeed, used simply in the translation of Lat. *bellum sociale*, the 'Social' War, that is, the War of the Allies, against Rome in 91–88 BC:

(11) la batalla **social,** de la qual auemos dicho, et la qual estada facta dentro Ytalia [...] (CORDE: Juan Fernández de Heredia, Traducción de *Breviarium ab urbe condita*, de Eutropio, 1377–99)[4]

the Social War, which we have spoken of, and which, having been fought in Italy [...]

[4] The significance of the works of Juan Fernández de Heredia (c.1310–96) in introducing cultured borrowings has been stressed by Dworkin (2010: 176). It is worth remembering in the context of transnational contact that Fernández de Heredia was a Grand Master of the Hospitallers, whose network transcended national boundaries for centuries.

Social widens its meaning and gains in frequency from the eighteenth century onwards (we shall examine this phase of its trajectory in a different context in the section 'Case study: *social*' below. But, besides this, its success is no doubt encouraged, as in the case of *existir*, by the presence of the morphologically related words *sociedad* (12) and *socio* (13) from at least the late fifteenth century.

(12) Assí que estos bienes temporales son buenos, & a la humana **sociedad** mucho aprouechan, quando son poseýdos por varones de prudencia. (CORDE: Hernando del Pulgar, *Claros varones de Castilla*, 1486)

So that these temporal possessions are good, and are of great benefit to human fellowship, when they are possessed by men of prudence.

(13) La blanca palomica
al arca con el ramo se a tornado;
y ya la tortolica
al **socio** desseado
en las riberas verdes a hallado. (CDE: San Juan de la Cruz (1542–91), *Poesía*, 1566)

The little white dove has returned to the Ark with its [olive] branch; and the little turtledove has found its desired mate on the green river banks.

Towards the end of the eighteenth century a morphological derivative *sociabilidad* appears (14), to be followed in the ninteenth and twentieth centuries by a large number of derivatives based on the root *socio: sociológico, socioeconómico, socialdemócrata* and so on.

(14) quedaron sofocadas para siempre aquellas preciosas semillas de libertad y obscurecidos tan luminosos principios de **sociabilidad**, de justicia y de derecho. (CDE: Francisco Martínez Marina (1754–1833), *Teoría de la Cortes o Grandes Juntas Nacionales*, 1794)

those precious seeds of liberty were stifled for ever, and such shining principles of sociability, justice and law were obscured.

Contact and convergence

A feature of cultured borrowings which cannot escape notice, and to which we have already referred, is the fact that they are widely shared among many European languages, especially (but not exclusively) the Romance languages and English. This is interesting in itself, since their large number and degree of diffusion have tended to bring about a good deal of lexical convergence among these languages. But it also raises the obvious question of the extent to which apparent cultural borrowing is in fact due to mutual contact rather than independent borrowing from Latin and Greek. We have been able to establish a number of histories of individual words which strongly suggest the latter and in which we even have some evidence of how such transnational diffusion might have taken place: the massive expansion of usage of *problem* and its congeners already referred to seems, for example, to be due to the recent influence of English rather than to any intrinsic process of cultured borrowing as such, as we shall see below. At the same time, it sometimes happens that cognate words, though having a good deal of shared history, ultimately take slightly different paths in different languages. The Spanish word *tópico* (from Gk. τοπικός borrowed into Late Latin as the adjective *topicus*, pertaining to a place) has as a noun developed the meaning of 'cliché', while Eng. *topic* is a 'subject' or 'theme' (corresponding to Sp. *tema*) and is not used in the same way. The recent historical trajectory of *tópico* can be appreciated from successive editions of the Real Academia dictionary, https://enclave.rae.es/ficha-palabra. Only in the 1884 edition is it first given as a noun, with the meanings of 'commonplace' and of a medicine applied externally (the latter follows from its earlier adjectival usage). The connection of the meaning of 'commonplace' with ancient rhetoric, where *τοπικός* / *topicus* was a convention or motif, is made clear in late twentieth-century editions.

Case study: *problema*

Problema and its congeners were almost certainly introduced into Western European intellectual discourse as a result of Bartolomeo da Messina's thirteenth-century translation of the *Problemata Aristotelis* from Greek into Latin and the subsequent commentary (*Expositio succinta Problematum Aristotelis*, also in Latin) by Pietro d'Abano, who, following Huggucio of Pisa, defines *problema* as 'Questio difficilis aliquod continens quod disputatione solvendum quod et voragine videtur' ('a difficult question containing something which is to be solved by disputation and appears to be a quagmire'; Van der Lugt, 2006: 79). The first attestation in French is in fact Evrart de Conti's translation of these two works:

(15) Chi comence li livres des **problemes** de Aristote, c'est a dire des fortes questions, translates de latin en francois. (http://www.arlima.net/eh/evrart_de_conty.html#pro, Evrart de Conti, post-1380, referred to in *TLF*)

Here begins the book of the 'problems' of Aristotle, that is to say, of the substantial questions, translated from Latin into French.

It is clear from the context of this example that *problemes* is an equivalence of convenience which is far from integrated even into cultured written language, since it needs explanation as 'fortes questions', and it therefore seems likely that it was not yet current in French at the time, despite French being regarded as the most apparent source for Chaucer, in whose work it appears with an apparently more general meaning of 'riddle' (16a), a sense also attested in fourteenth-century Italian (16b), and indeed in the use of *problema* in the Vulgate, which the early Wycliffite Bible renders as *probleme* as if it already had some familiarity in English (16c).

(16) a. How hadde this cherl ymaginacioun / To shewe swich a **probleme** to the frere? (*OED*: Chaucer, *The Summoner's Tale*, c.1382)

b. It.: e chiunqua passava quinde, costringea a solvere questo **problema** … (OVI: Francesco di Bartolo da Buti, *Commento al Purgatorio*, 1385–95)

and whoever passed by, he compelled to solve this riddle …

c. Judges 14:15:
Vulgate: blandire viro tuo et suade ei ut indicet tibi quid significet **problema**

Eng.: Fage to þi man & moeue hym þat he schewe to þee what betokneþ þe **probleme** (*OED*: Wycliffite Early Version, late 14th cent.)

Flatter your husband and persuade him to tell you what the riddle means.[5]

However, we have to wait some time for evidence of *problema* and its congeners being used outside specific reference to Aristotle's *Problemata* in the textual records of French and Castilian. In Castilian, the fifteenth-century poet Juan de Mena, an author celebrated for his innovative use of cultured borrowings, made a series of what may be seen as daring rhymes involving words of Greek origin (17), where *problema* may have been an intentionally 'difficult' word, suggesting something which hides the truth, maybe 'enigmatic expression':

[5] The medieval Spanish biblical translations, by comparison, do not make such an equivalence, preferring instead such renderings as *razon, adeuinança, apuesta, proposiçion, rrenuçio*: the Arragel Bible has *enduze al tu marido commo nos absuelua la proposiçion* (BM: Arragel, 1422–30). The corresponding section from E4 contains the extremely interesting form *metaforizaçion: enganna atu marido & notifique nos la metaforizaçion* (BM: 4, 13th cent.?).

(17) Usemos de los poemas
tomando dellos lo bueno,
mas fuigan de nuestro seno
las sus fabulosas temas;
sus fiçiones y **problemas**
desechemos como espinas,
por aver las cosas dinas
ronpamos todas sus nemas.

(CORDE: Juan de Mena, *Coplas de los pecados mortales*, before 1456)

Let us use poems by taking good things from them; but their fantastic subjects must be banished from our bosoms; we should cast away like thorns their fictions and 'problems', and break all their seals in order to possess the worthy things.

As the sixteenth century progresses, use of *problema* and its congeners appears to become more independent, and its meaning broadened to that of a more general question to be solved; but it does always seem to be associated with a question that is posed to which an answer is required, though not always a logical one:

(18) a. —Me doibz je marier ou non?

—Par les ambles de mon mulet (respondit Rondibilis), je ne sçay que je doibve respondre à ce **probleme**. (FRANTEXT: François Rabelais, *Gargantua*, 1542)

'Should I marry or not?'

'By the steps of my mule,' replied Rondibilis, 'I don't know what I should reply to this question.'

b. Y assí, acercándome más a la solución del **problema,** digo que el calor y humidad de toda esta tierra mana y procede de differentes principios. (CORDE: Juan de Cárdenas, *Primera parte de los problemas y secretos maravillosos de las Indias,* 1591)

And so, getting closer to the solution of the problem, I say that the heat and humidity of all this land stems and proceeds from different sources.

The semantic range of *problema* and its congeners extends during the seventeenth century to include specifically mathematical problems (19a–c), but the word still appears to be quite restricted in use. However, it seems quite clear that in this use the scientific community, now increasingly using the vernaculars as languages of publication and correspondence, maintained some transnational terminological commonality.

(19) a. Car la neufième question vous fournira d'idées pour examiner les plus sçavans analystes, qui se vantent de pouvoir resoudre toutes sortes de **problesmes** numeriques. (FRANTEXT: Marin Mersenne le Père, *Correspondance*, 1634)

For the ninth question will provide you with ideas for examining the most expert analysts, who boast of being able to solve all kinds of numerical problems.

b. y generalmente por esta práctica se medirán todas las distancias inaccessibles, que es **problema** universal, y escusa el individuar muchos casos particulares (CORDE: José Zaragoza, *Fábrica y uso de varios instrumentos matemáticos*, 1675)

and generally by this practice all inaccessible distances will be measured, which is a general problem and makes it unnecessary to detail particular cases

c. Ye variety of **Problems** that may be put about a right-angled triangle, divided into two right Triangles by a perpendicular falling from the right Angle in the Hypothenuse (*OED*: John Collins, 1673)

The eighteenth century brings some increase in frequency, perhaps due to a further broadening of meaning to 'difficulty to be overcome', as use of the word spreads to more general intellectual application (20 a–b):

(20) a. en fin, nació un **problema** pernicioso a la quietud de los reinos [...] (CORDE: Vicente Bacallar y Sanna, *Comentarios de la guerra de España e historia de su rey Felipe V, El Animoso*, mid-18th cent.)

in the end, there arose a pernicious problem for the peace of the kingdoms [...]

b. The grand political **problem** in all ages has been to invent the best combination or distribution of the supreme powers of legislation and execution. (*OED*: J. Otis, 1764)

Wider embedding clearly took place across the ninteenth and particularly the twentieth centuries, as can be seen in Figure 5, which echoes Figure 1. We may speculate that this phenomenon is a consequence of the Industrial Revolution, of the technologizing of Western society, and of the increasing availability of mass education.

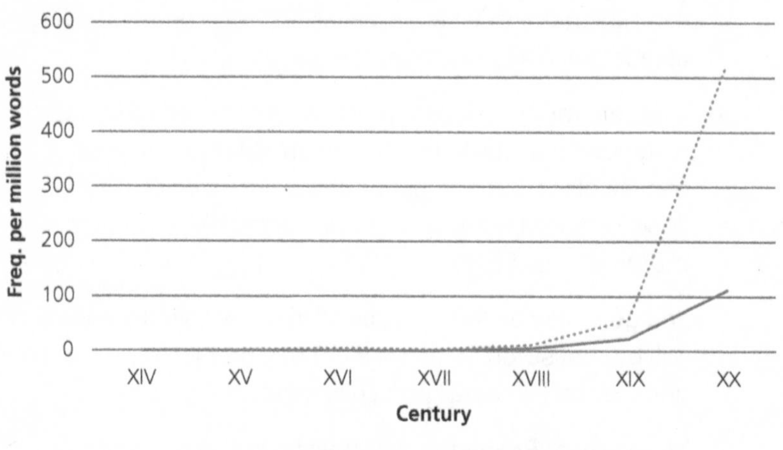

Figure 5. Frequency of Fr. *problème* (FRANTEXT) and Sp. *problema* (CDE).

But there is a further twist to be observed in the transnational story. The process of linguistic embedding has not only to do with widening of meaning and increase in frequency, but also with syntagmatic possibilities (see 'Participation in idioms and syntagms' in the third section 'Embedding' above). One very striking result of research in CDE, which permits such enquiry very easily, is the sudden growth in a number of specific constructions:

Table 2. *Problema* in certain syntactic contexts (Source: CDE).

	1200s	1300s	1400s	1500s	1600s	1700s	1800s	1900s
possessive + *problema*	0	0	0	0	0	1	14	143
es + possessive + *problema*	0	0	0	0	0	0	0	17
sin problema	0	0	0	0	0	0	0	12
tener + *problemas*	0	0	0	0	0	1	0	334
problema + adjective	0	0	0	2	0	12	71	528

TLF declares categorically that the nineteenth-century French *il n'y a pas de problème* (which it first attests in 1963) is a calque from Eng. *no problem*, and indeed it is possible that the example of English has been instrumental in the rise of all these new contexts (cf. *that's not your problem, no problem, to have problems, the terrorist problem*).

This is all enough to suggest that the attributions usually made concerning 'Latin' origin or 'mixed' etymology to *problema* and its congeners are rather bland, and that it is only in transnational terms that we can understand the intricate detail of (a) the origins, (b) the semantic development and (c) the linguistic embedding of a cultured borrowing in the course of what is actually a quite complex cultural history.

Case study: *social*

We contrast the development of *problema* with that of Spanish *social* and its congeners (already outlined in 'Derivational paradigms' in the third section 'Embedding' above), briefly recalling that the earliest usages of *social*, and so forth, refer to the *bellum sociale*. It is true that there are some very early examples in Italian and French of *social~sociale* used in the broader sense of 'pertaining to society' (21a–b), but this meaning appears to become more generally diffused only in the late fifteenth and sixteenth centuries, even though the frequency of the word still remains low.

(21) a. Et kistu esti lu plui raxunivili modu di pensari, ka l'omu sì esti naturalmenti **sociali**, amicabili et parintivili [...]. (OVI: Anonimo (Niccolò Montaperti o Casucchi?), *Sposizione del Vangelo della Passione secondo Matteo*, 1373)

And this is the most rational way of thinking, for man is indeed sociable, amicable and family-conscious [...].

b. Et pour vray la vie **sociale** ou compaignable est aux enfans moult couvenable, se la compaignie est bonne. (FRANTEXT: Jean Daudin, *De la erudition ou ensignement des enfans nobles*, 1360–80)

And truly, sociable or companionable life is very good for children, if the company is good.

In Spanish, Fray Bartolomé de las Casas (c.1484–1566), who was a pioneering advocate of humane treatment for the native peoples of America, seems to have favoured the word.

(22) los que, en gran parte y en munchas particularidades concernientes a la vida **social** y conversación humana, se rigen y gobiernan por razón. (CORDE: Fray Bartolomé de las Casas, *Historia de las Indias*, c.1527–61)

those who, for the most part, and in many details concerning social life and human conversation, are ruled and governed by reason.

But *social* almost certainly owes its diffusion in the second half of the eighteenth century and later to transnational factors which are relatively easily traceable: see also Álvarez de Miranda (2005: 1039–40). Corominas and Pascual (1980–91) call attention to the popularizing of Sp. *social* as a result of the impact of Rousseau's *Du contrat social* of 1761. CORDE and FRANTEXT allow us to analyse frequency by the decade, and indeed we can see (Figure 6) a sudden increase from precisely the 1760s onwards.

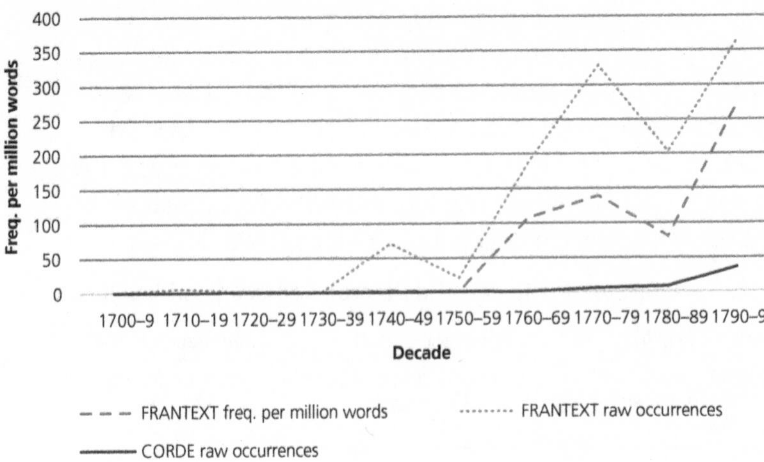

Figure 6. Eighteenth-century frequency of Fr. *social* and Sp. *social* by decade.

But it is important to scrutinize the eighteenth-century French record a little more closely. There are, as can be seen from Figure 6, a good number of attestations from the 1740s, and these are attributable in their vast majority to Diderot's *Essai sur le mérite et la vertu ou Principes de la philosophie morale*, which predates Rousseau's *Du contrat social* by 15 or so years. Now this text was in fact an adaptation of the Earl of Shaftesbury's *Inquiry Concerning Virtue*, in which Eng. *social* is regularly used (though examples in the *OED* suggest that it may have been in wider circulation in England before this time). The transnational impact of Shaftesbury's work, especially in France, Germany and the Netherlands, is well known. Rousseau's contribution to the story seems to have been to increase the range of collocations available to *social*. Diderot (and Shaftesbury) had used the word with generally positive connotations to indicate 'for the good of society': Diderot combines it (see Table 3) with such nouns as *affection, inclination, passion, penchant* and *sentiment*, and it also seems that the notion of *homme social* is due to Diderot's later works. Rousseau's collocations are more to do with the organization and structure of society: *contrat* itself, *pacte, ordre, corps, lien, loi, système* are among those he uses. And it is this kind of collocation which also characterizes the increasing use in Spanish in the late eighteenth-century enlightened authors Juan Meléndez Valdés (1754–1817) and Gaspar Melchor de Jovellanos (1744–1811), who in his *Informe de la Sociedad Económica de Madrid* of 1794 similarly combines *social* with such words as *orden, pacto, equidad, derecho* (these, and further, shifting connotations of *society* and *social* are outlined by Williams (1983: 205–8).

Table 3. Nouns used with *social* in Diderot, Rousseau and Jovellanos.

Diderot (1745)	Rousseau (1762)	Jovellanos (1794)
affection, inclination, passion, penchant, sentiment	*contrat, pacte, ordre, corps, lien, loi, système*	*orden, pacto, equidad, derecho*

From the turn of the eighteenth–nineteenth centuries onwards, the increase in relative frequency of Sp. *social* is again quite staggering. Figure 7 shows the profile returned by the CDE, for example.

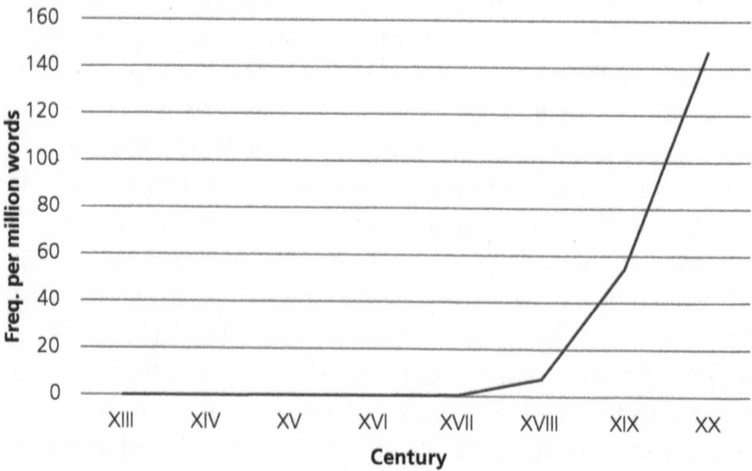

Figure 7. Frequency of *social* in the history of Spanish, based on the CDE (compare Figure 1).

On closer inspection, one factor which seems to be responsible for this growth is the proliferation of set phrases of noun–adjective combinations involving *social* as an adjective (Figure 8).

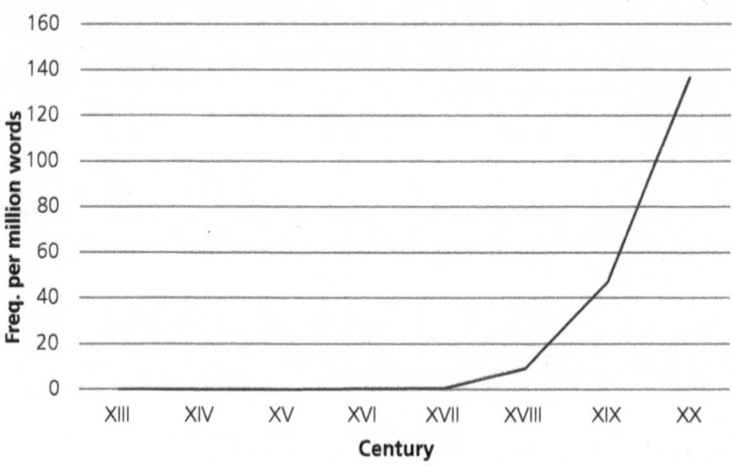

Figure 8. Frequency of N + *social* in the CDE.

The simple expedient of checking in *Linguee* (https://www.linguee.com) the usual translations of some of the combinations listed in the *OED* into French, Spanish and Italian reveals significant parallels across the four languages (Table 4). We should add that *Linguee* is a very significant source for our purposes because it reflects the work of modern translators and hence one of the main routes by which borrowing and linguistic embedding take place.

Replacement

A question which is raised by all borrowings which are ultimately successful in embedding in the host language is how the concepts they denote were previously expressed by speakers: this has been a particular concern of Dworkin (2000). Of course, it is sometimes new concepts which are being labelled, and this is particularly true of words which enter the language via scientific or technical discourse: there is a good deal of evidence that many cultured borrowings began life as straightforward adaptations of Latin originals in translations into the vernaculars, terms such as *horizon* (Gk. *ὁρίζων*, Lat. *horizon*) being clear examples. In some cases the borrowed word seems to have brought about the possibility of more nuanced semantic distinctions, as we

Table 4. *Social* and its congeners in set phrases in English, Spanish, French and Italian (Source: *Linguee*, http://www.linguee.com Accessed: 20 November 2016).

English	Spanish	French	Italian
social deprivation	penuria, etc., social	misère, etc., sociale	privazione sociale
social exclusion	exclusión social	exclusion sociale	esclusione sociale
social function	acto, función social	fonction sociale, rôle social	funzione sociale
social fund	fondo social	fonds social	fondo sociale
social history	historia social	histoire sociale	storia sociale
social housing	vivienda social	logement social	abitativa, edilizia sociale
social justice	justicia social	justice sociale	giustizia sociale
social ladder	progreso, promoción, escala social	ascension, promotion, échelle sociale	scala sociale
social life	vida social	vie sociale	vita sociale
social media	medios sociales	média social	*social media* (media sociali)
social medicine	medicina social	médecine sociale	medicina sociale
social sciences	ciencias sociales	sciences sociales	scienze sociali
social skills	habilidades, aptitudes sociales	compétences, aptitudes sociales	competenze, abilità sociali

have seen with Sp. *único* (Lat. *unicus*) (see 'Particular kinds of extension of meaning' in the third section above). But this is not always so: Sp. *último* 'last' seems in some ways an unnecessary borrowing, since Spanish already had the word *postrimero*, which it eventually replaced, with essentially the same meaning. The Spanish situation, essentially shared with Portuguese and Italian, is all the more surprising because it is not shared with French, where the notion of 'last' is rendered by *dernier*, from a conjectural Lat. **deretranu(m)* (a form very similar to the similarly conjectural **der(r)etrariu(m)* which was the origin of older Pg. *derradeiro*, an inherited rival of *postrimeiro*), and Fr. *ultime* is a rare word, appearing only in the nineteenth century, limited to literary language. We study the history of this semantic field in Pountain (2020a), concluding that it is perhaps its inherent complexity which favours such shifting preferences. Another cultured borrowing, *final* (Lat. *finalem*), is also involved: this word enjoys some currency in the fifteenth century in Spanish, only to decline in frequency thereafter until a sudden readoption in the nineteenth and then the twentieth centuries:

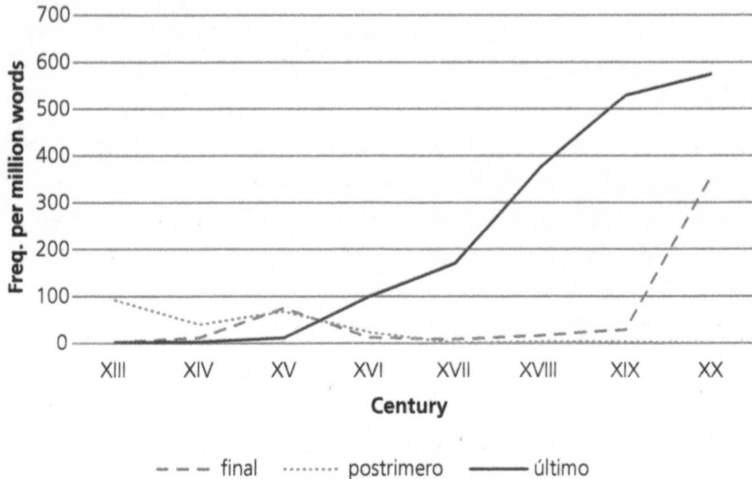

Figure 9. Sp. *final, postrimero* and *último* (CDE).

Structural impact

Following on from our observation (again, see 'Derivational paradigms' above) that the most successful cultured borrowings often form the basis of derivational paradigms, we have also been interested in the possible systematic impact of cultured borrowings on the morphological systems of their host languages.

Case study: Spanish *-ir* verbs

In Pountain (2020b) we examine the extensive borrowing of a number of verbs with the infinitival ending *-ir* into Spanish (e.g. *adherir* < Lat. *adhaerēre, adquirir* < Lat. *adquirĕre, exhibir* < Lat. *exhibēre*). While these verbs were sometimes simply assimilated into the patterns already established by inherited words (thus *describir, inscribir* and *suscribir*, together with the less common *adscribir, circunscribir, prescribir, proscribir, rescribir* and *transcribir*, are morphologically the same as the inherited *escribir*), others appear to join the *-ir* conjugation more spontaneously (e.g. *admitir*, *emitir*, *permitir*, *remitir* and *transmitir* show this development despite being historic compounds of Lat. *mittĕre*, which itself had developed as an inherited word to *meter*, to put). Most intriguing of all are *adquirir* and *inquirir*, which similarly join the *-ir* conjugation despite their historic association with Lat. *quaerĕre*, inherited as *querer*, to want; to love: these verbs actually create an anomalous morphological subtype, since in the present tense their stressed vowel undergoes the diphthongization normally associated with Lat. *ĕ* or *ae* (so *adquiere*, just like *quiere* itself, or like *siente* from *sentir*, to feel). Such cultured borrowings massively increased the number of verbs belonging to the *-ir* conjugation. While there is evidence for this conjugation having been quite productive at one time in the evolution of Latin to Spanish as a home for inherited Latin rhizotonic (stem-stressed) verbs (e.g. Lat. *petĕre* > Sp. p*edir*, to ask for) it is actually completely unproductive from the earliest documented stages of Spanish apart from the addition of such cultured borrowings. To try to quantify their impact, we have estimated that of the 164 *-ir* conjugation verbs listed among the 5,000 commonest words in Spanish by Davies and Davies (2017), 67 can be considered inherited words while the other 97, the overwhelming majority, are likely cultured borrowings. Most interestingly, then, these borrowings not only reinforced a minority morphological class but, as we have seen in the case of *adquirir* and *inquirir*, actually increased its complexity. In French, by contrast, despite the maintenance of a class of rhizotonic verbs (e.g. *mettre*, to put < Lat. *mittĕre*, *vivre*, to live < Lat. *vivĕre*), a large number of borrowed rhizotonic verbs are assimilated into the first, or *-er*, conjugation, for example Lat. *discutĕre* > Sp. *discutir*, Fr. *discuter*; Lat. *assistere* > Sp. *asistir*, Fr. *assister*; Lat. *constituĕre* > Sp. *constituir*, Fr. *constituer*.

Case study: present participles

In Pountain (forthcoming (b)), we look at the borrowing by Spanish of adjectives and nouns in *-nte* from Latin present participle forms (e.g. *patente* from Lat. *patentem*). While some of these were probably inherited words (e.g. *caliente* 'hot', *corriente* 'running'), their preservation perhaps provided the model for the very large number of subsequent cultured borrowings we have noted (116 in the 5,000 commonest words in Spanish according to Davies and Davies, 2017). The stock of such words seems to have been significantly increased in more recent times, not only by direct imitations of English words in *-ant*, such as *desodorante*, deodorant, *variante*, variant, *lubricante*, lubricant, and *-ing*, especially in collocations such as *cuestión candente*, burning question, *personal docente*, teaching staff, *vínculos existentes*, existing links, but by the ready use of a form in *-nte* to render many other technical anglicisms, such as *altoparlante*, loudspeaker, *comprobante de compra*, proof of purchase, *laxante*, laxative. Yet in spite of the undoubted creation by this means of a very productive suffix which typically denotes a function (*hablante*, speaker, *ayudante*, assistant), we cannot say that the suffix is totally productive. Far from all verbs have a corresponding form in *-nte* (e.g. *parecer*, to seem: **pareciente*, *sentar*, to sit: **sentante*), while conversely many forms in *-nte* do not have a corresponding verb (e.g. *suficiente*, *excelente*); the semantic relation between verbs and corresponding forms in *-nte* is not constant (*pariente*, relation does not necessarily imply the act of giving birth (*parir*)); forms in *-nte* do not even have a consistent syntactic function, since some are adjectives (*diferente*, *importante*), some are nouns (*ambiente*, atmosphere, *estudiante*), and some are both (*adolescente*, *constante*), while a very few have grammaticalized to still other functions (*durante*, during, *(no) obstante*, nevertheless). We certainly cannot speak of the restitution of a present participle as a part of speech, despite the wishful thinking of some grammarians (Real Academia Española, 1962: 428–9) and the attempts at the imitation of Latin syntax made by some creative writers in the fifteenth and sixteenth centuries:

(23) Ya passava el agradable
mayo, **mostrante** las flores

The pleasant [month of] May, showing the flowers, was passing.

(CORDE: Marqués de Santillana (Íñigo López de Mendoza), *Triumphete de amor*, c.1430)

and also in legal usage, presumably in imitation of Latin legal formulae:

(24) Et desi todo el capitol delos cano*n*ges dela dita igl*es*ia **capitulantes** et capitol **fazientes** & **Rep*re*senta*n*tes** todos concordes [...] damos et atorgamos [...] (CODEA+: Archivo Histórico Nacional | Clero, Zaragoza, carpeta 3625, nº 11, 28/03/1455)

And so [we], the whole Chapter of the canons of the said church, constituting the Chapter and making and representing the Chapter, all in agreement, [...] give and grant [...]

Conclusion

Through the various investigations we have undertaken in the course of this project, we hope to have suggested the following. First, we have underlined the importance of the adstrate role (the adstrate is a language that influences a neighbouring language) of Latin in an understanding of the history of the languages of Western Europe, especially the Romance languages (and that this is not restricted just to the history of the lexicon was made clear in Pountain, 2011), a process through which 'old' words belonging to a former stage of these languages are revived and become 'new'. Second, we have suggested that by looking at the historical trajectory of cultured borrowings following their initial appearance in the textual record, focusing on those which have been successful in achieving significant frequency in the modern language, we can come to appreciate the full impact that these erstwhile 'new' words have had on their host language as they have once again become 'old' (in the sense of firmly established and high in frequency). We have also shown that this impact is not only in the lexicon itself but may also impinge on morphology and syntax. Third, we have suggested ways in which the process of linguistic embedding should be conceived and studied. Fourth, we have demonstrated that what are sometimes labelled borrowings from Latin are in fact the result of transnational contact, not only in the Middle Ages and Renaissance but also in much more recent times, and that such contact is especially important for an understanding of the meanings and collocational possibilities of these words. We believe that we have made a case for the revival of interest in an area of historical linguistics which currently receives attention from only a small number of contemporary scholars, and, moreover, that it is one which lies at the heart of the linguistic representation of both new and old realities, the worldmaking that is the theme of our overall project.

References

Álvarez de Miranda, P. (2005) 'El léxico español, desde el siglo XVIII hasta hoy', in Cano, R. (ed.) *Historia de la lengua española*, 2nd edn. Barcelona: Ariel, pp. 1037–64.

Aut. = Real Academia Española (1963) *Diccionario de autoridades*, Edición facsímil. Madrid: Gredos.

BM = Enrique-Arias, A., and Pueyo Mena, F. J. *Biblia Medieval*. Available from: http://corpus.bibliamedieval.es (Accessed: 21 November 2016).

CDE = Davies, M. (2002–) *Corpus del Español (Genre / Historical)*. Available from: https://www.corpusdelespanol.org/hist-gen/ (Accessed: 20 September 2020).

CODEA+ = Sánchez-Prieto Borja, P. (coord.) *Corpus de Documentos Españoles Anteriores a 1700*. Available from: http://demos.bitext.com/codea (Accessed: 3 October 2019).

CORDE = Real Academia Española. *Banco de datos (*CORDE*). Corpus diacrónico del español.* Available from: https://www.rae.es/recursos/banco-de-datos/corde (Accessed: 15 May 2018).

Corominas, J., and Pascual, J. A. (1980–91) *Diccionario crítico etimológico castellano e hispánico.* Madrid: Gredos.

CORPESXXI = Real Academia Española. *Banco de datos (*CORPESXXI*). Corpus del Español del Siglo XXI.* Available from: https://www.rae.es/recursos/banco-de-datos/corpes-xxi (Accessed: 12 September 2020).

Covarrubias Orozco, S. de (1977 [1611]) *Tesoro de la Lengua Castellana o Española.* Madrid: Ediciones Turner.

Davies, M., and Davies, K. H. (2017) *A Frequency Dictionary of Spanish: Core Vocabulary for Learners.* London: Routledge.

Díaz-Bravo, R. (2015) 'Herramientas computacionales aplicadas al estudio de la Historia de la Lengua Española', in J. P. Sánchez Méndez, M. de la Torre, M., and V. Codita (eds) *Temas, problemas y métodos para la edición y el estudio de documentos hispánicos antiguos.* Valencia: Tirant Humanidades, pp. 377–93.

Díaz-Bravo, R. (2018) 'Las Humanidades Digitales y los corpus diacrónicos en línea del español: problemas y sugerencias', in E. Romero Frías and L. Bocanegra Barbecho (eds) *Ciencias Sociales y Humanidades Digitales Aplicadas: casos de estudio y perspectivas críticas / Applied Digital Humanities and Social Science: Case Studies and Critical Perspectives.* Granada and New York: Universidad de Granada and Downhill Publishing, pp. 562–86.

Díaz-Bravo, R. (2019a) *Francisco Delicado, 'Retrato de la Loçana andaluza': Estudio y edición crítica.* Cambridge: Modern Humanities Research Association.

Díaz-Bravo, R. (2019b) 'Study of medial and conceptional orality in the *Retrato de la Loçana andaluza*', *Bulletin of Hispanic Studies*, 96, 1191–217.

Díaz-Bravo, R., and Vaamonde, G. (2019–) *LD: Lozana Digital / DL: Digital Lozana: A Digital Edition of the 'Retrato de la Loçana andaluza'*. Granada: Universidad de Granada. Available from: http://corpora.ugr.es/lozana (Accessed: 1 September 2020).

Díaz-Bravo, R., and Vaamonde, G. (2020) 'Los cultismos en una novela dialogada del siglo XVI: un estudio de sociolingüística histórica', in C. J. Pountain and B. Wislocka Breit (eds) *New Worlds for Old Words: The Impact of Cultured Borrowing on the Languages of Western Europe*. Wilmington, DE: Vernon Press, pp. 211–229.

DLE = Real Academia Española (2014) *Diccionario de la lengua española, 23rd edn*. Madrid: Espasa. Available from: http://dle.rae.es/ (Accessed: 3 September 2020).

DTM = Real Academia de Medicina (2012) *Diccionario de términos médicos*. Madrid: Editorial Médica Panamericana. Available from: http://dtme.ranm.es/index.aspx (Accessed: 3 September 2020).

Du Cange, C., Henschel, G. A. L., Carpenter, P., and Adelung, C. (1883–7) *Glossarium mediæ et infimæ latinitatis*. Niort: Léopold Favre. Available from: http://ducange.enc.sorbonne.fr (Accessed: 5 January 2017).

Dworkin, S. N. (2010) 'Thoughts on the re-Latinization of the Spanish lexicon', *Romance Philology*, 64, 173–84.

Dworkin, S. N. (2020) 'Latinisms as lexical substitutes in late medieval and early modern Spanish', in C. J. Pountain and B. Wislocka Breit (eds) *New Worlds for Old Words: The Impact of Cultured Borrowing on the Languages of Western Europe*. Wilmington, DE: Vernon Press, pp. 135–156.

Esgueva, M., and Cantarero, M. (1981) *El habla de la ciudad de Madrid. Materiales para su estudio*. Madrid: CSIC.

FRANTEXT = ATILF-CNRS & Université de Lorraine. *Base textuelle FRANTEXT*. Available from: http://www.frantext.fr (Accessed: 21 November 2016).

Labov, W. (1994) *Principles of Linguistic Change. Volume 1: Internal Factors.* Oxford: Blackwell.

Lewis, C. T., and Short, C. (1879) *A Latin Dictionary.* Oxford: Clarendon Press. Available from: http://www.perseus.tufts.edu/hopper/text (Accessed: 12 February 2017).

OED = Oxford English Dictionary. Available from: http://www.oed.com (Accessed: 15 November 2016).

OVI = *Le Banche dati dell' Opera del Vocabolario Italiano Antico.* Available from: www.ovi.cnr.it (Accessed: 22 November 2016).

Pountain, C. J. (2006) 'Towards a history of register in Spanish', *Spanish in Context,* 3(1), 5–24.

Pountain, C. J. (2011) 'Latin and the structure of written Romance', in M. Maiden, Smith, J. C., and Ledgeway, A. (eds) *The Cambridge History of the Romance Languages, Volume I: Structures.* Cambridge: Cambridge University Press, pp. 606–59.

Pountain, C. J. (2020a) 'Mi "ultimo" saludo: historia de un préstamo culto', in Escobedo de Tapia, C., Bueno Alonso, J. L., and Taboada Ferrero, C. (eds), *Contigo Aprendí: Estudios en homenaje al Profesor José Caramés Lage.* Oviedo: Universidad de Oviedo, pp. 135–57.

Pountain, C. J. (2020 b) 'Cultured borrowing of verbs: the case of the Spanish *ir* conjugation', in Pountain, C. J. and Wislocka Breit, B. (eds) *New Worlds for Old Words: The Impact of Cultured Borrowing on the Languages of Western Europe.* Wilmington, DE: Vernon Press, pp. 173-189.

Pountain, C. J. (forthcoming a) 'Los cultismos de cada día', in *Actas del XI Congreso Internacional de Historia de la Lengua Española, Lima, 6–10 de agosto 2018.*

Pountain, C. J. (forthcoming b) 'The Romance "present participle": lexical elaboration of a morphosyntactic gap?'

Pountain, C. J., and García Ortiz, I. (2019) 'La investigación de las voces cultas a través de los corpus históricos', *Revista Internacional de Historia de la Lengua Española*, 14, 47–76.

Real Academia Española (1962) *Gramática de la lengua española.* Madrid: Espasa-Calpe.

TLF = *Trésor de la Langue Française informatisée* (2004) Paris: CNRS Éditions. Available from: http://atilf.atilf.fr (Accessed: 4 October 2016).

Ullmann, S. (1970) *Semantics. An Introduction to the Science of Meaning.* Oxford: Blackwell.

Van der Lugt, M. (2006) 'Aristotle's *Problems* in the West: a contribution to the study of the medieval Latin tradition', in P. de Leemans and M. Goyens (eds), *Aristotle's* Problemata *in Different Times and Tongues.* Leuven: Leuven University Press, pp. 71–111.

Weinreich, U., Labov, W., and Herzog, M. I. (1968) 'Empirical foundations for a theory of language change', in Lehmann, W. P. and Malkiel, Y. (eds), *Directions for Historical Linguistics.* Austin, TX: University of Texas Press, pp. 95–189.

Williams, R. (1983) *Keywords: A Vocabulary of Culture and Society*, rev. edn. New York: Oxford University Press.

7

Digital mediations and advanced critical literacies in Modern Languages and Cultures

Paul Spence and Renata Brandão

Overview

This chapter explores interactions and tensions between digital culture and Modern Languages research across numerous disciplinary and methodological perspectives, mapping a topography which is rich and complex, but from which we propose strategic directions for the acquisition of critical digital literacies in language education. We argue that digital mediation in language education does not just imply studying the digital transformations in Modern Languages, but rather a more collaborative (and bidirectional) engagement, which also involves bringing multilingual and transcultural expertise to bear on digital ecosystems and study objects. This leads to a series of mutual disruptions between the fields of Modern Languages and Digital Humanities in both pedagogy (engaging the dynamics of a multilingual and intercultural classroom) and research (designing transcultural and translingual methods and interfaces).

Introduction

'Coding, today's modern language' ran the title of an article in *Education Technology* magazine in 2015 (Armstrong, 2015a), and elsewhere, in an adapted version of the same post, the same commentator, Mark Armstrong, asked: 'Why learn French when you can learn to code?' (Armstrong, 2015b). In the timeframe since these opinion pieces were published there have been occasional, but recurring, debates about whether or not computer coding should fulfil the Foreign Language requirement at secondary school level in various US states, notably Florida in 2016/2017 (Clark, 2017) and more recently Maryland in 2019 ('Maryland Bill weighs coding as a language', Anon., 2019), and it is a debate which has had some traction in other English-speaking countries (Mason, 2017).

So far, most of these initiatives directly equating or connecting coding to Modern Languages (ML) in education policy have failed – through opposition from not just language educators but also often computing science advocates – but the fact that they are even taking place is, in itself, instructive. Beyond the observation that coding as a school subject is in the ascendant whereas Modern Languages are in decline in many countries, this episode opens up vital questions about the value and role of a Modern Languages education, the changing media expectations of our students, practice versus critical theory in education, the vocational concerns of students (and vocationally driven education policy) and the kinds of literacies we need to become effective professionals – and purposeful human beings – in the global, multilingual and transcultural dynamics of the twenty-first century. These expectations and concerns are firmly entwined with the project's notion of 'language acts' and the increasingly multimodal and collaborative worldmaking dynamics characterized by post-internet cultural engagement.

Thankfully, we have largely moved away from polarized views about the value of digital transformations in both academia and society as a whole, a cultural shift which also applies equally to the field of Modern Languages. In spite of that, as a survey we carried out in 2018 demonstrated, the relationship between digital cultures and Modern Languages is frequently not understood well, or is understood differently, across different areas or levels of language education (Spence and Brandão, 2019). This chapter charts an evolving debate about the nature and significance of digital mediations involving Modern Languages and Cultures and the critical competences required to negotiate them effectively. In so doing, we summarize conclusions from a series of surveys and experimental interactions exploring how Modern Languages and Cultures can be studied in hybrid digital/non-digital environments.

What are the basic digital literacies (in the plural) which would most benefit Modern Languages across different sectors, and how can linguists gain agency by developing a language-focused agenda for digital learning? What kind of resources are needed at higher education level (the main focus here, but also at primary and secondary levels) to support hybrid pedagogies? And what are the incentives and barriers to developing them? We consider characteristics of twenty-first-century learning which are likely to be increasingly important in Modern Languages education, such as peer-based and project-based learning, collaborative learning modes, the international classroom and learning beyond the classroom. We explore the kinds of literacies and pedagogies which are required, both to interpret Modern Languages using digital tools and to navigate digital culture from the perspectives of geographic and linguistic diversity.

On digital mediation

We chose the term 'digital mediations' for our research strand of *Language Acts and Worldmaking* not only to capture the breadth of interactions between Modern Languages and digital culture but also to connect our exploration with key debates in Modern Languages, Media Studies, Science and Technology Studies, and the Digital Humanities about the place of 'digital' and the effects it is having on identity creation and how we produce knowledge. 'It is commonly claimed that "everything is mediated",' remarked

Sonia Livingstone in 2009 (Livingstone, 2009), and certainly 'mediation' is an often used but loosely defined term which reflects the increasing variety and prevalence of media influencing our lives. Nevertheless, the term has a series of overlapping meanings which are useful to the discussion here: 'mediation' as a reconciliation of different stakeholders and ideas leading to negotiation and resolution; 'mediation' derived from media, a filtering medium through which information and communication pass and are transformed; and 'mediation' in a more social sense, 'as a transformative process in which the meaningfulness and value of things are constructed' (Silverstone, 2002: 761), and which in turn shape the 'construction and circulation of meanings' (Siapera, 2014: 540).

The experience of culture, communication and connectedness through digital media is as much social as technical, and Jones reminds us that digital media 'channel us into particular ways of being, ways of thinking and ways of relating' in a process which is ontological (influencing how we represent our understanding of the world), epistemological (affecting how we construct and justify knowledge based on this representation) and axiological (shaping our values) (Jones, 2020: 203–4). On one level, 'digital' mediation is just another form of mediation which should not be privileged over any other, but at this moment in time society in general, and Modern Languages in particular, are still grappling to engage fully and critically with the 'affordances' of digital devices – the qualities or properties which determine how they may be used – in a manner which privileges the social and cultural voice over techno-deterministic modes. Burdick et al. argue that 'the multiplicity of media and the varied processes of mediation and remediation in the formation of cultural knowledge and humanistic inquiry require close attention' and propose that we 'apply the same kind of rigorous media-specific, social, cultural, and economic analyses that we have honed to study print culture to understand the specificity and affordances of digital culture' (Burdick et al., 2012: 30).

The concept of mediation has also been very important in the field of Modern Languages, where 'intercultural mediation' has explored 'the ability to navigate and mediate between more than one culture' (Anon. 2016: 10) and where it contributes to 'sense-making' in a context of linguistic and cultural diversity (Liddicoat, 2009: 261). This finds echoes in sociolinguistics and discourse studies which explore digital communication practices that are firmly embedded in 'everyday life with language in superdiverse societies' and which aim to develop 'the theoretical vocabulary and methods of language and discourse studies in ways that integrate and merge media and mediation with linguistic repertoires, practices, and contexts' (Androutsopoulos and Juffermans, 2014: 5). These are debates which are largely disconnected from digital studies as a whole, which tend to be profoundly monolingual (and overwhelmingly Anglophone) and whose understanding of 'language' is often narrowly focused on the formal aspects of linguistics to the detriment of multicultural, plurilinguistic and transnational perspectives.

In *Mobile Literacies & South African Teens* in 2009, Marion Walton argued that 'unfettered, skilful mobility through vast online spaces of mediated culture is seen as the key to the power of cultural production, while there are potentially grave consequences for a cultural underclass, trapped on the wrong side of the "participation gap" and unable to participate in networked culture' (Walton, 2009). It should be added that the 'digital divide' was highlighted during the COVID-19 pandemic – between developed countries and developing countries; within countries, between urban and rural areas; between groups, levels of education and income; and in classrooms – but debates around global perspectives in Digital Studies (Galina Russell, 2014), multilingual digitality and digital cultural studies (Taylor and Pitman, 2007) had already started to coalesce. This chapter explores the connection between digital, intercultural and multilingual mediation in a number of educational settings.

Mapping Digital Modern Languages

Historical context

Digitally mediated practice is not new in Modern Languages – work on databases of medieval Spanish, Catalan, Galician and Portuguese literature started in the 1980s (http://bancroft.berkeley.edu/philobiblon/about_en.html) for example, and computer-mediated language learning has a similar depth of tradition. However, until recently, strong engagement with the 'digital' in languages-based education or research tended to be connected to specialist areas (such as digital art or digital editions) or related fields (such as translation or linguistics) where digital technology brought tangible transformations. Digital mediation as either a practice or an object of study in Modern Languages and Cultures historically grew from Digital Cultural Studies (https://latamcyber.wordpress.com/2012/04/23/digital-hispanism-at-the-ahgbi/) or the Digital Humanities (Gil and Ortega, 2016), but in recent years it has come into focus in Modern Languages through initiatives such as the writing sprint/publication on the 'Shape of the Discipline' convened by Taylor and Thornton (Taylor and Thornton, 2017), and the Digital Modern Languages seminar series in the UK (https://digitalmodernlanguages.wordpress.com/).

Meanwhile, digital research has increasingly moved from landmark resource-creation projects such as Philobiblon to collaborative community-led initiatives and to wider strategic assessments of the status of 'digital' within Modern Languages. Research and teaching increasingly take place in hybrid digital/non-digital environments and the media ecologies they operate in are increasingly filtered by networks, algorithms and data-informed views of the world. It is difficult to avoid acknowledging this fact in 2021, but what is in doubt is how language educators and researchers can or should engage with the technical (and cultural) machinery of these new 'media ecologies', a fact not lost on language professionals themselves.

Recent years have seen a steady stream of policy documents in some English-speaking countries about the crisis of Modern Languages, and the first stage of our research on Digital Mediations reviewed strategy documents relating to Modern Languages policy, in particular in the UK, and analysed the way in which digital mediation was defined and presented (for full information, see https://languageacts.org/digital-mediations/). We examined 21 documents relating to language policy in the United Kingdom, from 2004 to 2019, including education council and British Academy reports, publications by professional associations in the Modern Languages sector and official standards inspection reviews.

The first thing to say about the policy documents examined is how grave a picture they paint of the situation of Modern Languages in the UK. For example, the *Language Matters* position paper produced by the British Academy in 2009 warns that a 'whole generation risks being "lost to languages"' and that 'this will have a major adverse effect on the ability of the UK (and its citizens) to respond to many of the major challenges it faces today' (Anon. 2009: 8). Contrary to the common perception that Modern Languages is principally about learning a language, many of these reports emphasize that language and culture are inseparable, and that in an increasingly transcultural world, the field of Modern Languages has a wider connection to human 'processes, perceptions and self-expressions' (Ad Hoc Committee on Foreign Languages, 2007).

In the same period, Michael Worton's *Review of Modern Foreign Languages Provision in Higher Education in England* articulated a vision for Modern Languages at higher education level where the field would be 'proactive' in its own future, collaborating with other educational and external stakeholders to provide a 'clear and compelling identity for Modern Foreign Languages' and effective responses to a variety of complex needs among students, employers and others. The report outlined the challenges to be faced – including different perspectives based on language, disciplinary background and institutional role (notably the structural divide between language teachers and those teaching cultural or historical 'content') – while also saluting the increased collaboration and interdisciplinarity in the field (Worton, 2009).

What is most interesting to note for the purposes of this chapter is the degree to which Worton highlights the use of what he calls 'new technologies' and 'social networking tools' in helping to rethink how Modern Languages is delivered in teaching, in contrast to most of the policy documents we examined, which barely mention digital culture or technology at all (and where they do this is generally expressed as a set of external technical skills to 'innovate' current provision, rather than investigating their implications for culture, knowledge and pedagogy). While the language used to describe this activity in the Worton report – focusing on 'technology' and 'IT' over digital literacies, cultures or communication – betrays to some extent a technocentric view of digital culture predominant at the time, it nonetheless shows a level of imaginative engagement with digital mediation in curriculum design, assessment, peer-to-peer learning, online pedagogical resources and overall learning experience which remained largely absent from strategic discussions about Modern Languages (Worton, 2009).

Modern Languages course review

We followed this literature review of policy documents relating to Modern Languages with a study in 2018 on Modern Languages curricula in the UK, analysing where digital mediation was present and how it was represented in online public documentation about Modern Languages programmes at higher education level (Spence and Brandão, 2019). In this review, which took in 66 Modern Foreign Languages courses in the UK at undergraduate, Master's and doctoral level, we predictably found greater attention to 'digital' in Linguistics, translation courses and language courses than in courses looking at the culture and histories related to particular languages. Overall, we found explicit attention to new media landscapes in course content, and there was quite frequent reference to 'Computer Literacy' or 'Information Technology' skills in course aims or learning objectives, but available documentation did not give a sense that there was a coherent narrative about what these terms mean, or what the epistemological impact might be for Modern Languages. The general implied emphasis was strongly on technical skills rather than critical competence. 'Digital' was quite frequently mentioned as an object of study, but much less often as an actual substantive component in critical thinking, although there were some exceptions such as Kirsty Hooper's course on 'Cultural Connections, Digital Histories: Britain and the 19th-Century Hispanic World', which considered the communicative power of digital resources and developed critical collaborative digital skills to address Modern Languages research questions (https://warwick.ac.uk/fac/arts/modernlanguages/applying/undergraduate/hispanicmodules/hp313/).

Our conclusion from these two landscaping reviews was that information about digital engagement in Modern Languages was sparse and tends to focus specifically on 'digital technology', rather than facilitating a broader understanding of 'digital' as something which is profoundly cultural and embedded in knowledge systems, with interaction in both directions between the 'technological' and the 'social'.

First workshop

Our first workshop, 'Mapping multilingualism and digital culture', brought together 80 Modern Languages and digital practitioners to examine how digital mediation has transformed the way in which Modern Languages is carried out, evaluating the extent to which new research questions are articulated using digital media, and exploring the new research methods or research objects created as a result. In her keynote, Claire Taylor challenged the field to more actively engage with the digital as an object of study, to rethink 'existing literary and cultural formats', to reappraise 'geography and embeddedness', and to contribute to contesting anglophone models in digital culture (https://languageacts.org/digital-mediations/event/mapping-multilingualism-and-digital-culture/).

Presentations covered a wide range of themes including intermediality in the digital age, translingual dimensions to digital indigeneity, digitally mediated memory studies and the use of web archives to study language communities. These were followed by discussion groups between academics, digital practitioners and cultural sector respondents which looked at the degree to which networked communication, open culture and the so-called 'wisdom of the crowd' influenced the execution and transmission of Modern Languages research and the opportunities/barriers to wider adoption. While the heterogeneity in epistemological backgrounds and research design represented here was a challenge, the workshop also demonstrated a need (and hunger) for common methods, toolkits and training within Modern Languages. Discussion focused on four areas: expanded frames/scope, transferability, process and teaching/training.

The first point workshop attendees made was that the scope of Modern Languages research (and teaching) has been dramatically expanded by digital media in the last couple of decades: content is more abundant, less exclusively text-based and less controlled by cultural gatekeepers, and, in some respects, better reflects global diversity (although digital media bring new forms of filtering and ordering which researchers need to be aware of, and sometimes to subvert). We are starting to see the growing importance of what might be called 'short form scholarship' both in more traditional publication platforms and in new media forms (including blogs). But this expanded scope also leads to challenges in prioritization: with abundant content and a proliferation in methods, how do we manage research, how can we continue to be methodical?

The second topic was the transferability of tools and methods designed for individual projects in Modern Languages. This finds echoes in the early stages of the Digital Humanities, where there was considerable emphasis on creating experimental, and often ad hoc, responses to research questions, but in recent years there has been an increasing drive to build critical approaches and digital methods which can be extended to work across research themes and ecosystems and in low-resource environments. A challenge we currently face, then, is how to develop, document and critique broader frameworks for digital scholarship specifically appropriate for Modern Languages, which allow for innovation in a constantly evolving digital environment, but also normalize and integrate stable digital methods within current Modern Languages research planning and design. This will increasingly involve moving beyond critical digital literacies in the low-hanging fruit of digital culture as represented in popular social media, to more advanced, computationally driven methods (without requiring that everyone learns how to code!) which engage with the increasingly complex and technically opaque dynamics shaping transcultural and multilingual engagement in the world today.

The third theme related to what Taylor and Thornton have called 'the full cycle of research process' (Taylor and Thornton, 2017), from objects of study to research method articulation to 'final' publication (and beyond to archiving and reuse). Our workshop revealed the need for a better understanding of the flows and objects, the collaborative dynamics, ethics and sustainability of digital research from a critical Modern Languages perspective. It was clear from workshop responses that there is work to be done here – quite often 'digital' is seen as a purely technical modifier, which will make certain aspects of the research process 'quicker' or 'more efficient'; or as a 'black box', which is too complicated or too science-driven to be useful for languages-driven research. It is important to challenge these assumptions not least because Modern Languages, like other humanities fields, needs to urgently address the 'whole new dimension of historicity' produced by numerous forms of digital mediation, from digitized surrogates and their object metadata to the digitized annotations or interactions which often result (Kirsty Hooper in Taylor and Thornton, 2017). This might involve examining the pre- and post-digital traces of a literary work in studying its genealogy, for example, or interrogating the human and technical factors which help to shape a work's digital reception (through platform affordances, encoding choices or social media dynamics). Gradually, it is to be hoped, new critical and practical digital skills will become more embedded in Modern Languages research in a manner which constructively subverts the gatekeeping of large digital media companies and heightens the role and visibility of Modern Languages sensibilities in digital research design.

The final theme related to teaching and training, and specifically to what digital skills are helpful for the Modern Languages researcher of the twenty-first century, and how they connect to other growing Modern Languages-related research approaches such as ethnography (Wells et al., 2019). 'Now we need to be a different kind of researcher,' remarked one of the workshop attendees, and while it becomes easier to align teaching and research resources when information becomes digitally mobile, connecting research and education more closely nevertheless remains a challenge. That was the focus of our next initiative, a survey reviewing current attitudes towards digital culture and technology in Modern Languages education and research.

Attitudes towards digital culture and technology in Modern Languages

In the 'Attitudes towards digital culture and technology in the Modern Languages' study we sought to measure the degree of awareness (and integration) of digitally mediated methods and tools in Modern Languages research and education practice. Disseminated in a wide range of discussion lists and other fora dedicated to the study of Modern Languages and cultures, the study consisted of a detailed questionnaire survey covering four areas: the degree and nature of people's digital engagement, digital methods and tools, digital literacies and digital outputs/publication. The study report we published in 2019 summarizes the main findings from the study (Spence and Brandão, 2019), but here we wish to highlight outcomes which were common to education and research, and to explore further the connection between digital approaches to language learning and 'content'-based learning, which have historically been treated quite separately, as we saw earlier, and as noted in various chapters in this book.

The first thing to note is that there was considerable overlap in how digital affects 'research' and 'education' in the view of our survey respondents. In both cases they identified *increased access* (to learning materials / to primary sources), *more variety* (stronger visual focus in learning / new visual media as research objects), *greater authenticity* (videos, blog posts and social media with 'real' language for learning / 'real' language use 'in the wild' for research through social media and vlogs) and *networking potential* (new learner networks / potential for extensive online collaboration). While recognizing that the respondents generally demonstrated a high (and possibly higher than the norm) degree of digital engagement, it is important to note that those responding to the questions about education in particular claimed that we were witnessing a potentially profound transformation in the learning experience of Modern Languages students (whether studying language or 'content'), which might cater for different learning styles and provide a better response to intercultural and multilingual contexts. Many respondents argued that digitally mediated education might give students more agency through pedagogical models which encouraged greater student autonomy, project-based learning, peer-to-peer support, self-monitoring and smoother connections between 'language' and 'content'-based areas of the curriculum. They also saw potential in interactive, networked, multimedia and/or gamified learning, although this needed to be more closely (and critically) integrated into thinking about Modern Languages teaching. It is noteworthy that responses regarding Modern Languages research were somewhat more tentative, belying greater uncertainty and insecurity regarding the methods to use and outcomes which would be produced. In both cases, there was concern over a number of 'digital effects', such as the overdependence on screens and screen culture, the loss of interpersonal skills, the weakening of cultural-critical faculties and potentially catastrophic effects for some areas of the Modern Languages field and other language-based professions.

What practical consequences does this have for Modern Languages education today? Here it may be instructive to return briefly to the 'Mapping' workshop mentioned earlier, where a considerable amount of the discussion – in contrast to the invited presentations, which had a bias towards Modern Languages research and to the 'content' side of Modern Languages education – focused on implications for the Modern Languages syllabus. There were two sets of responses which are worth highlighting here. The first emphasized the need for better understanding of specific technologies such as machine translation, eye-tracking for online interaction, software facilitating language production or voice recognition technologies, and for greater discussion of how to integrate them into our teaching or learning. How should we incorporate Google Translate, Duolingo or multilingual versions of Wikipedia in our teaching, for example, and how can we foster critical perspectives on their usage in our students? The second aspect revolved around different levels of experience with digital culture and technology, manifested in perceptions (and myths) around 'digital natives' and 'digital immigrants' (Prensky, 2001) or 'digital visitors' and 'digital residents' (White and Cornu, 2011). Some attending the workshop argued that the radically altered landscape of language learning with apps, networked communication and strong emphasis on dynamically updated visual culture provided ample opportunities for 'two-way' teaching (between 'teacher' and 'learner') in digital literacies and encouraged 'co-creation' in a process which can effectively model real-world language practice. The next step, then, was to contemplate what kinds of digital competencies, or literacies, are needed by Modern Languages learners and researchers today.

Critical digital literacies in Modern Languages

What are digital literacies?

Despite a significant body of research into digital literacies, and a no less significant body of work on digital literacies in language learning, the concept and role of digital literacies are understood differently and with varying degrees of confidence in Modern Languages, a fact confirmed in various events we organized or took part in during the *Language Acts and Worldmaking* project. As a concept, 'digital literacies' has been inspired by wider scholarship on 'new literacies' made possible by new media realities (Lankshear and Knobel, 2003) as much as by specific waves of digital mediation, although the proliferation of terms for *functional* (information literacy), *digital-specific* (code literacy or data literacy) or *media-specific* (game literacy or multimedia literacy) literacies contributes to some of the confusion around the term (Spence, 2020: 474). In language learning, the term has been broadly conceived of as 'the modes of reading, writing and communication made possible by digital media' (Hafner et al., 2015: 1), but while some work has attempted to '(re)examine policies, practices, theories, and beliefs about digital literacies in foreign language education' (Guikema and Williams, 2014: 1), it has tended to focus more on language learning in the narrower sense (learning grammar and vocabulary of a language) than the wider interpretation (connecting a language to its wider cultural context).

It is likely impossible to define a single set of digital literacies which can be applied to the whole of Modern Languages, but it is instructive to observe how and where digital literacies are being enacted in the field at present. First, we should recognize the under-researched work being carried out (usually in low-resource conditions) in school-age education, in particular at secondary level, and visible through community-level initiatives such as the TiLT (Technology in Language Teaching) seminars (http://www.all-london.org.uk/site/index.php/webinars/) in the UK, #MFLTwitterati podcast (https://mfltwitteratipodcast.com/), or other social media streams from around the globe such as #langchat, #gilt_fb, #fslchat or #authres. This highlights an intersectoral disconnection on the topic which hinders a wider strategic view on digital literacies, and it is worth making the point that higher-level Modern Languages education (and higher-level digital literacies) has much to learn from digital pedagogies in pre-university education or language learning.

As noted, it has so far been sometimes difficult to discuss digital literacies in a joined-up/programmatic way – due to the combination of constantly evolving digital innovation, technical bias in how digital literacies are conceived, resource deficits and lack of strategic support from policymakers. Despite that, there has been considerable progress in a few areas where (1) the requirements and benefits are clearly defined, (2) technical adoption costs are low or sustainable and (3) a substantive body of research exists by way of pedagogical contextualization. This is the case, for example, in the use of telecollaboration for language learning, digital storytelling or visual/multimodal approaches to language learning.

Telecollaboration and virtual exchange provide language learners with the facility to expand their learning environments, while strengthening their intercultural and digital competences (Kurek and Hauck, 2014). Although dependent on effective scaffolding and mediated by digital equity factors such as internet access or varied opportunities for digital literacy (Müge and Hauck, 2020), virtual exchange nevertheless to some extent collapses geographical boundaries, and enables language learners to participate in their own digital worldmaking, which when practised effectively promotes critical reflection on their use of digital media. And gamified telecollaboration strategies such as that employed by the TeCoLa project combine video-based/virtual world interaction with the often elusive game-based element in digital pedagogies to facilitate student exchanges (at secondary school level throughout Europe), a potentially rich channel for intercultural negotiation and multilingual identity formation (https://sites.google.com/site/tecolaproject/).

The awareness that students are increasingly engaging with a wider range of semiotic resources (the materials that students encounter today include many signs and symbols to communicate information, including letters and words, drawings, pictures, videos, audio sounds, music, facial gestures and design of space) has heightened calls for greater 'visual literacies', more closely aligned to student experience and expectations shaped by an increasingly 'mobile first' cultural production model. There is still a shortage of published research on 'the use of film and audiovisual media and new techno tools' in language education (Herrero and Vanderschelden, 2019: xvi) and 'on the whole, our educational systems have been slow to respond to the ascendance of visual media in our society' (Donaghy, 2019: 4), but there is clearly great potential for using collaborative multimodal tools to foster digitally mediated intercultural communicative competence in language learning. This also applies in the more specialized study of language cultures, something we have started to see in Digital Humanities research projects, although the multilingual and intercultural aspects are generally under-theorized.

Similarly, digital storytelling (through which students co-create stories using a range of digital media, including film, audio and image-based content) represents for language education an area which embraces collaboration, critical digital competence and multimodal expression for the purpose of intercultural negotiation and multilingual identity formation. The Critical Connections/Multilingual Digital Storytelling Project (https://www.gold.ac.uk/clcl/multilingual-learning/criticalconnections/) stands out as a reference point for its cross-curricular, multi-genre, digitally experimental and project-based approach to language learning at school, in a model which purposefully breaks out of traditional institutional contexts. Again, the potential of digital literacies through digital storytelling is under-realized in more culture-focused and/or advanced areas of language education, although initiatives such as the recent African Digital Storytelling Symposium show the potential, across different narrative traditions and realized in a variety of forms (as archive, digital mapping, visualization or video game; https://africandh.ku.edu/digital-storytelling-symposium-2020).

Anderson and Macleroy demonstrate how multilingual digital storytelling challenges the concept of 'home languages' and 'monolingual ideology', providing a platform for multiliteracies which make 'critical connections' between digital literacies, learning environments and different educational sectors (Anderson and Macleroy, 2016).

Taken together, digital storytelling, virtual exchange and telecollaboration all suggest key foundational elements of a language-centric formulation of digital literacies: collaboration across existing educational or geographic borders, experimental/serendipitous interactions, learner- (or researcher-) driven digital mediation, peer-to-peer language learning worlds and the effective participation of language communities in a more equitable negotiation between global knowledge systems.

Acquiring digital literacies in Modern Languages

A key question here, then, is how people studying Modern Languages (and Cultures) can develop digital literacies, and how they can be embedded effectively within language education and research programmes. As noted earlier, while official policy documents and strategic reports in language education were generally silent or opaque on the topic, there is considerable practice-based activity in Modern Languages community-led initiatives and language pedagogies research. There is much less experience (and clarity) on the kind of advanced, culture-focused provision typified by so-called 'content' (in contrast to 'language') courses at higher education level. This is expected to change post 2020/21 pandemic where teachers, learners and researchers suddenly had to engage with online learning and remote collaboration through a myriad of tools and ecosystems. Hard empirical research and evidence-based study will fully evaluate the long-term impacts of changes brought about in the short and long term.

Digital methods training events we have been involved in have consistently shown participant interest in Modern Languages-focused digital methods courses which prepare researchers in how to work with data (discovering, processing, analysing and visualizing digital data) for Modern Languages research. This is no longer the preserve of the quantitative end of the field (corpus-based research), and now embraces increasingly ethnographic or culture-critical perspectives. Participants in events we attended as part of our project strand work have generally wanted both 'balance' in the digital methods they study (quantitative and qualitative methods, and often both) and 'variety', which typically includes topics such as comparative linguistic approaches to data; cultural analytics; network analysis; web archive-based studies of language communities; thematic analysis of spoken data; and methods for assessing digitally mediated linguistic complexity and creativity. There is a notable interest in methods commonly used in the social sciences, such as discourse analysis of social media production. Given the highly heterogeneous nature of Modern Languages research methods, it is difficult to come to general conclusions here, but we have found consensus in the desire for a language-aware and multilingually/transculturally focused perspective which is missing from general digital methods education programmes.

There is also the question of what vehicle(s) might be most appropriate to deliver the kind of critical digital literacies Modern Languages needs at this moment in time. Here we return to our survey again. There is a need for more detailed and focused research into the digital education requirements for different Modern Languages sectors (and different stakeholders), but our survey indicated strong support for greater programmatic development of digital competences in learners, teachers and researchers, such as data literacy; digital communication, collaboration and participation; or basic understanding of digital theory and practice. There was no strong consensus on the best way to achieve this, although there was generally strong support for all options we proposed, which included 'learning on your own'; through the 'school curriculum'; on a 'formal university module'; on 'formal research programmes or training'; and 'special training courses'. In all cases, it was deemed 'important' or 'very important' by more than 53 per cent of respondents. Formal/general provision (at school or university level) received slightly higher support than informal/specialized options (including 'learning on your own'). There are wider debates to be had on this topic, which go beyond the scope of this chapter, such as how to recover a digital 'deficit' in our critical and pedagogical skills while integrating digital literacies in existing programmes, and of balancing general provision (general critical digital competencies) with more focused offerings, but the survey did suggest some categories for thinking about the topic which we asked respondents to assess.

While there was a feeling that the field of Modern Languages as a whole mostly needs basic critical digital literacies in topics such as 'digital communication, collaboration and participation', 'information and media literacies' or 'basic understanding of digital theory and practice', the respondents themselves felt they would personally benefit from a balance of the topics we suggested, including options at the more computational end of the spectrum such as 'coding/programming for MFL (Modern Foreign Languages)' and 'advanced understanding of digital theory and practice'.

Following on from this, in July 2019 we convened an event called the 'Digital Modern Languages tutorial writing sprint' (https://languageacts.org/digital-mediations/event/writing-sprint/) to respond to one of our key findings in the 2019 survey – namely, that there was little evidence that respondents received institutional or any other kind of support as they attempted to engage with digital mediation in their learning/research practice. We describe the event and its outputs in more depth in 'Critical digital pedagogies in Modern Languages – a tutorial collection' (Spence and Brandão, 2020), the introduction to the set of self-guided tutorials which were the event's principal outcome, but it is worth briefly summarizing some key aspects in relation to debates around digital literacies in Modern Languages. First, the publication raised important questions about the relationship between text-based learning materials (which are sustainable and easier to produce) and visual materials (which can be more effective at illuminating some points and are closer to the media expectations of many of today's YouTube-reared learners). Second, the initiative, which was designed as much to study the 'process' of creating self-guided Open Educational Resources for Modern Languages (and Cultures) as to publish the tutorials themselves, illustrated the contrast between the creativity of Modern Languages educators and the validation/credit systems which exist to support that creativity. Finally, the collection represents to a large extent the areas often underrepresented in the digital mediation of Modern Languages education and research – namely, a focus on culture-focused 'content' modules and more advanced engagement with Modern Languages studies.

Advanced digital literacies in Modern Languages

In *The New Education*, a reappraisal of today's university 'for a world in flux', Cathy Davidson argues for eschewing the kind of 'technophobia' and 'technophilia' which characterized early responses to digital disruption, and proposes that we instead fully integrate digital literacies into the current education system in order to align with students' media expectations and the critical-practical digital skillset demanded in many professional environments. Davidson hints at an engagement which goes beyond basic (and technocentric) 'IT literacy' towards something more involved and integrated, training the learner to think actively and creatively through digital technology in a manner which becomes part of 'an intellectual toolkit of ideas and tactics that are as interactive and dexterous as our post-Internet world demands' (Davidson, 2017: 14, 90–1, 131).

This learning will become increasingly 'hybrid' in nature as learners and researchers become equally proficient in both 'online' and 'offline' spaces. Proponents of 'hybrid pedagogy' contrast *blended learning* ('an easy mixing of on-ground and online learning') with *hybrid pedagogy* (which 'is about bringing the sorts of learning that happen in a physical place and the sorts of learning that happen in a virtual place into a more engaged and dynamic conversation') (Stommel, 2012). In bringing together our real-life/digital experiences, hybrid pedagogy explores a number of intersections – among others, between 'garden-walled academia' and 'open education'; between 'institutional' and 'informal' education modes; and between 'learning in schools' and 'learning in the world' (Stommel, 2012). Theorists using the term distinguish between the narrower focus on learning 'process or practice' which blended learning suggests, and propose that we avoid polar online/offline comparisons and explore the wider pedagogical challenges which arise from constantly moving between digital and physical spaces.

This model of learning implies a more advanced engagement than is currently typical for language education – advanced in terms of its study focus (Modern Languages and Cultures), its methods, its (often digitally mediated) objects of study and the digital/hybrid literacies it requires. And central to achieving this is the concept of learner autonomy. In *Aprender a aprender en la era digital* ('Learning to learn in the digital era'), Román-Mendoza argues that 'learning to learn autonomously ... is one of the most important skills' in the twenty-first century (Román-Mendoza, 2018: 2, author translation from the Spanish original). In a comprehensive study of digitally mediated learning environments, the author charts the sometimes bewildering number of acronyms surrounding digital pedagogy and focuses on what she calls 'Tecnologías del Aprendizaje y el Conocimiento' ('Learning and Knowledge Technologies') as a more active means for capturing the combination of collaboration, community-building, connective participation and critical digital literacies required to foster learner agency and autonomy. These frequently step out of the often inflexible and overly traditional Learning Management Systems imposed by institutions for teaching to instead draw on an assorted combination of open-source and professional tools, or tools which students use in their everyday lives. This student-led approach to acquiring digital literacies for language education is principally applied to (Spanish) language learning in Román-Mendoza's work (Román-Mendoza, 2018: 11), but there are analogous approaches in content-focused pedagogy, notably in the Digital Humanities.

The field of the Digital Humanities, despite its transnational pretensions, has not generally interacted as much with Modern Languages as fully as it has with other fields such as English, History or Classical Studies. And although 'DH', as it is often called, is profoundly transdisciplinary, typically drawing together an eclectic mixture of epistemologies and practices, the field has also been criticized for its anglophone bias, which routinely privileges countries from the Global North (Fiormonte, 2017). Recent years have seen numerous attempts to refocus the Digital Humanities to become more linguistically and geoculturally inclusive (https://languageacts.org/digital-mediations/event/disrupting-digital-monolingualism), and some of these have explored the mutual interactions between Digital Humanities and Modern Languages in an anglophone context. In their call for a 'hybrid "critical DHML"', Taylor and Pitman (2007) propose closer collaboration between Digital Humanities and Modern Languages in addressing transcultural and translinguistic research challenges.

This has been apparent to some extent in events such as the publication section co-edited by Paul Spence and Naomi Wells on Liverpool University Press's Modern Languages Open publishing platform (https://liverpooluniversitypress.blog/2019/11/13/modern-languages-open-launch-of-the-digital-modern-languages-section/) and panels convened by Élika Ortega at the Modern Languages of America (MLA) conference. Across three panels – 'Digital Hispanisms' and 'Digital Humanities and Modern Languages' at MLA2019 and 'Critical engagements between Modern Languages and Digital Humanities' at MLA2020 – participants explored a range of DH–ML interactions at higher education level, bringing multilingualism and (trans)cultural criticism to bear on a more culturally complex and computationally intensive set of digital mediations. In appraising 'geopolitical asymmetries' in digital culture in her introduction to the 'Digital Hispanisms' session, Ortega alluded to 'a range of digital schisms that extend to the Hispanic world'. These became the target for the panel, which emphasized the importance of creativity as a complement to critical thinking, 'narratives of cultural encounter and cultural mixing' and the kind of cross-border thinking which typifies Modern Languages expertise (https://mla.hcommons.org/groups/digital-humanities/forum/topic/mla19-582-roundtable-digital-hispanisms-2/). This was extended at the MLA2020 panel by Eduard Arriaga in a talk titled 'Expanded digital infrastructures in teaching Latin American and Hispanic cultures' which connected visions of infrastructure in Modern Languages and Digital Humanities (Arriaga, 2020).

At the same 2020 panel, Bilis and O'Brien presented 'The Modern Language classroom as DH laboratory', a pedagogical approach aimed at 'redrawing the lines around DH and modern language practices' and moving beyond treating 'texts, cultural artifacts and digital media on [ML] syllabi' simply as a means of facilitating language acquisition, towards an approach treating them 'as objects of study in and of themselves'. Bilis and O'Brien point out that Digital Humanities curricula tend to be more 'in flux' and 'responsive' than more established Modern Languages syllabi, mouldable to specific student requirements and to 'questions that emerge out of their engagement with a wider range of methodologies, materials and genres'. Here, the Modern Languages classroom brings transcultural perspectives to multimodal representation or data-driven analysis and visualization (Bilis and O'Brien, 2020).

Melinda Cro's book *Integrating the Digital Humanities into the Second Language Classroom* invokes the experimental, content-driven, public-facing and 'tinker-centric' (using a term invented by Sayers (2011)) nature of the Digital Humanities in proposing a student-led and project-based pedagogy which not only advances their understanding of target languages and cultures but also typically creates an outcome which 'impacts the fabric of the world and cultures studied' (Cro, 2020: 38, 19). This repositioning of the student from 'consumer' to 'generator' of digital media provides them with the critical and technical skills to engage with a wide range of media, semiotic resources and creative tools and in so doing to develop the kind of advanced language-centric digital literacies embodied by deep DH–ML engagement. The increased agency which comes with this model of digital Modern Languages learning, built on personal learning environments/networks and the integration of in-class/out-of-class experience, both generates 'a meaningful bridge between classroom experience and professional endeavour for students across L2 curricula' and creates highly critically-technically literate plurilingual agents capable of analysing and responding to evolving digital literacy needs (Cro, 2020: 19, 38).

Conclusions

'Digital mediations' set out to explore interactions and tensions between digital culture and Modern Languages research, partly in order to point to some possible strategic priorities in fomenting the critical application of digital literacies, digital pedagogies and digital methods in language education. These mediations occur within a broad and complex zone of interaction, involving multiple actors and institutional roles, but which underpins how multilingualism, intercultural exchange, and language-focused 'worldmaking' can be understood in an increasingly digital age.

We found that digital culture and technology have had a major impact on the study of Modern Languages, but this process has been uneven, disconnected across different *sectors* (secondary/higher education), *areas of focus* (language learning/content-based learning), *languages* and *fields of study*. Digital mediation has fostered optimism (around authentic materials/interactions, visually rich materials and digitally augmented methods) but also concerns (about job security, disciplinary identity and critical skills). It still sometimes receives polarized responses – technophilia and technophobia – which cloud meaningful engagement with digital methods, tools and content. This chapter has attempted to signal some fruitful ways of exploring digital mediations in Modern Languages and of developing the kinds of digital literacies the field needs as a result. Digital mediation has profoundly affected a whole host of areas where Modern Languages has an important role to play, including cultural complexity, global divides and intercultural exchange. And advanced critical digital literacies will become a key prerequisite for sense-making in human environments increasingly characterized by rich media, algorithmically filtered communication flows and digitally mediated transcultural/translingual interactions.

We tentatively proposed some features of 'Topographies of Digital Modern (Foreign) Languages research' in a presentation at the Digital Humanities 2019 conference in Utrecht, The Netherlands. These included mutual disruptions between Modern Languages and Digital Humanities both in pedagogy (the international and plurilingual classroom) and in research (geocultural and linguistic diversity, transcultural/translingual interfaces, and multilingual digital methods and tools) (https://dev.clariah.nl/files/dh2019/boa/0245.html). These gesture at some of the more advanced critical-computational challenges facing Modern Languages in the future, and the notion of digital literacies in Modern Languages, will need to be expanded to enable students and researchers to engage with these new sites of multilingual and intercultural encounter.

In her introduction to this book, Catherine Boyle describes the origins of the worldmaking concept which was central to our project design, and it seems apt that Goodman's ideas entered our collective thinking via an encounter between Modern Languages and Digital Humanities researchers. Digital Humanities and Modern Languages education both depend on the kind of messy, experimental, transdisciplinary, peer-to-peer and intercultural interactions which we have explored in this chapter. Our project mission statement speaks of 'language as a material and historical force which acts as the means by which individuals construct their personal, local, transnational and spiritual identities', and it has been our contention here that we need to perform these 'language acts' across different media, and that we require new critical literacies and pedagogies which operate across multiple online and offline worlds.

References

Ad Hoc Committee on Foreign Languages (2007) 'Foreign Languages and higher education: New structures for a changed world', *Profession*, 234–45. Available from: https://www.mla.org/Resources/Research/Surveys-Reports-and-Other-Documents/Teaching-Enrollments-and-Programs/Foreign-Languages-and-Higher-Education-New-Structures-for-a-Changed-World (Accessed: 2 December 2020).

Anderson, J., and Macleroy, V. (eds) (2016) *Multilingual Digital Storytelling: Engaging Creatively and Critically with Literacy*. London and New York: Routledge.

Androutsopoulos, J., and Juffermans, K. (2014) 'Digital language practices in superdiversity: Introduction', *Discourse, Context & Media*, 4–51–6 [Online].

Anon. (2016) *Born Global: Implications for Higher Education* [Online]. Available from: https://www.thebritishacademy.ac.uk/publications/born-global-implications-higher-education/ (Accessed: 2 December 2020).

Anon. (2009) Language Matters [Online]. Available from: https://www.thebritishacademy.ac.uk/publications/language-matters/ (Accessed: 2 December 2020).

Anon. (2019) 'Maryland Bill weighs coding as a language', *Language Magazine* [Online]. Available from: https://www.languagemagazine.com/2019/04/21/maryland-bill-weighs-coding-as-a-language/ (Accessed: 2 December 2020).

Armstrong, M. (2015a) 'Coding, today's modern language', *Education Technology* [Online]. Available from: *https://edtechnology.co.uk/comments/coding-todays-modern-language/* (Accessed: 2 December 2020).

Armstrong, M. (2015b) 'Why learn French when you can learn to code?' *LinkedIn* [Online]. Available from: https://www.linkedin.com/pulse/why-learn-french-when-you-can-code-mark-armstrong/ (Accessed: 2 December 2020).

Arriaga, E. (2020) 'Expanded digital infrastructures in teaching Latin American and Hispanic cultures', paper presented at MLA2020 conference.

Bilis, H., and O'Brien, L. (2020) 'The Modern Language classroom as Digital Humanities laboratory', in de Medeiros, A. and Kelly, D. (eds), *Language Debates: Theory and Reality in Language Learning*. London: John Murray Learning, pp. 257–71.

Burdick, A. et al. (2012) *Digital Humanities*. Cambridge, MA: MIT Press [Online]. Available from: https://mitpress.mit.edu/books/digitalhumanities (Accessed: 2 December 2020).

Clark, K. M. (2017) 'No more foreign language swap in Legislature's coding bill', *Miami Herald* [Online]. Available from: https://www.miamiherald.com/news/politics-government/state-politics/article141026108.html (Accessed: 2 December 2020).

Cro, M. A. (2020) *Integrating the Digital Humanities into the Second Language Classroom: A Practical Guide*. Washington, DC: Georgetown University Press.

Davidson, C. N. (2017) *The New Education: How to Revolutionize the University to Prepare Students for a World in Flux*. New York: Basic Books.

Donaghy, K. (2019) 'Using film to teach languages in a world of screens', in C. Herrero and I. Vanderschelden (eds), *Using Film and Media in the Language Classroom: Reflections on Research-led Teaching*. Bristol, Blue Ridge Summit: Multilingual Matters, pp. 3–18.

Fiormonte, D. (2017) 'Digital Humanities and the geopolitics of knowledge', *Digital Studies/Le Champ numérique*, 7(1), 5 [Online].

Galina Russell, I. (2014) 'Geographical and linguistic diversity in the Digital Humanities', *Literary and Linguistic Computing*, 29(3), 307–16 [Online].

Gil, A. and Ortega, É. (2016) 'Global outlooks in Digital Humanities: Multilingual practices and minimal computing', in Crompton, C. et al. (eds) *Doing Digital Humanities: Practice, Training, Research*. New York: Routledge, pp. 22–34.

Goodman, N. (1978) *Ways of Worldmaking*. Indianapolis, IN: Hackett Publishing.

Guikema, J. P., and Williams, L. (eds) (2014) *Digital Literacies in Foreign and Second Language Education*, CALICO Monograph Series 12. Durham, NC: CALICO.

Hafner, C., A. et al. (2015) 'Introduction', *Language Learning & Technology*, 19(3), 1–7.

Herrero, C., and Vanderschelden, I. (2019) 'Introduction', in *Using Film and Media in the Language Classroom: Reflections on Research-led Teaching*. Bristol, Blue Ridge Summit: Multilingual Matters, pp. xv–xxii.

Jones, R. H. (2020) 'Mediated discourse analysis', in Adolphs, S. and Knight, D. (eds), *The Routledge Handbook of English Language and Digital Humanities*. Abingdon, Oxon, and New York: Routledge, pp. 202–19.

Kurek, M., and Hauck, M. (2014) 'Closing the digital divide: A framework for multiliteracy training', in Guikema, J. P. and Williams, L. (eds), *Digital Literacies in Foreign and Second Language Education*, CALICO Monograph Series. Durham, NC: CALICO, pp. 119–40.

Lankshear, C., and Knobel, M. (2003) *New Literacies: Changing Knowledge and Classroom Learning*. Buckingham: Open University Press.

Liddicoat, A. J. (2009) 'Communication as culturally contexted practice: A view from intercultural communication', *Australian Journal of Linguistics*, 29(1), 115–33 [Online].

Livingstone, S. (2009) 'On the mediation of everything: ICA Presidential Address 2008', *Journal of Communication*, 59(1), 1–18 [Online].

Mason, S. (2017) 'The coding versus language debate', *MLTAQ Journal*, 16623–8.

Müge, S., and Hauck, M. (2020) 'Exploring digital equity in online learning communities (virtual exchange)', in de Medeiros, A. and Kelly, D. (eds), *Language Debates: Theory and Reality in Language Learning*. London: John Murray Learning, pp. 272–92.

Prensky, M. (2001) 'Digital natives, digital immigrants Part 1', *On the Horizon*, 9(5), 1–6 [Online].

Román-Mendoza, E. (2018) *Aprender a aprender en la era digital.* London and New York: Routledge.

Sayers, J. (2011) 'Tinker-centric pedagogy in literature and language classrooms', in McGrath, L. (ed.), *Collaborative Approaches to the Digital in English Studies*. Logan, UT: Computers and Composition Digital Press, pp. 279–300 [Online]. Available from: https://ccdigitalpress.org/book/cad/index2.html (Accessed: 2 December 2020).

Siapera, E. (2014) 'Tweeting #Palestine: Twitter and the mediation of Palestine', *International Journal of Cultural Studies*, 17(6), 539–55 [Online].

Silverstone, R. (2002) 'Complicity and collusion in the mediation of everyday life', *New Literary History*, 33(4), 761–80.

Spence, P. (2020) 'English language and digital literacies', in S. Adolphs and D. Knight (eds), *The Routledge Handbook of English Language and Digital Humanities*. Abingdon, Oxon, and New York: Routledge, pp. 472–93.

Spence, P., and Brandão, R. (2019) *Attitudes towards Digital Culture and Technology in the Modern Languages* [Online]. Available from: https://kclpure.kcl.ac.uk/portal/en/publications/attitudes-towards-digital-culture-and-technology-in-the-modern-languages(cf43a369-e1d2-4091-9738-4b65df80f115).html (Accessed: 5 May 2020).

Spence, P., and Brandão, R. (2020) 'Critical digital pedagogies in Modern Languages – a tutorial collection', *Modern Languages Open*, (1), 38 [Online].

Stommel, J. (2012) 'Hybridity, pt. 2: What is hybrid pedagogy?', *Hybrid Pedagogy* [Online]. Available from: https://hybridpedagogy.org/hybridity-pt-2-what-is-hybrid-pedagogy/ (Accessed: 3 December 2020).

Taylor, C., and Thornton, N. (2017) 'Modern Languages and the digital: The shape of the discipline', *Modern Languages Open* [Online]. Available from: http://www.modernlanguagesopen.org/articles/10.3828/mlo.v0i0.156/ (Accessed: 9 June 2017).

Taylor, C., and Pitman, T. (eds) (2007) *Latin American Cyberculture and Cyberliterature*. Liverpool: Liverpool University Press.

Walton, M. (2009) *Mobile Literacies & South African Teens: Leisure Reading, Writing, and MXit Chatting for Teens in Langa and Gugulethu* [Online]. Available from: https://www.bibsonomy.org/bibtex/26f01d8a635dc83de99484c057fed724f/yish (Accessed: 3 December 2020).

Wells, N., et al. (2019) 'Ethnography and Modern Languages', *Modern Languages Open*, (1), 1 [Online].

White, D. S., and Cornu, A. L. (2011) 'Visitors and Residents: A new typology for online engagement', *First Monday*, 16(9) [Online]. Available from: http://firstmonday.org/ojs/index.php/fm/article/view/3171 (Accessed: 10 March 2015).

Worton, M. (2009) *Review of Modern Foreign Languages Provision in Higher Education in England*. Bristol, UK: Higher Education Funding Council for England (HEFCE) [Online]. Available from: http://www.hefce.ac.uk/pubs/hefce/2009/09_41/ (Accessed: 3 December 2020).

Glossary

activism the use of direct action to bring about political or social change

affordances (of digital devices) the qualities or properties which determine how (digital devices) may be used

assimilationist someone who participates in or advocates for cultural or racial integration

asymmetries when two halves of something have different shapes; in this context, not being equally available to two people or groups

chronotopic of or related to a specific time or place

cognate words or languages which are cognate have the same origin or source; having qualities in common

congener a person or thing of the same kind or class as another

conjuncture a particular combination of circumstances or events

derivational relating to that which is derived (e.g. develops from the original form or meaning)

diachronic occurring or changing along with time; in this context, concerned with linguistic features

diacritics special distinguishing marks such as accents to indicate different pronunciation, stress, tone or meaning

diaspora (diasporic) a group of people who spread or are dispersed from their original homeland to other countries and the community and culture which subsequently forms

diffusionist someone who supports the theory of diffusionism: i.e. that changes in one culture are caused by diffusion of ideas from another; the theory that diffusion is the main force in cultural change and innovation

digital 'deficit' a significant gap in going or being digital (of people or organizations)

digital literacy an individual's ability to critically assess and use digital media in its various forms, often involving multimodal competence, developing new dynamics of identity creation or connecting to autonomous, personalized and peer-to-peer modes of learning

digital mediation the way in which life is mediated through digital media, in this context connected to young people engaging, learning and developing in technology-rich environments

digital residents a term used for those who live, interact socially with friends and share information about their social life on the web rather than just use it for browsing in a functional way

digital storytelling the practice of ordinary people using digital means to tell and share their stories; can also be in an interactive form

digital transformations process of change brought about by digital culture and technology, including new tools, methods and ways of working

digital visitors a term for those people who browse the internet functionally and are concerned about privacy and therefore do not leave comments or opinions online

diphthongize (diphthongization) to make a simple vowel into a diphthong: a single syllable vowel sound in which the tongue changes position while it is being pronounced so the beginning of the sound is different from the end of the sound: the sound glides from one vowel sound to another

disruptions a widely used term (influenced by the work of Clayton Christensen and others) to describe a process by which an innovation displaces an established business paradigm using a new market and value network; it has come to be used as a term for any new technical (or other) change which is assumed to be destined to supplant existing frameworks

doublet two or more different words of same derivation but having different meanings and phonological forms

embed to fix something firmly and deeply into a substance or structure

epistemology the theory and philosophy of knowledge, distinction between opinion and fact, what can or cannot be known, how we construct and justify knowledge

etymology a study of the origins/roots of words and how their meaning changes over time

extractivist seeking to extract as much of a high-demand resource as possible; it has come to describe a way of running the economy in resource exporting countries, especially in Latin America

geocultural related to geography and culture; the ways in which cultural practices and attitudes can be connected with geographic places and regions and the cultural sphere

geopolitics the study of the way a country's size and position influence its political relationships and its power relations with other countries; international relations influenced by geographical factors

hermeneutic philosophical study of interpretation, the way meanings gradually change

historicity historical authenticity

historiography the study of history and how it is written

hypotactic use of a conjunction to make one clause subordinate to another; syntactic subordination of one clause to another

interculturality the interaction of people from different cultural backgrounds using authentic language in an appropriate way which demonstrates knowledge, awareness and understanding of the cultures; the possibility of generating shared cultural expressions through dialogue and mutual respect

intermediality (in the digital age) interconnectedness of modern media of communication and the way different media interact

intersemiotic cultural communication using language, image and other semiotic resources to explain, translate and circulate ideas

lexical convergence the way in which languages come to resemble one another structurally or change linguistically as a result of prolonged language contact and mutual interference (whether or not those languages belong to the same family)

linguaphobia fear of unknown or foreign languages

loanwords a word taken from one language and used (e.g. 'borrowed or loaned') in another

'mediation' as a reconciliation of different stakeholders and ideas leading to negotiation and resolution; in a more social sense, as a transformative process in which the meaningfulness and value of things are constructed

metadata a set of data that describes or helps you to use other data or information

metalanguage a set of symbols or specialized form of language used to describe or discuss the structure of another language

minoritarian someone who holds a minority view; supporter or member of a minority group especially in the political sphere – in this instance in the linguistic sphere

morph (morphing) to gradually change or to change someone or something from one thing to another, to take on a different appearance

morphology (morphological) the study of words and parts of words (morphemes), looking at how they are formed – their internal structure

multimodal having or using a variety of methods (modes) to do something

neologism (neologistic) creation or use of a new word or expression in a language or a new meaning for an existing word

paradigm (paradigmatic) a clear and typical example of something; serving as an explanatory pattern or a model

paratactic using a style in which sentences (or elements within sentences) are set down with little or no indication of their relationship

paratext material associated with, but distinct from, the main body of a film, book, game, text, typically created or supplied by someone other than the original author

peer-to-peer learning when students learn from other students, especially when the teaching student has a deeper knowledge of the subject

periphrastic (of a case or tense) formed by a combination of words rather than by inflection (e.g. 'did go' or 'of the family' rather than 'went' and 'the family's') or formed by the use of function words or auxiliaries instead of by inflection

phonological the sound system of a language or study relating to the sounds in languages/science of speech sounds, especially history or theory of sound changes in a language or related languages

plurilingual someone with the ability and competence to switch easily between multiple languages, depending on the situation, for ease of communication

polycentric having several or many centres

register the style of language, grammar and words used for different situations according to the user's communicative purpose, social context and standing (determined by the degree of formality and choice of vocabulary, pronunciation and syntax)

rhizotonic a linguistics term: an inflected form whose stressed syllable is in the stem

semiotics exploration of how meaning is created and communicated, especially how signs and symbols create meaning (e.g. emoticons, traffic lights)

synchronicity when two or more similar or related events happen by chance at the same time, a deeply significant coincidence

syntagm (syntagmatic) the way different linguistic units can be combined to make well-formed language structures

taxonomy a classification scheme: a system for naming and organizing things (i.e. plants, animals) into groups which share similar qualities

techno-determinism a theory that assumes that a society's technology determines the development of its cultural values and social structure over other factors

telecollaboration a form of network-based language teaching which brings together classes of language learners through computer mediated communication to promote learning through social interaction and collaboration

transcultural cross-cultural; relating to or involving more than one culture

translanguaging instead of trying to use a single language, a multilingual speaker will use their full linguistic repertoire to communicate (often using several languages at once)

translingual involving more than one language or occurring in more than one; also ability to switch effortlessly from one language to another when speaking or writing

transnational going beyond national boundaries; extending operations across different nations

twenty-first-century learning developing learning, literacy and life skills as a part of the classroom experience including skills such as creativity, digital literacy, critical thinking, problem solving, collaboration and communication

virtual exchange a facilitated education programme which uses technology to allow people to communicate and interact with each other although geographically separated, combining the deep impact of meaningful intercultural exchange with the broad reach of new media technology

visual literacies how meaning is made in still and moving image 'texts': closely examining diverse visual texts across a range of types

xenodochial friendly to, hospitable to strangers – compare *xenophobia*, fear of or hostility to the stranger or the foreigner

Index

About the contributors

Dr Inma Álvarez is a Senior Lecturer in Spanish at the Open University (UK). She is currently Director of Postgraduate Research Studies, and her research is on the links between the performance of language(s) and culture(s) and the arts in different contexts and practices. She was Co-Investigator, with Mara Fuertes Gutiérrez, of the Diasporic Identities and the Politics of Language Teaching research strand of the *Language Acts and Worldmaking* research project.

Catherine Boyle is Professor of Latin American Cultural Studies at King's College London where she is also the Director of the Centre for *Language Acts and Worldmaking*. Her research and practice is based in connections between cultural history and translation and on methodologies for theatre translation in research and performance, and she was Principal Investigator for the *Language Acts and Worldmaking* research project.

Dr Renata Brandão is a Lecturer in Multimedia Journalism in the School of Arts and Creative Industries at the University of East London and a Visiting Researcher at King's College London on *Language Acts and Worldmaking* for the Digital Mediations strand on which she was previously a Postdoctoral Researcher. Her research focuses on the uses and representation of data across media outlets. Her work demonstrates how digital data enhances and expands Modern Languages research and learning in meaningful, creative and accessible ways.

Isabel Cobo Palacios has taught Spanish in UK universities for more than a decade. Currently, she is teaching Spanish at the University of Warwick and conducting her PhD research at the Open University, within the *Language Acts and Worldmaking* project, where she is investigating higher education language teachers as mediators in the classroom and their perceptions and reflections on this process.

Dr Rocío Díaz-Bravo is a Lecturer in Spanish Language at the University of Granada and a Visiting Researcher at King's College London, where she is a member of the Loaded Meanings team, researching cultured borrowings in the *Retrato de la Loçana andaluza*. Her study and critical edition of this work is published by the Modern

Humanities Research Association, and together with Gael Vaamonde she is developing *Lozana Digital*, a digital edition which will enable the linguistic investigation of this Golden Age text. Her doctoral thesis was a linguistic study of the orality of this work. She also holds Masters degrees in both Digital Humanities and in the Teaching of Spanish as a Foreign Language. Her current research is on the application of Digital Humanities to Spanish language, the teaching of Spanish and the history and varieties of Spanish.

Ella Dunne is completing her PhD within the *Language Acts and Worldmaking* project at King's College London. Focusing on the work of Peruvian José María Arguedas (1911–69), she uses translation to bring his texts to an English-language interlocutor and to provide close readings of the post-colonial, multilingual text.

Dr Mara Fuertes Gutiérrez is a Senior Lecturer at The Open University (UK). She is currently the Head of Spanish. Over her career, she has conducted extensive research in the areas of Spanish Language Teaching, Historiography of Linguistics, Applied Linguistics and Sociolinguistics. She was Co-Investgator, with Inma Álvarez, of the Diasporic Identities and the Politics of Language Teaching research strand of the *Language Acts and Worldmaking* research project.

Isabel García Ortiz is a doctoral student at Queen Mary, University of London within the *Language Acts and Worldmaking* project. Her research focuses on the borrowing and embedding of scientific and medical loanwords from Latin into the Western European languages. She holds a BA in Translation and Interpreting and an MA in Hispanic Linguistics from the University of Granada and is currently also studying for an MA in Compulsory Secondary Education at the University of Almería.

Debra Kelly is Professor Emerita in Modern Languages, School of Humanities, University of Westminster, London. Her recent research concerns the historical and contemporary presence of the French and Francophone communities in London and she is co-editor of *A History of the French in London: Liberty, Equality, Opportunity* (2013) and author of *Fishes with Funny French Names: The French Restaurant in London from the Nineteenth to the Twenty-First Century* (2021). She is also Visiting Senior Research Fellow at King's College London working with the Centre for *Language Acts and Worldmaking*. She was Co-investigator, with Ana de Medeiros, of the project's Language Transition research stand.

Dr Ana de Medeiros is Director of the Modern Language Centre at King's College London. Her work examines questions of identity in life writing with a particular focus on the works of Marguerite Yourcenar, Assia Djebar and, more recently, Marie Nimier. *Marie Nimier: Le Sujet et ses écritures/The Self in the Web of Language* (Peter Lang, 2021) is the latest collection of essays which she co-edited with David Gascoigne. She was Co-Investigator, with Debra Kelly, of the Language Transitions research strand of *Language Acts and Worldmaking*.

Dr Carlos Montoro is a Learning Designer at The Open University (UK). He has done research in Language Teaching, Educational Technology and Organization Studies. His most recent work focuses on the politics of language teaching in the UK using an activity-theoretical, worldmaking framework. He was a Postdoctoral Researcher for the *Language Acts and Worldmaking* project on the Diasporic Identities research strand.

Christopher Pountain is Emeritus Professor of Spanish Linguistics at Queen Mary University of London and a Life Fellow of Queens' College, Cambridge. He has published over 50 articles in the field of the history of the Romance languages and is author of *A History of the Spanish Language through Texts* (London: Routledge, 2001) and *Exploring the Spanish Language* (2nd edn, London: Arnold, 2016), as well as being co-author of several Spanish pedagogical works. He was the Co-Investigator of the Loaded Meanings strand of the *Language Acts and Worldmaking* project. His current research interests are the impact of Latin on the Romance languages and sociolinguistic variation in the history of Spanish.

Donata Puntil is the Programme Director for the Modern Language Centre at King's College London, where she is responsible for internal and external staff development and intercultural training. Donata has extensive teaching and research experience in Second Language Acquisition, Intercultural Studies and Applied Linguistics. She is conducting her PhD research at the Open University within the *Language Acts and Worldmaking* project.

Dr Rachel Scott is Lecturer in World and Hispanic Literatures at Royal Holloway University of London. She was previously a Postdoctoral Researcher for the Travelling Concepts research strand and remains a Visiting Researcher at the Centre for *Language Acts and Worldmaking* at King's College London. She publishes on medieval and early modern Iberian literatures in their transnational and global contexts and is the author of *Celestina and the Human Condition in Early Modern Spain and Italy* (2017) and co-editor of *Al-Andalus in Motion: Travelling Concepts and Cross-Cultural Contexts* (2021).

Paul Spence is a Senior Lecturer in Digital Humanities at King's College London. His work focuses on digital publishing, global digital humanities and multilingual digital practice. He was Co-Investigator for the Digital Mediations strand for the *Language Acts and Worldmaking* project. He researches digital transformations in how we engage with Modern Languages, while also analysing the power of language to disrupt digital monolingualism in knowledge infrastructures, methods and data. Paul co-convenes the 'Digital Modern Languages' Section on 'Modern Languages Open' (www.modernlanguagesopen.org) and the 'Digital Modern Languages' seminar (https://digitalmodernlanguages.wordpress.com/).

Dr Sophie Stevens is a Leverhulme Early Career Fellow in the School of Literature, Drama and Creative Writing at the University of East Anglia (UK). Her research project investigates the work of Latin American women dramatists in order to explore links between activism, performance, digital networking and translation. She was previously a Postdoctoral Researcher for the *Language Acts and Worldmaking* project on the Translation Acts research strand.

Juan Luis Suárez is Professor of Digital Humanities and Computer Science at Western University, Ontario, where he is also the Director of the CulturePlex Lab, one of Canada's leading centres for digital research and innovation within the Humanities.

AbdoolKarim Vakil is Lecturer in Contemporary Portuguese History in the Departments of History and of Spanish, Portuguese and Latin American Studies at King's College London, and Co-Investigator, with Julian Weiss, of the Travelling Concepts strand of *Language Acts and Worldmaking*. He is co-editor (with S. Sayyid) of *Thinking through Islamophobia: Global Perspectives* (2010), and co-author (with Fernando Amaro Monteiro and Mário Artur Machaqueiro) of *Moçambique: Memória Falada do Islão e da Guerra* (2011). With S. Sayyid he has published 'Reports of Islamophobia: 1997 and 2017' (Islamophobia Research and Documentation project, UC Berkeley/*ReOrient: Journal of Critical Muslim Studies* blog, 2018), and the 'Preface' to

Defining Islamophobia (Muslim Council of Britain, 2021). *Al-Andalus in Motion* (co-edited with Rachel Scott and Julian Weiss) was published by KCL CLAMS in 2021.

Mary Ann Vargas is a practice-based doctoral researcher working with the *Language Acts and Worldmaking* project at King's College London. Her thesis investigates questions and redefines ideas and practices related to re-enactments of belonging away from home.

Julian Weiss is Professor of Medieval and Early Modern Spanish at King's College London. He has held positions at the Universities of Liverpool (UK), Virginia (USA) and Oregon (USA), where he was Head of Romance Languages. He is also a member of the international research group Seminario de Poética Europea del Renacimiento, based at the Universitat Autònoma de Barcelona, and one of the partners of *Language Acts and Worldmaking*. His research and teaching interests range widely across medieval and early modern Iberian literatures: he has published numerous books and articles on such topics as medieval poetic theory, medieval and Renaissance lyric, clerical narrative, theories of gender, early modern censorship, manuscript studies and the history of the early printed book.

Dr Bozena Wislocka Breit is currently a Lecturer in Technical English at the Polytechnic University of Madrid and was a Postdoctoral Researcher on the *Language Acts and Worldmaking* project for the Loaded Meanings strand. She holds a PhD in Linguistics as well as a postgraduate Diploma in Translation. She has taught at the Jagiellonian University, Cracow, and at the Instituto Universitario de Lenguas Modernas y Traductores at the Complutense University of Madrid. Her recent research has focused on the impact and presence of cultured borrowings in the contemporary Spanish language.